# A GOOD MONTH FOR MURDER

# A GOOD MONTH FOR

# MURDER

## THE INSIDE STORY OF
## A HOMICIDE SQUAD

## DEL QUENTIN WILBER

HENRY HOLT AND COMPANY   NEW YORK

Henry Holt and Company, LLC
*Publishers since 1866*
175 Fifth Avenue
New York, New York 10010
www.henryholt.com

Henry Holt® and ® are registered trademarks of
Henry Holt and Company, LLC.

Library of Congress Cataloging-in-Publication Data

Names: Wilber, Del Quentin, author.
Title: A good month for murder : the inside story of a homicide squad /
 Del Quentin Wilber.
Description: New York : Henry Holt and Co., 2016.
Identifiers: LCCN 2015036515| ISBN 9780805098815 (hardback) |
 ISBN 9780805098822 (electronic book)
Subjects: LCSH: Homicides—Washington Metropolitan Area. | Criminal
 Investigation—Washington Metropolitan Area. | BISAC: TRUE CRIME / Murder
 / General. | BIOGRAPHY & AUTOBIOGRAPHY / Law Enforcement. | SOCIAL
 SCIENCE / Criminology.
Classification: LCC HV6534.W18 W55 2016 | DDC 363.25/95230975251—dc23
LC record available at http://lccn.loc.gov/2015036515

Our books may be purchased in bulk for promotional, educational, or business use. Please
contact your local bookseller or the Macmillan Corporate and Premium Sales Department at
(800) 221-7945, extension 5442, or by e-mail at MacmillanSpecialMarkets@macmillan.com.

The names of some persons described in this book have been changed. In each case,
the use of a pseudonym has been noted.

First Edition 2016

Map by Gene Thorp

Designed by Kelly Too

Printed in the United States of America
1  3  5  7  9  10  8  6  4  2

*To the men and women who toil in
the heart of darkness so the rest of us don't have to*

*Police work is fueled by blood, sweat, caffeine, and mothers' tears.*

—Edward T. Norris, former Baltimore police commissioner

# PRINCE GEORGE'S COUNTY HOMICIDE UNIT

## • FEBRUARY 2013 •

### SUPERVISORS

Captain George Nichols
Lieutenant Billy Rayle
Lieutenant Brian Reilly

### M-10 SQUAD

Sergeant Tony Schartner
Mike Barnhardt
Joe Bellino
Ben Brown
Jonathan Hill
Billy Watts

### M-20 SQUAD

Sergeant Trevel Watson
Andre Brooks
Mike Delaney
Paul Dougherty
David Gurry
Paul Mazzei

### M-30 SQUAD

Sergeant Kerry Jernigan
Victoria Bracey
Mike Ebaugh
Jeff Eckrich
Eddie Flores
D. J. Windsor

### M-40 SQUAD

Sergeant Joe Bergstrom
Jamie Boulden
Joe Bunce
Mike Crowell
Sean Deere
Allyson Hamlin

### M-90 SQUAD

Sergeant Greg McDonald
Kenny Doyle
Spencer Harris
Wayne Martin
Marcos Rodriguez
Denise Shapiro

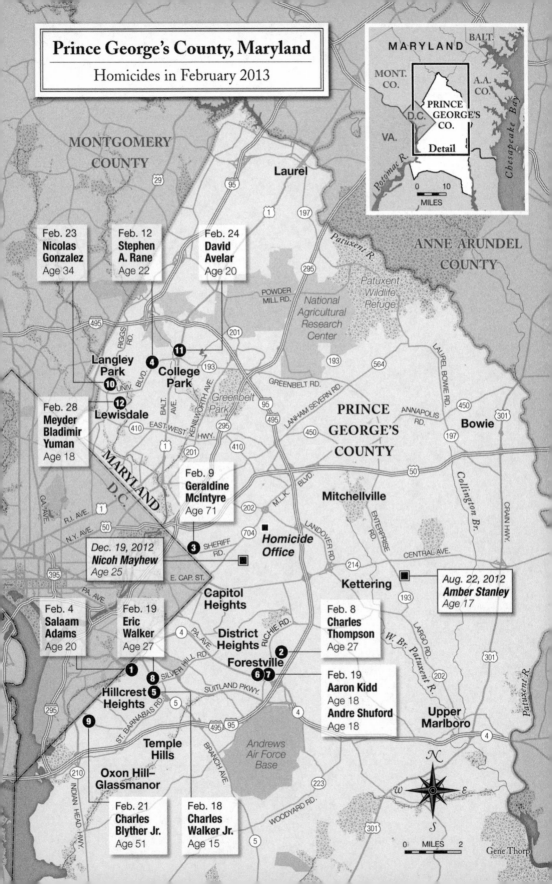

# Prince George's County, Maryland
## Homicides in February 2013

MARYLAND
BALT.
MONT. CO.
D.C.
A.A. CO.
PRINCE GEORGE'S CO.
VA.
Chesapeake Bay
Potomac R.
Detail
0    10
MILES

MONTGOMERY COUNTY

Laurel

ANNE ARUNDEL COUNTY

Patuxent R.

Patuxent Wildlife Refuge

POWDER MILL RD.

National Agricultural Research Center

Feb. 23
**Nicolas Gonzalez**
Age 34

Feb. 12
**Stephen A. Rane**
Age 22

Feb. 24
**David Avelar**
Age 20

Langley Park

College Park

Greenbelt Park

GREENBELT RD.

PRINCE GEORGE'S COUNTY

Bowie

Feb. 28
**Meyder Bladimir Yuman**
Age 18

Lewisdale

EAST-WEST HWY.

Mitchellville

Feb. 9
**Geraldine McIntyre**
Age 71

MARYLAND
D.C.

Dec. 19, 2012
*Nicoh Mayhew*
*Age 25*

SHERIFF RD.

**Homicide Office**

Kettering

Aug. 22, 2012
*Amber Stanley*
*Age 17*

Capitol Heights

Feb. 4
**Salaam Adams**
Age 20

Feb. 19
**Eric Walker**
Age 27

District Heights

Forestville

Feb. 8
**Charles Thompson**
Age 27

Hillcrest Heights

Feb. 19
**Aaron Kidd**
Age 18
**Andre Shuford**
Age 18

Upper Marlboro

Temple Hills

Andrews Air Force Base

Oxon Hill–Glassmanor

Feb. 21
**Charles Blyther Jr.**
Age 51

Feb. 18
**Charles Walker Jr.**
Age 15

WOODYARD RD.

N
W    E
S

0    MILES    2

Gene Thorp

# A GOOD MONTH FOR MURDER

# · PROLOGUE ·

Stooping over the dead man, Detective Ben Brown notes a large bulge under the left eyebrow, most likely caused by a bullet that entered the back of the victim's skull. The man is lying faceup, his half-open eyes staring vacantly into the freezing predawn darkness. Brown inspects the victim's attire: thick black jacket, gray sweatshirt, gray pants, and spotless Timberland boots, one of which still has its leather tag. *At least he died in new shoes,* thinks Brown. Standing straight again, he sniffles and jams his hands deeper into the pockets of his black overcoat.

The investigator's eyes trace two long rivulets of blood that run from under the man's head down the sloping road that wends through the large apartment complex. For a few moments, Brown stares at the blood, until his attention is drawn to a white plastic grocery bag that's been picked up by the whipping wind. As he watches, the bag flutters over the corpse, pirouetting in the glare of floodlights powered by hammering generators. The detective turns slightly to the right, shifting his focus to the broader scene: a single trash can, the back wall of one of the apartment buildings, a long metal fence bordering the access road.

From behind, Brown hears leather soles scuffing on concrete. A moment later he's joined by his sergeant, Tony Schartner, who comes to a stop by his left side.

"It's f-f-fucking cold," says Schartner, who has a pronounced stutter.

"It's cold to the bone," says Brown, his whispery voice almost lost in the wind.

The two men step back and watch an evidence technician photograph the victim. Brown is blinking hard against the pulses of incandescent light when a patrol officer approaches. The officer tells Brown that the area has been secured and no witnesses have come forward. He points to his right, past the fence, and says he found the victim's parents standing just beyond the police tape. Pulling out a notebook, he provides Brown with the dead man's name and age.

Brown thanks the officer and jots down the information in his own notebook. A name and the presence of next of kin are the first pieces of good news the detective has received since being awakened at 3:15 a.m. and alerted to the homicide—*his* homicide— in Forestville, a working-class neighborhood in Prince George's County, Maryland, on the outskirts of Washington, DC. The fatal shooting, he was told, occurred just fifteen or so minutes earlier on the 3300 block of Walters Lane. Brown knows the neighborhood well: he has investigated at least eight murders in the area, and none has been easy to solve. Why should it be otherwise? Walters Lane, a jumble of boxy apartment buildings and strip malls, is governed by the code of the street—*Do not snitch*—and police officers spend an inordinate amount of time simply trying to find witnesses willing to give their real names.

As he drove to the scene, Brown thought about one of his first

homicides in the neighborhood: the shooting of a female drug cou-
rier in her sports car. In the weeks following the crime, Brown had
developed her dealer as a suspect but had been unable to turn up
even a single good witness. Seven years later, his most vivid memory of the case is that of police officers struggling to pry the three-
hundred-pound victim from behind the wheel of her car. Brown has
never forgotten the lesson of that night: Not even the dead cooperate on Walters Lane.

Trim and fit, with slicked-back salt-and-pepper hair and deep
crow's-feet framing his hazel eyes, the forty-four-year-old detective
is an Eagle Scout, the father of two Eagle Scouts and a Boy Scout,
and a faithful Catholic. He believes that he does God's work, and
his right bicep bears a tattoo of the archangel Michael, patron saint
of police officers. But a decade of murders has hardened him to
death—a not uncommon occurrence in his profession—and he
rarely feels much empathy for his victims. In truth, it's been a year
and a half since a homicide really got to him: in the boiling summer of 2011, a Washington, DC, police officer shot and killed his
mistress in a park and left their eleven-month-old daughter to roast
to death in her mother's Kia. After conducting an experiment that
proved that the interior of the car had reached 125 degrees, Brown
could no longer control his emotions, and he broke down crying.

Most homicide cases, however, do not involve such innocent victims, and now, as he stands at the scene, Brown suspects that this
one is likely to be far more typical. After all, what kind of person
would be out on the street at such an hour in such a dangerous
place? *It's fucking Walters Lane,* he thinks. *Just one shit bag killing
another.*

As Brown and Schartner watch the evidence technician take
photographs and inspect the scene, they are joined by Detective Jonathan Hill, a rookie homicide investigator who has been canvassing
neighbors and talking to the responding police officers. Hill tells
Brown that no one has admitted to seeing anything or has provided

any useful information. He then steps around Schartner for a closer look at the body. The rookie—known for his sarcastic wit—frowns, clears his throat, and speaks in a mock-anchorman voice:

"Here is yet another young black man who voted for our beloved president and now, sadly, won't be able to attend his inauguration."

The two veterans smile: in just seven hours, Barack Obama is scheduled to deliver his second inaugural address on the west steps of the U.S. Capitol. As white men, Brown and Schartner could never get away with Hill's joke. But Hill, an African American who is the son of one of the DC police force's first black officers, is quick to find humor in almost any situation.

All three detectives are fairly certain that their victim had no intention of attending the ceremony that will take place just seven miles from where they are standing. A line drawn from the crime scene in suburban Maryland to the inauguration's majestic venue would cut through neighborhoods both run-down and quaint, busy avenues and quiet residential streets, the polluted Anacostia River and the tony row houses on Capitol Hill. At one end of that short distance there is hope—the nation's first black president will once again take the oath of office—while at the other is a familiar and ignominious reality: yet another black man has been murdered on the streets of a crime-plagued neighborhood.

PRINCE GEORGE'S COUNTY is a microcosm of the new America, a suburban sprawl of nearly 900,000 residents to the east of the nation's capital. Spread over 485 square miles, it is one of the most diverse collections of communities in the country. Its population is 65 percent black, 14.5 percent white, and 16 percent Hispanic. It encompasses farmland, low-income apartment complexes, traffic-clogged highways, middle-class subdivisions, and affluent enclaves. It is home to big-box retailers, mom-and-pop stores, and countless strip malls filled with nail and hair salons, convenience stores, and churches. It is both poor and prosperous. With a median household income that is $20,000 greater than the U.S. average, it is the highest-income majority black county in the nation. Yet it has extreme pockets of poverty, especially inside the 87 square miles enclosed by the Capital Beltway.

High crime rates and underperforming schools have cast Prince George's County as the ugly stepchild of the Washington region. It has little of the luster of the gentrifying District, the charm of historic Alexandria, Virginia, or the leafy suburban aura of either Maryland's Montgomery County or Virginia's Fairfax County. In 2011, when former Prince George's county executive Jack B. Johnson pleaded to corruption charges, admitting he had accepted hundreds of thousands of dollars in bribes while in office, and was sentenced to seven years in federal prison, the region reacted with a shrug: *Well, that's PG for you.*

For years, the county has also endured far too many killings. From 2001 through 2011, PG tallied at least 90 homicides a year, a staggering toll for a suburban jurisdiction of its size. As recently as 2005, the county recorded 169 murders, a per capita rate that far outstripped the country as a whole. That pace finally slowed in 2012, when 64 people were slain. The reasons for the drop are complex and will long be debated; PG's police department credits several of its most successful initiatives, including a more intensive focus on particular hot spots, the closing of troublesome nightclubs linked to many violent confrontations, and better integration of other county agencies into the fight against crime.

As 2013 began, the twenty-five detectives and five sergeants in the PG Homicide Unit took some comfort in the recent slowdown in the county's killing machinery. Lately they have had more time to work their cases; they have even begun to dig into a number of old files. But they have also been feeling apprehensive. They've seen such lulls before: two years earlier, in January 2011, they were hit with twelve murders in just eleven days, a spate that followed a brief respite not unlike this one. As they raced from body to body that January, the unit's detectives were forced to skip anniversaries, birthdays, school plays, and youth hockey games. They still recall that period—a savage test of their endurance and abilities—with horror and reverence. And they wonder if another test is coming.

WHEN BEN BROWN returns to the office about twelve hours after standing over his victim on Walters Lane, he is anxious. *Clearing this murder has been way too easy,* he thinks. In quick succession, he interviewed the dead man's parents, extracted the name of a key witness, interviewed the witness, and identified the killer, who was then arrested in northwest Washington. After driving into the District, and despite the congestion caused by the president's inauguration, the investigator found a parking space right in front of the DC homicide office. And minutes after Brown introduced himself to the suspect, the man confessed that he had killed the twenty-one-year-old victim to steal his backpack and take revenge for an earlier act of violence. Improbably, the case had gone from a stone-cold whodunit to what PG detectives call a "smoker" in less than a day.

Brown is superstitious; he's convinced that because he caught this easy-to-solve case, his next one will be colossally difficult. So he's not happy when he finishes up a report, looks around the PG homicide office, and sees that the place is buzzing. Detectives are talking loudly into their phones, questioning witnesses in the office's three interview rooms, and hurrying out to their cars. Brown's killing is the third in just four days; it's been months since the unit has handled so many murders in such a compressed span, and everyone is hustling.

Brown thinks back to a comment made by his lieutenant the previous month. One night, as Lieutenant Billy Rayle was holding court with several investigators not far from Brown's desk, he said that things had been too quiet for too long. Rayle—a hard-living, fun-loving cop whose appendix would burst a few days later, keeping him out of work for four months—seemed to have a sixth sense for when a run of killings would commence. Rayle had been a supervisor in the Homicide Unit for six years, and that night he told his detectives that the tide was about to turn; there was simply too much pent-up violence on the streets, and it needed an outlet. The unit was due.

"We'll catch a few more this month," Rayle predicted on that calm December night. "And in January, it will get busier. But February—watch out. Be ready for February. It will be a good month for murder."

# · CHAPTER 1 ·

On a frigid midwinter day, Mike Crowell slows his Chevy Impala to a stop and turns his domelike head from left to right, scanning the street for the man he thinks is a killer. But Central Avenue is devoid of people, even of stray dogs, and all Crowell spies are bare trees, beat-up houses with rusty chain-link fences, and scruffy yards covered in the remnants of an early-morning dusting of snow.

His eyes trained on the street, the detective feels for a soft pack of Marlboro Silvers in the pocket of the driver's door, jiggles the last cigarette free, sticks it between his lips, and tosses the empty pack onto the passenger-side floor, where it joins another. He lights the Marlboro, lowers the window a couple of inches, and exhales a plume of smoke, which momentarily swirls in the cold wind before whipping back into the car. He takes another drag, his left foot tapping the floor, his right pumping the brake, his fingers drumming the steering wheel.

*Where is he? He must be around here somewhere,* thinks the

detective, yanking his smartphone from its belt holster and scanning his e-mail messages. It's been like this for the last two hours: Crowell has been aggressively crisscrossing Prince George's County and pulling over every ten minutes to check for an e-mail that he hopes will pinpoint the location of Jeff Buck,* a twenty-three-year-old suspect in a murder investigation that hangs over the Homicide Unit like a shadow at dusk.

The e-mails are from Buck's cell-phone carrier, and they provide "hits"—longitude and latitude coordinates of the suspect's location. The last position was in the heart of the county, but the hit was hardly precise, having a margin of error of plus or minus thirteen hundred yards, or three-quarters of a mile. Crowell has received several dozen of these e-mails; after each, he raced to the assigned spot and hunted side streets and thoroughfares in an ever-expanding circle until the next e-mail arrived. The hits started near where Crowell believes Buck's girlfriend lives and have gotten progressively closer to the DC-Maryland line. Crowell figures that Buck, a well-known street thug and drug dealer, is either on a bike—unlikely in the cold weather—or making stop-and-go narcotics deliveries.

Seeing no new e-mail, Crowell closes his smartphone's screen and adjusts his wraparound sunglasses to ward off the glare from the bright winter sun.

"Where are you?" he wonders aloud, his gaze sweeping the street.

To his right, a black car speeds toward the intersection and then suddenly slows; the driver has clearly spotted Crowell's unmarked cruiser. A beat-up black Lincoln with flashy rims and heavily tinted windows, the car is of the sort favored by young men in the drug trade, what police call a "battle wagon." As the Lincoln rolls slowly past, the driver's silhouette becomes visible through the darkened

---

*Not his real name.

glass: short, slim, close-cropped hair, baseball cap. Crowell knows that the driver is not the suspect; the detective is looking for a tall man with dreadlocks. Even so, Crowell eases his foot off the brake. He lets the Impala slip into the intersection and turn ever so slightly toward the battle wagon.

Crowell can't help himself. For more than a decade, he roamed the streets with an elite robbery-suppression unit that investigated and tried to prevent street crimes. The work is embedded in Crowell's DNA—a double helix of high-speed pursuits, wrestling matches with men bent on fleeing, and aggressive interrogations. But those days are over. Crowell has been a homicide detective for two years; this job requires him to wear a suit and engage a more cerebral set of skills. He often spends hours at a desk, poring over cell-phone records, social-media postings, crime-lab reports, and interview summaries. This morning, however, he feels like his old self. Wearing his bullet-resistant vest, jeans, a gray fleece jacket, and sneakers, he is on the hunt. A grin spreads across face, and his grip tightens on the wheel. He lets the cruiser slip farther into the intersection.

*Bet there's a gun in there,* Crowell thinks. *And drugs—there are definitely drugs.*

Pulling the driver over would be no challenge at all. Crowell would follow the man for thirty seconds, find one of a thousand pretexts to stop him, and then persuade the guy to allow his car to be searched.

Crowell watches as the battle wagon accelerates away to his left. His right hand *thwack-thwack-thwack*s the wheel. *Fuck. Fuck. Fuck.* His Robbery Unit self is screaming for him to chase the car. But the homicide detective in him—still learning to be patient— whispers that he should let the Lincoln go, that he has more important work to do.

*Chase or not chase? Chase or not chase?* The battle wagon is nearly out of view. *Shit.* Exhaling a plume of smoke, Crowell stomps the brake, bringing the cruiser to a full stop. He watches the car vanish down a side street.

Shaking his head, he pulls out his phone again and checks his in-box.

*Come on! Where are you?*

The next hit suggests that the suspect is still making his way toward the DC line, so Crowell heads in that direction, motoring through a blur of neighborhoods. He jacks up the volume of the car stereo when he hears his favorite song, "Figured You Out," by the rock band Nickelback. "I like your pants around your feet," the singer belts. "And I like the dirt that's on your knees."

When the song ends, Crowell switches to a rap station, and soon angry lyrics and a thudding bass line are pulsing from the speakers. The detective's taste in music is eclectic—he likes everything from classical to rock to heavy metal to hip-hop. But when he's chasing suspects, rap seems best, and now the detective pumps his balding head to the heavy beat.

As he checks his phone for the next hit, Crowell hears a gravelly voice crackle from the police radio in a pocket of his bullet-resistant vest: "I'll be in the AO in five mikes."

It's Sean Deere, Crowell's squad mate and the lead detective on this case, the investigation into the murder of an innocent seventeen-year-old named Amber Stanley. Crowell chuckles and keys the microphone: "Command post copies."

*Fucking Deere, acting all military,* thinks Crowell. Deere is definitely not military. A former undercover narcotics investigator, he is as laid-back as Crowell is aggressive, as methodical as Crowell is impulsive. And because he is chronically late, Deere's nickname is "Detective En Route."

Crowell and Deere are friends, though earlier that morning there had been a testy exchange that highlighted their differing approaches to police work. Deere had obtained a court order compelling a communications company to provide Jeff Buck's phone records and the data the detectives needed to track his phone. The department has a cell-phone-locating truck, a technological marvel that can pinpoint a phone in continuous real time by zeroing in on its signal. But to the great frustration of the PG homicide detectives, the truck has been out of service for six months, meaning they have to rely on other agencies to help them track fugitives. Crowell and his partner, Joe Bunce, had arrived early that morning to begin the search for Jeff Buck and wanted to catch the suspect quickly. After a string of grueling weeks, the two men had hoped to enjoy some time on a quiet Friday evening with their wives, Beth and Debbi.

"Beth said she would be waiting upstairs for me," Crowell told Bunce, egging his fellow detective into calling the head of the DC police department's phone-truck squad. "They'll find the guy a lot faster than we will."

"But Sean wants us to grab Buck ourselves—quietly," Bunce said.

"Fuck it," said Crowell. "I want to get some ass tonight."

When Deere finally walked into the office, at 11:00 a.m., he scowled at Bunce's mention of the DC request. "I don't want them involved right now. I don't want a bunch of guys on the street scaring this guy," said Deere, adding he would prefer to rely on the less precise tracking method of hopscotching from e-mailed location to e-mailed location. "I want to take him nice and quiet."

"Sean, they do this all the time," Crowell said. "They don't cause a scene. They are good."

"No, I want to do this my way," Deere insisted. "And that is nice and quiet."

Crowell wasn't happy with the decision, but he said nothing further. This was Deere's case, so Deere's word was law.

WITH A CIGARETTE dangling from his lips, Sean Deere drives toward the AO—the area of operations—zigzagging through Capitol Heights, a 4,000-person town of single-family homes, town houses, and apartment buildings squeezed into less than a square mile next to the DC line. He, too, is dressed casually: black boots, blue jeans, long-sleeved black T-shirt, black police jacket. Country music blares from the stereo of his loaner, a car so beat-up that its glove box is secured by duct tape. His usual ride, a blue Impala with 121,000 miles on the odometer, is getting a tune-up at the department's maintenance shop. Six months into his investigation of Amber Stanley's murder—the most difficult case of his career—the detective feels as rundown as his Impala and as rickety as his loaner.

Deere regrets having snapped at Mike Crowell and Joe Bunce earlier, but he had his reasons. For one, the stakes are high, and he can't afford to take the risk that another department's officers will screw up his investigation. For another, the warrant he has for Jeff Buck's DNA is rather thin. To emphasize this point to the ever-impatient Crowell, Deere that morning had waved his hands over the document like a wizard. "It's all rumor and magic," he half-joked to Crowell, "and it might get tossed by a judge. So I want to keep it in my pocket. I want him to consent."

In the heart of Capitol Heights, Deere drives slowly down avenues and up side streets. He scans sidewalks but sees no one who matches the description of his target. As he cruises through another alley, he feels his smartphone vibrate. He pulls the cruiser to a stop and reaches for his belt holster. Scrunching his eyes, he studies the e-mail on his smartphone. He smiles.

"You see this?" Crowell blurts over the radio.

Deere keys his mike and tells Crowell that the hit has a variable radius of only about a hundred feet. "He must be out in the open." Deere knows that hits get more precise when suspects are on the phone and outdoors.

Placing his radio back on the passenger seat, Deere enters the longitude and latitude into a mapping program on his phone, and out pops the location: a half mile away near Eastern Avenue, a dividing line between PG County and the District. The detectives were right: Buck has been moving toward the line. If they're lucky, they will catch him with a gun or drugs, giving them leverage in the interrogation room.

Deere slams the accelerator, and the battered cruiser roars to life. The detective races up Southern Avenue and swerves onto Eastern Avenue, a blur of town houses, vacant lots, squat apartment buildings, and parked cars flashing past his window. A moment later, he spies a tall man in a leather jacket sauntering down the sidewalk, a grocery bag in his right hand. It's Jeff Buck—no question.

*Got you,* thinks Deere, grabbing his radio and relaying Buck's location. "Sixty-second and Eastern."

"On my way," says Crowell.

Hanging back a bit, Deere watches Buck stride into an apartment complex's parking lot. A moment later, the detective pulls into the lot, comes to a quick stop next to Buck, and leaps from the car. "Put your hands on the hood!" Deere shouts.

Buck spins toward Deere, his dreadlocks flailing under a dark ball cap as his eyes search for an escape route. Deere knows from having read reports and spoken to fellow officers that Buck is not afraid to run from the police.

"Don't," says Deere. *"Don't!"*

Buck and the detective lock eyes for a moment, both men utterly still. Finally the suspect frowns and gently sets the grocery bag on the ground. Swiveling, he places his hands on the car's hood.

"I've been trying to get in touch with you for a little bit," Deere tells Buck, running his hands up and down the man's sides and over his legs, checking for weapons. Finding none, he pats Buck on the back, prompting him to spin around.

Over the past two months, Deere has often eyed Jeff Buck's mug shot, and now he is not surprised by what he finds in front of him. The twenty-three-year-old has a long, sloped face, a flat nose, and a goatee. A Pittsburgh Pirates cap covers his thick dreadlocks, and he's clad in camouflage pants and a clashing red-and-black leather jacket. Leaning back against the car, Buck jams his hands into his jacket pockets and sneers, clearly unhappy about being stopped and frisked in public.

"I have to take you back to the office," Deere says. In his peripheral vision, he catches Crowell's Impala pulling into the lot. A moment later, his fellow detective stands at his side.

"What the fuck? I'm just bringing these things to my baby's momma," Buck says, nodding toward the plastic bag at his feet.

Deere glances at the bag and sees that it contains cleaning supplies and diapers. Off to his right, he hears a door open, and a woman in a blue bathrobe emerges from a ground-floor apartment. The woman briefly surveys the scene before taking a few angry steps toward the investigators. She must be the baby's mother, Deere thinks, so he holds up his right hand, a signal for her to halt.

She complies, puts her hands on her hips, and begins to scream.

"You can't take him!" she shouts. "You need a warrant! You need a warrant! Let him go!"

"No, I can," says Deere.

"Is he going to be all right?" the woman asks. "Give me your card. What is your badge number? Give me your badge number!"

"We'll give it to him," says Crowell. "He'll be fine—he's with the police!"

"Fuck you!" the woman yells. "Fuck you all! Jeff, don't say a word! Fuck you all!"

"He's an adult," Deere says, too quietly for the woman to hear, as he opens the front passenger door of the cruiser.

"You can come with us if you like," he says to Buck. Then he grabs the man's left arm with his right hand and guides him around the door. Before his suspect can object, the detective spins him into the passenger seat and slams the door.

———

THE PHONE CALL that ushered Sean Deere into a personal hell came six months earlier, at 11:10 p.m. on August 22, a warm and muggy Wednesday. Deere was at home; half-asleep on his couch, he was watching the late news. When he answered his cell phone, the midnight-shift detective told him a teenage girl had been slain in her own bedroom. The murder, the detective said, had occurred in Kettering, a suburban subdivision featuring tree-lined streets with genteel names like Burleigh and Princeleigh and Wimbleton.

A neighborhood of ramblers, split-levels, and colonials built in the 1960s and 1970s, Kettering was east of Washington's Beltway—which in PG County is generally considered the highway's "good side"—making it a somewhat unusual venue for a homicide. But after having spent five years investigating murders all across the sprawling county, Deere was keenly aware that even the most placid neighborhoods can hold deadly secrets. As he drove toward Kettering, his mind ran through the typical reasons a teenager might be killed in such a place: she was a prostitute, a gang member, the girlfriend of a drug dealer, or the resident of a narcotics stash house. All were grounds enough to be slain in PG County.

Deere arrived in Kettering just after midnight and soon turned onto Chartsey Street, a curving road lined with homes on small but neat grassy lots. He passed a dozen PG patrol cars and evidence vans before stopping in front of the victim's house, a split-level with beige siding, burgundy shutters, and a red mailbox. The investigator got out of his car, ducked under police tape, and found Andre Brooks—the midnight-shift detective who had called him an hour or so earlier—chatting with Deere's sergeant, Joe Bergstrom. The investigators told him what they knew: someone had kicked in the front door of the house, climbed to the second floor, and fatally shot Amber Stanley in her bedroom.

Brooks told Deere that Amber Stanley's mother, older sister, and foster sister had already been taken to the homicide office, where investigators were quizzing them. The older sister, Brooks said, reported being in her basement bedroom with her four-year-old son and hearing Amber scream; she then heard a gunshot, more screams, and more gunshots. The sister ran to the first floor and dipped her head around a corner. Looking up the stairs to the second floor, she saw a man leaving Amber's room. He was wearing a dark sweat-shirt and a dark mask; in his right hand he was holding a semiauto-matic pistol. Before the gunman could react, the sister dashed downstairs to her room and slammed the door. She blocked it with a filing cabinet, snatched her son, and climbed out a back window.

Deere jotted down some notes, then walked to the front door of the house. It had clearly been smashed in—the dead bolt was extended, and the jamb was cracked—but he saw no evidence of shoe or boot imprints. Shifting his gaze, he spotted a mangled bul-let three feet in, on the entryway's hardwood floor; five feet beyond that was a shell casing.

Deere stepped into the house and took the stairs on his right to the second floor. Amber Stanley's room was just off the landing; slipping across the threshold, he found the murdered girl. Clad in a baby-blue sleeping T-shirt, looking tiny and delicate, she lay crum-pled over a pillow on her bed. Under her face was a pool of con-gealing blood. A jarring mix of scents—perfume, hair spray, gun powder—filled the small white room.

On the bed's bright green comforter, Deere noticed several shell casings; he also saw a casing was on the floor to his right. Nearby were a pile of clothes, a small dresser, and a set of white shelves filled with books and pink baskets containing hair spray, brushes, mousse, and creams. Pink curtains covered the far window. In one corner of the room was a jewelry box, in another an electronic music keyboard. On the wall was a dry-erase board with a to-do list: "book reflection, two essays, binders, sheet protectors." Under it was a cal-endar; in the box for Monday, August 20, bracketed in blue and red marker, were the words "First Day."

Deere's stomach clenched. His victim was not involved in the drug world; a dirtbag's girlfriend does not highlight the first day of school, and certainly not with enthusiasm. In her bedroom and then elsewhere in the house, Deere studied photographs of the girl, every one of which was striking. With soft, round cheeks and glimmering brown eyes, Amber Stanley had been beautiful—later, Deere would learn that she was a part-time model and an honor student who dreamed of becoming a geneticist.

A stream of investigators and evidence techs came and went from Amber's room. There was no banter at the victim's bedside; to the officers present, this girl could have been a sister or a daughter. Deere was as hardened as any of them, but as he leaned close to the girl he felt a surge of sadness, his thoughts drifting to images of his four children, two of them girls.

Working deliberately, Deere noted several wounds to Amber's head and face, the position of her body, the type of shell casings, the lack of other physical evidence. This didn't feel like a robbery: a plastic bag of cash, apparently Amber's, lay at the foot of the bed. It didn't seem like a domestic dispute, either. It felt like an execution, which made no sense. *Nobody executes honor students,* Deere thought. *Not like this.*

While searching the rest of the house, Deere was momentarily puzzled by a black footprint on the door of a second basement bedroom, this one normally occupied by the foster sister. The door had been kicked in, but Deere quickly realized that the damage wasn't the work of the killer. Instead, the footprint had been left by the shoe of an officer frantically hunting for the gunman or any survivors. When Deere entered the foster sister's rather plain room, he found a twin bed, a dresser, and a desk covered with journals and diaries. He collected the brightly colored volumes as evidence, but nothing else in the room caught his attention.

Deere spent the next few hours working closely with evidence technicians and forensic investigators. It was his responsibility to make sure they did their jobs properly; he observed them photographing the victim and the scene, collecting potential evidence, and, finally, placing the body into a zippered bag. Just as the sun rose above Chartsey Street, Deere left the house and drove to the office, where he would spend much of the next forty-eight hours. Already, he was deeply worried; this was not a typical homicide. He could feel it in his bones.

OVER THE NEXT several days, Deere reviewed the autopsy results, the evidence collected by the techs, and the interviews with the victim's family members. He soon put together a plausible scenario of what had happened in the house that night: the gunman had kicked in the front door and startled Amber Stanley, who was standing just ten feet away in the front hallway. The killer fired his first shot; the round struck the teen in the left arm, breaking it. Chased by her assailant, Amber fled upstairs and ran to her bedroom. There she took refuge on her bed, next to her stuffed animals. The gunman followed her into the bedroom, stood over her, and fired several more times, hitting her in the face and head. Then he raced back down the stairs and out of the house.

But the killer's motive—not to mention his identity—remained a mystery. Within hours of Amber Stanley's murder, the case had begun to attract a huge amount of attention from both the PG police department's higher-ups and the media. It was a classic "red ball": a high-profile murder that *must* be solved, and solved yesterday. (The police took the nickname from the railroad business; red balls were trains carrying priority items.) As Deere knew, the gunman had killed more than just a pretty teenager: Amber Stanley— an honor student with a bright future—was a living emblem of hope in a county too often defined by shattered dreams.

Under intense pressure to find her killer, the PG police department hurled plainclothes officers, drug investigators, and dozens of detectives into the case. Days became weeks, but still the case remained unsolved. Now, six months after the murder, Deere struggles to believe that he's making any real progress. He often feels like a lifeguard being dragged under by a drowning swimmer.

With thinning brown hair, sallow cheeks, and puffy bags under his eyes, Deere looks a decade older than his forty-four years. He has put on at least thirty-five pounds since catching the case, erasing the gains of a months-long diet that combined a strict vegan regimen with the regular consumption of appetite-suppressing cigarettes.

Possessed of an innate curiosity and a superb memory, Deere is a whiz at trivia contests and an enthusiastic student of history. The son of a DC firefighter, he grew up in Prince George's County, did well in school, and attended junior college with the idea of going into real estate. But public service was in his blood, and he quickly grew bored with his studies. Changing course, he applied to the PG police department and became an officer in 1990, at the age of twenty-one. Like all rookies, he started in patrol before spending a decade as an undercover narcotics investigator—a job that taught him patience, since complicated drug probes can take years to build. In 2008, looking for a new challenge, he won an assignment to homicide, policing's most dynamic and intellectually challenging assignment.

After five years in the crucible of murder investigation, Deere thought he had seen everything—until he caught the red ball express the night Amber Stanley was killed. Since then, he has worked an almost endless string of sixteen-hour days, conducting scores of interviews, compiling hundreds of reports, filling seven binders with meticulous dossiers on witnesses and suspects. He has listened to mind-numbing recordings of phone calls from jail, delivered at least three detailed briefings to the police chief, and passed far too many nights staring at the bedroom ceiling, fretting over what crucial piece of evidence or information he has missed. Though he blames his weight gain on the long hours and the abrupt demise of his vegan-and-cigarettes diet, the real culprits were stress and anxiety. With twenty-three years on the force, Deere is nearing retirement; for better or worse, his reputation will ultimately be defined by this one case.

Deere is well aware that some of the county's most infamous red balls have never been solved. In fact, the twentieth anniversary of one such case is fast approaching. In May 1993, ten-year-old George Stanley Burdynski Jr. left his family's white bungalow on his bicycle in the working-class town of Brentwood, never to be seen again. For months, Junior's disappearance was a major news story, with reporters chronicling the frantic efforts by the police to find the boy, or at least his missing red bicycle. For a while, investigators suspected that a ring of pedophiles was responsible, but eventually that trail went cold. On a number of anniversaries of Junior's disappearance, the department has displayed thousands of pages of reports to prove to reporters how hard the case has been worked, as if the stacks of dusty documents demonstrate anything other than the obvious: despite enormous effort, no killer has ever been brought to justice.

Five years after Junior's disappearance, fifty-year-old Sherry Crandell was discovered bound, raped, and strangled in her office at Prince George's Hospital Center. The crime shocked the DC region: was the county so dangerous that hospital employees were not safe at work? The police promised a quick arrest; they believed the killer was a thief who had assaulted Crandell after she surprised him while he was rummaging through her office. Not only had the killer left behind his DNA, the hospital also boasted security cameras that were likely to have captured crucial evidence. Yet the investigation went nowhere, and now, nearly fifteen years after Crandell's death, the investigation's lead detective remains tormented by the failure.

These murders haunt the PG police force like phantoms. In particular, they plague Sean Deere, who yearns for Amber Stanley's case—his investigation—to be solved. In his darkest moments, he imagines a painful phone call ten or twenty years hence, from some young detective who brazenly asks how he had missed an obvious piece of evidence. This is his waking nightmare: that the answer to the Amber Stanley riddle lies somewhere in his seven binders, that he has somehow missed the critical clue among hundreds of facts and rumors, reports and scribbled notes. The clue waits there, unseen and uncaring, and it will wait there as he retires, grows old, and dies.

TEN MINUTES AFTER grabbing Jeff Buck, Deere parks his Impala behind police headquarters, leads the suspect through a set of double doors and down a long hallway, and then turns left into the unmarked door of the homicide office. They pass one closed door before Deere opens a second one—this is Interview Room 2. He deposits Buck inside, telling him that he and Detective Crowell will return in a few minutes.

After closing and locking the door, Deere shuffles through the 1,350-square-foot squad room. The low-ceilinged space is crammed with five rows of workstations, each topped by a filing cabinet decorated with work schedules, family photos, and sports logos. The room's fluorescent lights are harsh, and though one wall has five windows, they are small and their curtains are drawn, so almost no natural light enters the room. On each desk, a whirling fan circulates the stuffy air, which smells of stale pepperoni pizza and fried chicken, the last two meals devoured by investigators.

Deere passes between two rows of desks piled high with case files, papers, and boxes. His is the last desk in the last row; it sits next to a concrete wall so thick that it blocks most cell-phone signals from the bunkerlike room. A moment later, Crowell arrives and takes a seat at his desk, which is next to Deere's. For five minutes, the two detectives silently review notes and check e-mails.

Then Deere stands and signals for Crowell to follow him. It's time.

The detective walks to the interview room and presses his right eye to the peephole. Jeff Buck has removed his leather jacket and is now down to a black sweatshirt. With his hands deep in the pockets of his camouflage pants, he is half-sitting, half-lying in a plastic chair, his eyes closed. He appears to be asleep.

*The felony nap,* thinks Deere.

As every homicide detective in the unit knows, only the guilty sleep in the windowless, eight-by-eight-foot interview room known as "the box." The innocent pace, bounce on their toes, sob, even piss their pants in fear. Who wouldn't in this grim enclosure, with its gray walls, flickering lights, heavy door audibly locked from the outside, and black video orb mounted in an upper corner? No, the innocent do not nap.

The guilty, however, sprawl out on the wooden table or the dingy tile floor or in one of the hard plastic chairs. They sleep, or pretend to. Within the Homicide Unit, explanations for this behavior abound: maybe some kind of circuit breaker has tripped in their minds; maybe they are simply acting. Sean Deere has his own hypothesis: the guilty, the true killers, are reptilian motherfuckers who don't give a shit, either about the life they have taken or the one they might be about to lose.

Stepping back from the door, Deere runs a hand through what remains of his hair and rubs the bags under his eyes. He takes a deep breath; glancing over his right shoulder, he spots Crowell checking the wall clock and jotting down the time on his notepad.

"Ready?" Deere asks.

"Let's do this," says Crowell.

Deere does not want to show Buck the flimsy warrant for collecting his DNA, partly because it will alert him to his status as a suspect, partly because Buck could challenge it and prevent jurors from hearing the evidence Deere hopes to collect. So the detective wants to keep the interview low-key for as long as possible and eventually persuade Buck to consent to giving them his DNA. The results of that test will either confirm that Buck is a serious suspect or force Deere to reevaluate two months of work. Deere also hopes to convince Buck to surrender his cell phone and its potential trove of e-mails, texts, photographs, videos, and social-media postings.

As Deere and Crowell step into the interview room, the detectives are assaulted by the pungent smells of marijuana and body odor. On the ten-minute ride to the station, Deere had sniffed the skunklike smell of weed emanating from Buck's clothes. Now that aroma has merged with the stink of the room's most recent occupant, most likely a homeless man. Deere wonders whether they should move Buck to a better room but decides against it. The detectives will get used to the smell; they always do.

"You got weed on you?" Crowell asks, his voice muffled by a golf-ball-sized plug of sunflower seeds in his right cheek.

"I don't think so," the man says.

"Are you sure you don't have a J on you?" asks Deere.

"We don't care," Crowell says. "If you do, we're just going to get rid of it."

"Do you smoke?" asks Deere, referring to marijuana.

Buck laughs—of course he does.

"This morning?" Deere says.

"Yeah, this morning."

Deere wonders if the man is too impaired by the drug to continue but decides that he's reasonably lucid and presses ahead. The detective doesn't like the way the furniture is arranged in the box, so he and Crowell move the table away from the wall, into the center of the room. Deere takes a seat across from Buck, while Crowell sits in one corner of the cramped room, his right knee two feet from Buck's left knee.

Deere begins the interrogation with straightforward questions about the man's background. Buck is twenty-three and says he lives with his "baby's momma"—the screaming woman from earlier that afternoon—in an apartment on Eastern Avenue in Capitol Heights, on the line between PG County and the District.

After he finishes with Buck's background, Deere asks where he was last night and this morning. It's a test, a question to which Deere and Crowell think they know the answer. They have spent weeks learning everything they can about the suspect, and for the past few days they've tracked his cell phone. They believe he spent the night at another girlfriend's apartment, about three and a half miles from where they nabbed him.

Buck says he slept at his baby's momma's house and, before that, was with a friend on Southern Avenue. In other words, he was nowhere near where his cell phone was pinging. He says he had just left a grocery store on an errand for his baby's momma when the detectives found him. That part was no doubt true—he'd been carrying a shopping bag filled with the expected supplies—but it seems more likely that he had popped into the store on his way home from his other girlfriend's apartment, or perhaps after conducting a few drug deals.

When Deere asks Buck why he went to the grocery store, Buck says his baby's momma had run out of soap for her washing machine. He also says he needed cigarettes and bought two.

"You buy cigarette singles?" Deere asks.

"Yeah," Buck says. "The guys around here sell them in singles."

"How much is a cigarette?"

"Fifty cents."

"Fifty cents for one?" Deere asks in the hoarse voice of a smoker who inhales a pack a day of Camel Blues.

"Yeah, two for a dollar."

"You get a better deal with two for a dollar," Deere deadpans.

Buck's brow creases; he is perplexed. "It's the same thing," he says.

Deere laughs. "The more you buy should be cheaper. Hey, a carton is cheaper than a pack."

"I'm trying to cut down," Buck says. "But as many singles that I smoke, I should buy a pack."

Deere taps pen to paper once, twice, a third time. The preliminaries are over. He asks Buck about his last visit to this office, five months earlier. Like a number of others who live in or near Amber Stanley's neighborhood, Buck had been questioned about the murder. Deere has read the department's report on the interview, and from what he can tell, the detective who interviewed Buck did a decent job. But the detective clearly hadn't been particularly familiar with the details of the case; besides, in light of what Deere has recently uncovered, he couldn't possibly have known the right questions to ask.

When Buck replies to Deere, his tone is casual: "He asked me if I knew her, who I think did it. He asked me a lot of random questions. I really can't remember—it was a couple months back. He was asking me if I know the girl."

"What did he say happened?"

"He didn't tell me. He wanted my story first."

"What did you hear?" asks Deere.

"Basically, some guys came into a house. I think they said three guys came into the house. They shot the girl while she was sleeping in her bed and left."

The two detectives exchange quizzical looks. It is the first time Deere has heard anything about three men being involved; he also wonders if the confidential detail about Amber Stanley being slain in her bed has leaked out. He knows Buck has at least one fact wrong, however: Amber Stanley wasn't sleeping when she was killed.

"Three guys came into the house and shot her while she was sleeping?" asks Deere, making sure he has the story straight.

"Yeah."

Deere is quiet for a moment, again tapping his pen to paper, nodding slightly in thought.

"You knew her?" he asks.

"No, but I knew her sister."

Deere and Crowell exchange another look. Good: Buck has admitted that he knows the sister. Not the older sister—the foster sister. Looking back at his suspect, Deere thinks, *Okay, now it's time*.

FROM THE FIRST, Deere was all but certain that Amber Stanley was an innocent victim who had done nothing to deserve her fate. The murder had to be about something else, or somebody else. That somebody, Deere felt, was probably Amber's foster sister, Denise Garner,* a known prostitute who was a magnet for trouble.

A thin, pretty teenager, Denise seemed mentally unstable and had endured a deeply troubled childhood and adolescence. When she was three, her mother, a prostitute, was found sexually assaulted and beaten to death. Until she was thirteen, the girl lived with various family friends and relatives, including an aunt. She then moved through a succession of foster homes, finally arriving at Amber Stanley's parents' house eight months before the murder. Her new situation suited her; in fact, she described living with Amber Stanley's mother, Irma Gaither, as the best experience of her life. Even so, the most recent move had apparently done little to improve Denise's behavior. As police investigators quickly discovered, she was selling sex for cash, marijuana, and cigarettes.

Denise, who turned eighteen not long after Amber's slaying, soon became the focus of Deere's investigation. She had a lengthy list of clients who needed to be tracked down, but Deere was particu-

---

*Not her real name.

larly interested in learning more about a violent incident that might be related to the killing. Just five days before Amber's murder, her foster sister had reported having been raped.

According to Denise, she had been walking home from a friend's house at about 8:00 p.m. on August 17 when she was pulled into some bushes by a man wielding a knife. After forcing her to the ground and threatening to kill her, the man sexually assaulted her. "I almost died in the dark, all alone, in the grass somewhere," she told sex-offense investigators a few hours after the assault. She initially denied selling herself to the man, but investigators were well aware of her background and suspected that she was lying about what had happened.

Soon after Amber's murder, Deere talked with the sex-offense investigators who had interviewed Denise. They expressed considerable doubt about the teenager's story: under questioning, Denise had changed several details of her account, and by the end she'd decided that she didn't want to report the crime. The investigators came away from the interview feeling somewhat skeptical that a rape had taken place; their guess was that a client had probably refused to pay and brandished a knife when Denise got angry.

Deere came to a different conclusion. Early on in their investigation of Amber's murder, Deere and Crowell interviewed Denise and felt she was being honest about the rape. Though she admitted to selling sex for money, she was persuasive when swearing that she had not filed a false report to punish a client who'd refused to pay. The detectives inspected several cuts and small bruises on her arms, knees, legs, and hands, physical evidence that corroborated her description of struggling with a man threatening her with a knife. And Deere took note of two other salient facts: not only had her attacker used a condom, he'd also worn gloves, despite the summer heat. He had seemed to go out of his way to make sure that he didn't leave any forensic clues behind—behavior that was hardly typical of a random trick gone bad.

Ever since learning of the assault, Deere had been guided by the wisdom of a former sergeant: "There are no coincidences in homicides." Though Deere believed that his victim had not played a role in her own demise, her foster sister was a prostitute who had been raped a few days before the murder. The investigator's suspicion that the sexual assault and the murder were connected gained credence as detectives learned more about Denise's actions in the days after the rape. Soon after the assault, she had taken to Facebook to taunt her assailant, at one point writing, "ALL I GOTTA SAY IS LET ANOTHER PERSON HIT ME OR TRY TO. ITS GOING DOWN! BECAUSE NIGGAS COMING OUTSIDE WITH KITCHEN KNIVES AND BLACK GLOVES, NIGGA I WILL GET YOUR ASS SHOT!"

Given that Denise was displaying such bravado on the Internet, her attacker could have concluded that she'd also talked to the police about the rape. To Deere, that suggested a motive for shooting Denise, which in turn suggested that Amber Stanley could have been slain in error. Now Deere had a scenario that seemed plausible: desperate to stop Denise from talking further to the police or broadcasting details of the rape on social media, the rapist had gone to Denise's house, kicked down the front door in a fury, and shot the young woman standing in the hallway. As he'd watched Amber run up the stairs, he might or might not have realized that he had shot the wrong girl. To Deere, it didn't matter: the killer had to finish what he'd started, so he'd followed Amber up to her room and murdered her in her bed.

As Deere dug into the details of Denise's rape in the days following Amber's murder, he came across an intriguing piece of evidence: after the assault, a small spot of blood had been discovered on Denise's shirt. The attacker had been careful, but Deere wondered if perhaps he had been cut during the encounter. Though the detective scoured the reports, he found no mention of Denise having been injured beyond scratches and bruises—certainly nothing that would explain the spot of blood. Further confirmation came from the injuries he and Crowell had noted when inspecting Denise's extremities: none were terribly serious, though they were extensive enough to convince Deere that they corroborated her story of fending off an attacker.

In mid-October, Deere received the DNA test results on the blood and learned that it had indeed been spilled by a man. Now Deere believed he'd found another piece of the puzzle, a deduction that Denise would later confirm: during the assault, the teenager had wrestled the knife away from her assailant long enough to turn it on him. If the detective could locate the man whose DNA matched the blood found on Denise's shirt, he might also have Amber's killer.

That fall, Deere pursued a number of leads and theories, but none pointed to a likely suspect for either Amber's killer or Denise's rapist. Then, in early December, Deere got the tip that led him to Jeff Buck. A Maryland State Police detective told Deere that one of his informants had pinned Amber's murder on a gang operating near her neighborhood. Actually, "gang" was too strong a term—as Deere came to understand, the crew was a loose-knit group of hoodlums, drug users, and marijuana dealers who chilled on porches and in parks, smoked lots of their own product, and committed crimes ranging from breaking into cars to armed robberies. Jeff Buck was the group's leader; a street tough whose criminal record included arrests on such charges as drug distribution and assault, Buck was known by the police to be a marijuana hustler. The informant said that Buck had raped Denise and ordered a friend, his gang's enforcer, to silence her. After the killing, the gunman had supposedly fled to California.

This lead seemed especially promising. Not only were the informant's details specific, but Deere was able to establish that Denise had frequently hung out with the gang's members, putting her in close proximity to the new suspects. Deere would have liked to interview Denise about Jeff Buck and his gang, but for the moment that wasn't possible. Earlier that fall, she had been whisked out of town and placed in a residential mental-health facility in the Midwest. Access to her was severely restricted: no calls in, no calls out, and very few visitors. Deere hoped he'd get the chance to speak with Denise at some point, but in the meantime he turned his attention to Buck and his crew.

Just before Christmas, Deere and Crowell went hunting. First they found the alleged triggerman, Buck's enforcer. Though he denied killing Amber, the man acknowledged having traveled to California in the weeks after the murder—an unwitting confirmation of information provided by the informant. After only a little prodding, the enforcer provided a DNA sample. Several weeks later, Deere learned that the sample didn't match the blood on Denise's shirt—hardly surprising, since the informant had said the shooter had played no role in the rape. By this point, Deere knew that the only way to find out whether the enforcer was involved was to question the man who'd supposedly ordered the hit.

Deere spent a good part of January learning everything he could about Buck's history and his current operations. The detective was particularly eager to get his suspect's cell-phone records, since they would provide a trove of details about his daily activities. When the records finally landed on Deere's desk, he went straight to the information about Buck's calls on August 22. Suddenly the new lead looked even better: the records showed that Buck's phone was in Amber's neighborhood at the time of the murder.

SITTING ACROSS FROM Buck, Deere jots an occasional note as he listens to the suspect talk about his friends in Amber's neighborhood, including Denise. He's glad Buck has fessed up to knowing the foster sister—he thought he might have to waste time pressing Buck to admit that he was friends with, or at least an acquaintance of, the teen. As the interrogation rolls on, Deere and Crowell ask Buck for more details about his relationship with Denise.

"She was loose," Buck says, shrugging. He explains that another neighborhood girl had approached him and asked if he would pay fifty dollars to have sex with Denise. He is friends with the pimp's boyfriend, who drives an unlicensed taxi and gives Buck rides in exchange for gas money. Deere jots down the information—two more people to track down.

"She wanted to sell her body or something," Buck adds. "All I know is that it's beneath me. I would never pay for no pussy."

Crowell chuckles. "Oh, you pay for it."

"Huh?"

"You are paying for it," Crowell says, winking.

After a moment, Buck gets the joke, but he barely cracks a smile. "In a way," he replies, "but I'm not putting a dime in her pocket. I might pay for dinner or something of that sort. I feel like I'm showing a female a good time. But I don't put money in her pocket."

Changing tack, Deere asks Buck whether he chills out at a house that has a recording studio in the basement. It is a well-known hangout; Deere would love to search it and guesses he would find guns or drugs. Buck acknowledges spending time in the studio; he says he's cut a song there and hopes to produce another one that will earn him $2 million.

Deere pivots again, asking in a friendly way whether Buck and his friends enjoy "the purple drink," a combination of Sprite and strong cough syrup that for some reason is consumed separately, in two cups.

"I'm going to put my beer in two cups so people think I'm drinking the purple drink," Deere jokes, hoping to set Buck further at ease.

The banter has the opposite effect. Buck's eyes narrow; he looks up at the wall as if to find a clock and check the time, but there is no clock in the box. He is clearly annoyed by these two uncool detectives trying to be hip. They can't even pronounce the name of the drink right: on the street, it sounds like "purple drank."

"How much longer am I going to be here?" Buck asks. "I have some things I have to—"

"You are going to be here a minute," Deere interrupts, his voice harder now.

Bearing down, Deere begins questioning Buck about the murder. For the most part, the suspect deflects and evades, though he does provide what Deere considers helpful insights. He says he originally believed that the foster sister was the one killed. A week or two before the murder, Buck says, Denise had told him that "somebody had tried to rape her, or did rape her when she was walking home."

Crowell asks Buck what else Denise said about the assault.

"She got to running and he got to grabbing her and she was fighting back," Buck replied. "She thought the person was going to kill her, and she let him take it. After it was over, the nigga was like, 'You shouldn't be walking out this late at night because people out here like me are going to get you.'"

"He had a knife?" asks Deere.

"Yeah."

"Where did she say it happened?"

"On the way home."

"Did she always walk by herself?" Crowell asks.

"Yeah, she was always by herself."

"Did you ever walk her home?" Deere asks.

Buck shakes his head; then he says that because the girl wore such skimpy clothes, she deserved what she got.

"You told her that?" Crowell asks.

"No. I was thinking it. I'm not that coldhearted a person."

Deere purses his lips, thinking, *Oh really?* Then he asks, "Did you ever talk about it after that, since the murder?"

"No."

Deere is quiet for a moment. He considers asking Buck more

questions about Denise but instead decides to focus on the murder, hoping to learn more about what Buck knows or is trying to hide.

"What's the rumor on the street about what happened—what does everyone think happened to her?" Deere asks casually. He leans back in his chair, his hands clasped on top of his head, as if the question is unimportant.

"Who?"

"The girl who got killed."

"Somebody came in," Buck says, "and shot her in the face."

FIFTEEN MINUTES LATER, after deciding to leave Buck alone in the box for a bit, the two detectives are huddled in the alcove just outside the back door of the Criminal Investigation Division's wing of police headquarters. Puffing on cigarettes, they plot their next angle of attack.

The police headquarters building is located in Palmer Park, a working-class neighborhood just inside the Beltway and south of bustling Route 202, about nine miles northeast of the U.S. Capitol. A former middle school, the building was renovated in the late 1980s to house the headquarters and one of the county's six district-level police stations. In recent years, the building has fallen into disrepair: wires hang from ceilings, and the interior walls are painted a mishmash of yellow and grayish brown, a shade one detective likened to "faded manila envelope." The headquarters's exterior is beige, and in several places it is smeared with a substance that resembles tar or tire streaks. Here and there, fist-sized chunks of the wall are missing.

Deere, Crowell, and the other detectives could smoke standing outside the front door, but that would afford them no privacy, given the steady stream of sex and gun offenders reporting to the department to be included on public registries. There's also the ever-present danger of getting splattered by the droppings that rain down from the gang of birds that roost in the awning above the entrance. Thus the small alcove behind the building is where much of the department's work gets done, in a haze of cigarette smoke and bullshit.

At 2:40 p.m., as Deere and Crowell are having a smoke, their sergeant, Joe Bergstrom, slips out the double doors. Thrusting his hands into his pants pockets, the slight, bald fifty-year-old paces inside the alcove, occasionally kicking at a wind-blown pile of dead leaves. On the force since 1990, Bergstrom spent eleven years investigating homicides before being promoted to sergeant. He has led Deere's five-detective squad since June.

The squad's moniker is M-40. Like the other four homicide squads, Bergstrom's is identified by the letter *M*, and a number that's a multiple of ten. Each squad has its own personality: M-10 is the ultra-serious student who always sits in the front row; M-20 is the grumpy uncle; M-30 is the goofball; M-90 is the poet. And to Bergstrom's never-ending frustration, M-40 is the class clown. Like cut-ups in high-school biology class, the four senior detectives in M-40 sit next to one another in the squad room's last row, their backs to the concrete wall. Boisterous, ill-mannered, and overly fond of bad jokes and annoying pranks, the squad's behavior is a constant source of irritation to the other detectives in the cramped homicide office.

Because of his low-key, by-the-book manner, Bergstrom was tapped to take over the M-40 squad; the commanders figured he might be able to keep the rowdy detectives in check. Bergstrom's days as an investigator are behind him—in many police departments, sergeants are assigned homicides, but in PG County they mostly fulfill administrative functions. Their job is to get detectives the resources they need, process pay slips, sooth fragile egos, and make sure investigations don't get screwed up. As the command staff has taken an ever greater interest in the Amber Stanley murder, Bergstrom has been keeping closer tabs on his investigators' lines of inquiry. But he rarely intrudes; he knows they are working hard and doing all they can.

While Bergstrom paces and kicks at the pile of leaves, Deere and Crowell continue smoking and talking about their interrogation of Jeff Buck.

"Nobody knows she was shot in the face," Crowell says.

"Unless he was in her bedroom," says Bergstrom.

"I don't know," Deere says, crossing his arms against the cold and thinking hard about Buck's comment. "I—I have heard that before from someone, I think."

Deere has been so deluged by reports and interview summaries that he finds it difficult to recall whether anyone else talked about Amber Stanley's wounds with such specificity. Publicity and rumor can ruin an investigation, especially in a case as big as this one. Commanders, politicians, reporters, columnists—all have opined on the murder, making it impossible for detectives in the age of social media to keep track of what was said about the crime, when it was said, and whether it is true. In the old days, a detective merely collected copies of the articles that ran in the *Washington Post,* the *Washington Times,* and the local weeklies; with those in hand, he could feel reasonably sure that there was only one way a suspect could know an unreported detail: he had been at the scene.

Deere and Crowell talk a bit about Buck's demeanor—tough, not too helpful—and agree that they need to advise him of his rights while hoping that he waives them and continues to talk. That outcome is far from assured: Buck is smart and has had extensive dealings with the criminal justice system, so he knows how the game is played.

"Getting him to waive will be a real challenge," Crowell concedes.

"Yeah, it will be," says Deere. "I'm not saying he doesn't have rights, but I need him to talk. I need him to say something. Even if he doesn't waive, we should keep him talking."

As Deere knows, he can continue questioning a suspect even after he declines to speak with investigators, as long as the interview is clearly voluntary. Though statements made during these conversations are barred from being introduced during a prosecutor's case at trial, they can still be helpful to the police.

"He knows something," says Crowell.

"I *need* something," says Deere.

The doors crack open and out pops Joe Bunce's basketball-sized head. Wearing a wide smile, Bunce looks around until he spots Crowell.

"Mike, your wife called," Bunce says.

Crowell frowns. "What did she say?"

"Not much. I told her I would swing by for that booty call because you can't make it," Bunce answers, laughing.

"Shit," says Crowell. "What did you really say?"

"I said you were in the interview room."

"What did she say?"

"She said, 'Okay.' "

"That's it?"

"Yeah."

"She seem annoyed?"

"Yeah. She seemed kind of pissed."

"*Shit,*" Crowell says, slapping a fist into his palm.

"Sorry, Mike," says Bunce, his head vanishing back through the door.

Crowell laughs. "Well, I won't be getting any ass tonight."

"No, you won't," says Deere.

Bergstrom grins at Crowell's frustration, kicks a dry leaf, and follows Bunce inside.

Deere flicks his cigarette butt onto the ground and says, "Let's hope he gives us his phone and the DNA."

"He will," says Crowell.

"I really need him to talk," Deere says.

Crowell takes a last drag, tosses the butt to the ground, and enters the building.

Before following Crowell inside, Deere lingers for a moment, staring at the gray sky, thinking: *I need something.*


NINETY MINUTES LATER, Deere has something: after another round of questioning, Jeff Buck agreed to voluntarily give up his DNA and his cell phone. It's a big victory, but it's not everything. Despite their best efforts, Deere and Crowell failed to get their suspect to waive, though he seemed to leave the door open for further questioning. When Buck asks to use the bathroom and smoke a cigarette, Deere agrees, hoping a new venue will encourage Buck to decide to provide a statement after all. If he does, Deere is confident that a judge would conclude that Buck had had sufficient time to think over his initial refusal before changing his mind and waiving his rights.

Deere and Crowell escort Buck into the bathroom. They would never allow a suspect to take a piss alone.

"I feel like my time is being wasted here," Buck says, standing at a dingy urinal. He looks over his right shoulder at Deere, who is propping the bathroom door open with his foot. Crowell stands just behind Buck's left shoulder.

"We're doing stuff," says Deere, unable to contain the frustration in his voice.

"We are trying to figure out who did this," says Crowell. "What if you did it? What if you had something to do with it?"

Buck points out that he didn't run when Deere confronted him earlier that afternoon. "You never would have had a chance to stop me if I did," he says.

"You haven't seen this guy run," Crowell says, jerking a thumb in Deere's direction.

"Who, him?" Buck says.

"He's an Olympic track star," Crowell deadpans.

Buck's eyes trace Deere's less-than-impressive physique from foot to head. "Nah," he says, grinning. After zipping his fly, he strides toward the door, a cocky roll to his gait.

Deere puts up a hand; he doesn't like the swagger. "Wash your hands," he says, nodding toward the sink.

After Buck has finished, Deere directs him out the door, saying, "Okay, let's go smoke."

The detectives walk across the hall and steer their suspect through a rusty steel door posted with a sign that reads, NO SMOK-ING, EFFECTIVE 2-20-94. A dusty former evidence bay, the room is now used for storage and cigarette breaks. It's filled with decrepit decades-old filing cabinets, boxes of records from the Financial Crimes Unit, and several broken chairs. The air is stale, but it also carries a slight scent of death; after a brief search, Deere spots a decomposing bird between two stacks of boxes. Most likely the bird entered through a faulty ventilation shaft and was unable to escape.

Buck sits in a rolling chair while the two detectives alternately pace in small circles and lean casually against the filing cabinets. Deere and Crowell often bring suspects into this semi-secure room; smoking sessions can sometimes be critical components of interrogations. They ease tension, reward suspects for cooperating, and allow detectives to engage in off-the-record banter that might prove helpful later, during the taped interrogation.

"All I'm saying, if I did something wrong, I wouldn't have answered any of your questions," Buck says, removing a Newport from his jacket pocket. He lights it and takes a drag as Deere and Crowell puff on their own cigarettes. The room quickly fills with an acrid haze.

"We're just trying to get to the bottom of it," says Crowell.

"We are talking to lots of people," says Deere, staring down at Buck.

"I don't know anything," Buck says.

Deere wants to learn more about what Buck was doing on the night of the murder. Earlier in the interrogation, Crowell asked Buck how he'd spent the evening of August 22; Buck replied that he thought he'd spent it with some "lady friends." Now Deere asks again: who was he hanging out with that night? Buck thinks hard before responding and then says he was chilling with a girl, hanging out at a friend's house, or smoking weed in a park. He names the park; it is located just to the east of the dead girl's subdivision. Deere pushes a bit about the friend, and Buck responds by saying that in fact he's pretty sure he was hanging out with him. He gives the detectives his friend's name and address; like the park, the house is not far from Amber Stanley's neighborhood.

Not wanting to press too hard in this informal setting, Deere decides to move the conversation toward lighter topics. Crowell picks up on the tactic, and soon the three men are chatting about the neighborhood, basketball, the Redskins, and the upcoming Super Bowl. Deere and Crowell talk in circles, leading Buck away from the murder and then returning to it.

After a while, Buck seems to forget that he is being interrogated and begins talking freely about the neighborhood drug trade. Deere takes advantage of the opening and asks him about the alleged triggerman, the friend and enforcer suspected of killing Amber Stanley.

Buck nods and then smiles; he seems to be enjoying himself. He mentions that he heard a rumor that the enforcer had killed the girl. "I even asked him about it, and he said he heard the same thing."

Deere and Crowell are stunned. Is Buck really passing along a rumor, or is he trying to cover up something by claiming it's a rumor? Or perhaps the cigarette break has lowered his defenses and he's providing a partial confession.

"Why didn't you tell us that before?" Crowell asks. "We talked about this! You ain't fucking dumb."

"You were being an asshole," Buck replies, glaring at Crowell. "And you didn't ask me."

"We have to ask you precisely the right question?" Deere asks, frustrated.

Leaning back in his chair, Buck smiles again and says nothing.

"I just want you to do the right thing," Deere says. "I need to know these things."

"I'm letting you get my DNA, the swab thing, and even letting you go through my phone," Buck says. "What else do you want from me?"

"I need to know what happened," says Deere. "I need the truth."

Buck shrugs and holds his palms up in the air. The detectives stare at him in silence, finish their cigarettes, and wait for Buck to take his last draw.

When their suspect flicks his butt to the floor, Deere taps him on the left shoulder. "Let's go," he says.

Buck slowly rises from the chair. The detectives escort him back to Interview Room 2 and lock the door after him. For the next hour or so, they will let him stew.


By 6:45, Deere and Crowell agree it's time to press Buck hard. The games are over: they're convinced that Buck knows something. He may have actually played a role in the rape or the murder, but at the very least has heard things on the street.

Back in the box, Deere sits down next to Buck, and Crowell takes the chair across the table. They start in on him right away, hoping to throw their suspect off balance, asking him again and again about his whereabouts the previous night and earlier this morning. Buck continues to claim he was with a friend and his baby's momma. The detectives don't believe him but can't shake his story.

Shifting gears, Crowell asks Buck about a friend of Denise's named David Norris* who works as a grocery clerk. On the night of the rape, Denise said she had been attacked after leaving Norris's house; at the hospital, she told a nurse that she had been assaulted while "walking home from a friend's house, or at least I thought he was a friend." The statement suggested that Denise was angry at Norris, perhaps because he had played some role in the rape. Early on, Deere had speculated that Norris might have pimped for Denise and arranged a trick with Buck; it was even possible that the assault had occurred in his house. And in mid-January, when Deere finally got Buck's cell-phone records, his interest in the grocery clerk was piqued further: the records showed nearly a dozen calls between Buck and Norris in the days before and after the rape and murder.

But now, when asked about Norris, Buck says he never hung out with him, barely knows him, and certainly never called him.

Crowell shakes his head; he places a set of cell-phone records on the table and points to a column of numbers. "Outgoing, from your number to his number," Crowell says.

Buck leans over and looks at the records. "Someone else probably used my phone."

Crowell points out that Buck told them earlier that his phone had never left his possession. Growing stern, Crowell says, "These records don't lie. We have discredited some of your stuff. And we are going to keep discrediting your stuff."

Someone knocks on the interview room's door, and a moment later Joe Bunce enters and hands a stack of papers to Crowell. Bunce tells his colleagues that he's been reviewing the complete phone records and looking for other calls between Buck and Norris. "There are tons of calls," Bunce says.

"You want to keep doing this, man?" Crowell asks, leaning across the table and staring hard at Buck.

---

*Not his real name.

"Oh, my man, I have gotten myself in some shit," Buck mutters.

"You did, buddy," Crowell says. "We have come to a fork in the road. You are at the point where you are going to possibly affect the rest of your life. This is way bigger than calling someone. Do you know what we are investigating?"

"A real live murder," Buck says, sounding resigned.

Crowell nods; Deere leans forward in his chair.

"You told us some shit, and we proved it wrong," Crowell says. "Don't play with us."

Crowell and Buck spend several minutes arguing back and forth about the calls and their meaning. Clearly perturbed that someone would suggest that he was buddies with the grocery clerk, Buck insists that he was only returning Norris's calls, never initiating them. Ultimately he admits that Norris was calling him because he wanted to smoke marijuana and Buck knew how to get it for him.

"So, you hooked him up?" asks Deere.

"That's basically all it was," he replies. "I just know where to go get it."

*Bullshit,* thinks Deere. He is all but certain that Buck is actually Norris's drug supplier.

"You have me nervous as shit in here," Buck says, his tone increasingly anxious.

Deere exchanges a glance with Crowell, who picks up the cue. It's time to drop their best piece of evidence: the records showing that on the night of the murder, Buck's phone was in Amber Stanley's neighborhood, not in his normal hangout a bit farther north. The records also revealed that he was speaking to his enforcer, as well as two other men, just before and after the homicide. The detectives know that phone location data can be misleading: it's possible that Buck was merely driving through the area or sitting in the park smoking weed when the tower grabbed his cell signal, but they won't tell Buck that.

"Let me show you something, son," Crowell says. Pulling out a map that displays an icon of a cell tower and an outlined, cone-shaped area, he explains that the cone indicates where Buck's phone was located on the night of the murder.

After using a pen to draw a circle around Amber Stanley's neighborhood, Crowell says, "Your cell phone is in this area at the time of the murder. How do you explain that?"

Buck becomes confused about which neighborhoods appear on the map, so Deere stands up and begins pointing out the various roads and landmarks.

"I might have been there," Buck says, gesturing to an area outside the cone.

"You couldn't have been," says Crowell. "Do I think for a second you pulled the trigger in this house? No. Do I think you have some involvement in this? Absolutely."

"I don't even know what I'm looking at," Buck says, becoming agitated. "This is crazy."

"It is," Crowell says.

"You are trying to get me to lie. I ain't going to go like that."

"Then explain it to us," says Deere.

"You tell me my phone is hitting here," Buck says angrily. "I don't remember what I was doing at the time of the murder." Yelling now, he argues with the detectives about the names of towns on the map, in an attempt to prove that he wasn't in Amber Stanley's neighborhood on the night she was killed.

Finally Buck takes a deep breath and leans back in his chair. "This don't make no sense," he says.

"How would you spell this out logically?" Deere asks.

"I really think I'm going to go down for a murder," Buck says, his tone a mix of resignation and exasperation.

"He just said he doesn't think you are the one who pulled the trigger or nothing like that," Deere notes, as calmly as possible. His hope is that Buck will point the finger at someone else. If he can get his suspect to snitch on his enforcer, he'll be snitching on himself, too.

But Buck won't take the bait. Soon the interrogation devolves into another sparring match over town locations and postal designations on the map. At one point Crowell uses his pen to point to the area where Buck's cell phone pinged off a tower. "There is no question you are here," the detective says.

"I don't care if you believe me or not," Buck replies.

"Tell the truth," Crowell says.

Buck is silent for a moment, and then his face contorts in anger. Deere sees immediately that he's had enough.

The suspect thrusts his chair back against the wall. "You are blowing me!" he yells. "I'm trying to answer your shit, and you are blowing me. I'm not answering any more questions. Get the fuck out of my face. Take me to jail then. Prove it. Fuck it! Take me to jail!"

DEERE KNOWS HE can't hold Buck much longer, much less take him to jail. Eager to cool things off, he declares that it's time for another break. He and Crowell take Buck into the old evidence bay again, but this time Deere asks the squad's rookie, Jamie Boulden, to join them. Boulden has spent part of the past couple of hours watching the interrogation on a video monitor located in a closet-like space in the Homicide Unit that houses a number of computer servers.

Buck takes a seat on a swivel chair and looks down at the floor. Deere slumps into a hard plastic chair. Crowell is too fidgety to sit; instead he paces in circles while throwing a ball made of rubber bands against the wall. Boulden scoots a rolling chair up to Buck's knees and hands him one of his Newports; he knows it's Buck's brand, too. All four men light up and begin puffing. For a minute, the tired detectives and their suspect say nothing as they savor their cigarettes.

Boulden is acquainted with Jeff Buck from his days as a street cop patrolling the neighborhoods not too far from Amber Stanley's home. Earlier, during one of the interrogation's breaks, Boulden told Deere he would be happy to take a crack at the suspect, and now he has his chance. Right away it's clear that he and Buck have a mutual respect and rapport. Clad in a wrinkled, ill-fitting suit, Boulden casually crosses his right leg over his left, leans back in his chair, and reminisces with Buck about their epic foot chases, as if he were bullshitting about an old high school basketball rivalry.

Buck relaxes; he even laughs at a couple of Boulden's lines. But just when he starts arguing playfully with Boulden about his foot speed, the detective leans forward again and suddenly turns serious.

"This ain't about playing craps, and this ain't about selling drugs," Boulden says, sitting knee to knee with Buck and looking him straight in the eye. "This is about a fucking murder. We need to know where you were that night. No bullshit."

"I was smoking," Buck says, meaning he was getting high. "I don't know. Listen, I understand what you are trying to do."

"We want the truth," says Boulden.

"I told you the fucking truth," says Buck. "I am not making anything up."

When Boulden doesn't reply, Buck turns to his left and stares Deere down. Then he asks, "Where were you on September twenty-second?"

"Probably here," Deere replies.

"See, you don't know for sure. So how can I be sure about where I was on August twenty-second?"

*If I'd killed an honor roll student,* thinks Deere, *I'd know exactly where I was.*

For the next few minutes, all three detectives pepper their suspect with questions. They go round and round, rehashing the same questions raised earlier—questions about calls to and from the grocery clerk, the cell phone pinging off the tower the night of Amber's murder, Buck's friend passing along the gruesome rumor.

"We discredited your shit," says Crowell.

"Stop lying to us," says Deere. "We just want the truth."

"This ain't about drug dealing," Boulden points out again.

But Buck just shakes his head. "If you have me, take me to jail," he says, his voice flat now. "Just take me to jail."

"Doesn't work that way," says Deere. "Why would you want to go to jail?"

"Sleep—and I can watch ESPN."

Deere, taking a deep drag on his third cigarette, stretches his legs and rests them on an upside-down desk. Boulden leans back in his chair and stares at the white ceiling. Crowell fires the rubber-band ball against the wall.

*How do we keep him talking?* Deere wonders to himself.

"Listen, we know you didn't kill her," Deere says. "Maybe—"

"I'll take a lie detector," Buck interrupts. "Give me a test. I pass, and I can go home. Promise me I can go home if I pass it, and I'll take one."

The words strike the detectives like lightning. Deere takes his legs off the desk; Boulden leans forward in his chair; Crowell turns to Buck and flubs a rebound, the rubber-band ball falling to the floor and rolling under a cabinet.

Deere can't believe what he's just heard. *Did he just say that? Can we be that lucky?*

"Fuck it—I'll take a lie detector test," Buck says. "Give me one!"

"Sure, we can do that," says Deere. "We can do that right now."


DEERE BRISKLY ESCORTS Buck back to Interview Room 2, locks the door, and goes to find Joe Bunce.

Bunce, a stout forty-three-year-old former bartender with a receding crew cut, comes from a police family. His father was an air force investigator, his grandfather was a New York City police officer, and his younger twin brothers are also on the PG force. For the better part of his fifteen-year career, Bunce labored to reach the Homicide Unit, a goal he finally achieved about a year earlier. He is a solid investigator and a decent interrogator, but he is truly gifted at mining computer databases for clues. He's also been trained to use the Computer Voice Stress Analyzer and has more experience with the technology than anyone else in the squad.

Not fifteen minutes after Buck's unexpected request, Bunce is sitting across from the suspect in the box. Bunce pulls a laptop from a bag and places it on the table, attaches a microphone cord to the laptop, and clips the microphone to Buck's shirt, explaining that the device is a "next-generation" lie detector; it works by measuring stress in a person's voice as he answers yes-or-no questions.

Because lie detector results are not admissible in court, the detectives mostly use the machine to try to scare people into telling the truth. Its success depends on a detective's ability to sell its infallibility, and Bunce is a very good salesman.

"This machine is one hundred percent," Bunce tells Buck. "It does not fuck up."

Once Bunce has loaded the appropriate program into the computer, he begins asking Buck basic questions. Is this the month of February? Is today Friday? Bunce tells Buck to lie in response to queries about his name and his birthdate, to help calibrate the machine. Then come the real questions.

"Did you kill Amber Stanley?" Bunce asks.

"No," Buck says.

"Do you know who killed Amber Stanley?"

"No."

"Do you suspect someone of killing Amber Stanley?"

"No."

After running through the same questions a second time, the

detective takes a minute to study the results displayed on the laptop's monitor. He sighs dramatically and shakes his head.

Buck is leaning forward across the table, eager to learn the results.

Bunce swivels the laptop around so Buck can see the monitor. He points to one of its fourteen charts.

"This is what the truth looks like: up and down like a Christmas tree," Bunce says. Using a finger, the detective traces the graph's jagged lines, which rise sharply to a peak before abruptly descending.

Buck nods.

"See, this is what it looks like when you lie," Bunce continues, pointing to a second graph, this one depicting one of Buck's intentional lies. It resembles the jagged hairdo of the cartoon character Bart Simpson.

Buck nods again, but he's becoming wary.

Bunce scans the remaining charts and purses his lips. He points to another jagged graph. "That looks like a lie, too," he says, shaking his head sadly. "I can already tell that something is not right here."

"What question is this?" Buck asks, pointing to a third jagged graph.

Bunce swivels the laptop to better see the image. He frowns. Then he leans forward and stares Buck in the eye.

"'Do you know who killed Amber Stanley?'"

# · CHAPTER 2 ·

Bracing his shoulders against a stinging wind, Detective Eddie Flores slams shut his car door. He walks fifty yards across worn grass and past three barren trees, then slips under police tape and takes his place at the head of the corpse. The sky is overcast and the neighborhood is quiet, except for the distant, riverlike rush of highway traffic whispering through a copse of trees.

Flores scans the scene, a community park, from left to right. He notes a picnic table, a barbecue stand, several green trash cans, and a plastic and metal playground set. He surveys the landscape again, hoping to spot a security camera. Nothing.

The investigator steps to his right and greets Wayne Martin, the first detective at the scene. A nine-year veteran of the Homicide Unit, Martin is cool and low-key; he's been to dozens of scenes like this one. Blowing into his hands, Martin turns and nods at Flores. His eyes missing nothing, he quickly assesses the twenty-eight-year-old rookie, who joined the unit only three weeks earlier.

Outwardly, Flores appears professional and ready. His ears are protected by a black headband, and not a single strand of his carefully coifed dark hair is out of place. His hands are casually thrust into the pockets of a black overcoat, known among the detectives as a "murder coat," and his steno pad is jammed expertly under his right arm. He looks as if he, too, has done this many times before.

But Martin sees it right away: the nervousness, the fear. It's there in Flores's eyes. They look as big as half-dollars, and they are dancing. Martin decides to take it easy: no jokes. This is Flores's first murder, after all.

"You have a whole lot of nothing right now, buddy," Martin tells the rookie. "A black male with apparent head trauma."

Flores drops his gaze to the dead man at his feet. Lying faceup on bloodstained dirt, the victim is a slight man clad in a black sweatshirt and blue jeans. His face is caked with drying blood that must have gushed from his nose and mouth; his left eye is bulbous, as though swollen from a vicious punch. A half-open right eye stares into the steel sky. Flores feels a pressing weight on his shoulders— he had not expected the intensity, or the intimacy, of this moment. Realizing that he is about to begin an investigation into the violent death of a human being, he suddenly imagines the victim's sobbing mother.

*Fuck,* he thinks. *This is no training exercise. This is a real murder.*

Shaking the vision from his head, Flores swivels to check the park's access road for the maroon Impala driven by his veteran partner, Jeff Eckrich, who is on his way to the scene from the Eastern Shore of the Chesapeake Bay. Attracted by the relatively inexpensive real estate and the distance from their day jobs—"You don't want to eat where you shit," one detective explained—eleven of Eckrich's neighbors are in local or federal law enforcement. But having a large house, a pool, and a nice yard on a cop's salary in the DC region comes with a trade-off: an hour-long commute over the traffic-clogged Bay Bridge. At rush hour, it can take two.

*Where are you, Jeff?* Flores wonders. *Hurry up, man.*

Flores doesn't want to be alone when his hulking, gritty-as-a-rusty-nail sergeant appears. Sergeant Kerry Jernigan is not only gruff, he truly understands the job, having spent fifteen years as a homicide investigator before being promoted to the supervisory position in December. Flores knows he cannot snow Jernigan.

"The body was found by a guy walking his dog," Flores hears Martin saying, and the rookie again focuses on the corpse at his feet. "The guy says he's out here every day. There were no reports of gunfire, and no witnesses. No ID on the victim, or of him, as far as we can tell. We haven't rolled him yet, obviously, so he might still have something in a back pocket."

*Crap,* thinks Flores, *a John Doe in the park.*

There's a good chance the body was dumped, in which case the actual murder scene is elsewhere, possibly trampled or torched, like the car from the murder his partner caught in July. Given the early hour, Flores's victim was probably killed or discarded in darkness, perhaps during the Super Bowl, which had been played the night before. This increases the odds that there are no witnesses: who in his right mind would be spending time outside, hanging around in the cold in this dangerous neighborhood in the middle of the night? For a moment, Flores wonders if the dead man might be a San Francisco 49ers fan who lost a bet—the Baltimore Ravens won the tight game, which included a freakish power outage.

Unlikely, Flores decides, but then again, this park, Oxon Run, is in the northern corner of Hillcrest Heights, a 2.4-square-mile patch of violence on the DC line. The neighborhood recorded four homicides the previous year, plus scores of other violent crimes. Any motive was possible.

Flores should be groggy, exhausted even. He and Eckrich are in the midst of a seven-day tour on the midnight shift, and the rookie had just climbed into bed when his cell phone rang with the news of this killing. But Flores is wired, running on first-case adrenaline, and he is eager to get started.

A moment later, he sees Sergeant Jernigan's Impala sweep down Oxon Run Drive, pull onto the park's access road, and roll into the lot. *Fuck,* Flores thinks. *Hurry up, Jeff. Hurry up.*

As if in answer to Flores's silent plea, Eckrich's maroon cruiser tears down the access road and comes to a hard stop next to Jernigan's car. The investigators get out of their Chevys and shake hands. The two men chat for a moment before Eckrich makes a beeline for his rookie partner, while the bearlike Jernigan lumbers to the outer edge of the crime scene. Flores feels an intense jolt of respect for his new boss, who as a detective openly disdained meddlesome supervisors. In taking his place next to a nearby tree, Jernigan is sending a clear message: *I'm not going to intrude, but I'm here if you need me.*

Eckrich ducks under the tape and comes to a stop a foot from Flores's left side. The veteran detective is PG's version of Joe Friday—utterly ordinary, a forty-one-year-old of average height and weight, with a round face and thick black hair speckled with gray. Clad, like Flores, in a black overcoat, Eckrich sighs, creating a plume of condensation. He rubs his burning eyes; he has done the job for too long to be energized by a case, even a big one, and he is exhausted from the midnight shift. Actually, his fatigue runs much deeper: he hasn't slept well in years due to a mangled back, which he injured in 2005 in an on-duty car crash. To make it through each day, Eckrich consumes at least a half dozen Coca-Colas; he has already chugged two bottles on the drive to the scene.

"How's it going, Eddie?" he says, smiling wanly. "That sure was a great night of sleep, right?"

Flores grins but quickly reaffixes his "case face," a serious expression worn by all the unit's detectives when working a crime scene. Nobody wants to get caught by a news photographer smiling over a corpse—not that there are any television cameras or newspaper photographers recording the first minutes of this investigation. Though reporters were told about the discovery of a body when they made their morning checks, the department's PR office has not disclosed that police suspect the man was murdered, creating enough ambiguity to keep inquisitive journalists away.

"Like I was telling you, I always get my cases on midnights," Eckrich says, shaking his head. "Fucking midnights." Eckrich, who has been a member of the unit since 2008, has caught at least four murders on the graveyard shift.

Feeling more confident now that Eckrich is here, Flores watches his partner step closer to the corpse and bend down as far as his sore back will allow.

"Shit, Eddie—you see how it looks like he was making a snow angel?" he says, pointing to winglike patterns in the dirt near the man's arms. "That means he had a very slow, painful death."

Flores nods, his mind conjuring an image of the man's arms flapping as he died.

"It looks like he was kicking the dirt, too," Eckrich observes.

Flores sees that the soil around the victim's feet has been disturbed; his right sneaker has come off and lies on the ground a few inches away. Flores speculates that the man got into a fight and lost.

"Probably got bashed in the head," Eckrich says, studying the swollen eye.

"Jesus," says Flores.

Eckrich tells the county's evidence technicians to "bag the guy's hands"—the killer's skin or DNA might be under his fingernails. Next he summons the state medical examiner's forensic investigator to roll the body to see what is under it and to inventory the dead man's pockets before she carts him away to the morgue.

As the investigator begins her work, Eckrich leans to his right and inspects Flores's empty notebook. "Write down what he was wearing, his exact tattoos, who the forensic investigator is, and who the lead evidence technician is," Eckrich says.

Flores jots a description of the scene, noting that the man is lying faceup and is clad in a black hooded sweatshirt, a Blue Jays ball cap, blue jeans, red socks, and Nike Air shoes.

The forensic investigator—a tiny woman in her mid-forties wearing latex gloves and a thick black jacket over her gray ME polo shirt—lifts up the man's sweatshirt. After recording the fact that his victim is also wearing a white undershirt and a gray T-shirt, Flores leans closer to the corpse to better read a tattoo scrawled across the man's stomach. "Departed But Still United" frames the number "1400."

The rookie mulls over its meaning and then says, "Probably a gang sign. Maybe the block he hung out at."

"Possible," says Eckrich.

Flores also spots a tattoo of a teardrop under the victim's left eye, often a memorial to a slain gang brother or the "tally mark" of a kill. Later, after the body is fully disrobed at the autopsy, he will learn that the man has two more tattoos on his arms: "Murder" and "ABK," which stands for "A Bloods Killer." Only a member of a serious gang would risk antagonizing the ultraviolent Bloods with such artwork.

The forensic investigator grabs the victim's left shoulder and hip and gently lifts the body toward Eckrich and Flores. As the man rolls over, Flores sees a bloody mess of dried leaves and prickly sweet-gum pods sticking to the back of his sweatshirt—and a nickel-sized hole at the base of his skull. Even Flores can tell that the large amount of blood on the ground strongly suggests his victim was killed, not dumped, here. And this was no fight: it was an execution.

"He's been shot," Eckrich says, a note of surprise in his voice. Turning to Flores, he says, "Make sure you write 'defect'—don't say gunshot wound or entrance wound if he looks like he's been shot. Just say 'defect.' "

Eckrich has already explained the importance of this to Flores:

you don't want to mistake an exit wound for an entrance wound in your notes. It will only cause problems if the case goes to trial. It's best to let the autopsy report speak for itself.

Flores dutifully writes, "Defect: rear of head."

The two detectives examine the bloody ground but see no shell casing. Either the man was shot with a revolver, which doesn't eject casings, or the killer picked up the casing before running. It's also more than possible that it has been trampled by responding officers and is now hidden under the park's detritus of leaves and seed pods. "Better sweep the area with a metal detector," Eckrich tells an evidence technician, who heads to her van to retrieve the equipment.

As Flores watches, the forensic investigator searches the man's clothing. She comes up empty except for a folded piece of paper that she plucks from the right rear pocket of his jeans. Gently cradling it in her gloved hand, she holds it out to the detectives.

Flores and Eckrich huddle over the paper, which is damp and seems to be smeared with bodily fluid. Flores is able to make out the words "www.coachusa.com" and what appears to be a reservation number.

*A bus ticket,* he thinks.

"Does it have a name?" Flores asks, watching eagerly as the investigator flips the paper back and forth.

"No," she says.

Flores sighs. He might as well have caught a pile of bones.

AFTER FINISHING HIS work at the murder scene, Flores drops by the nearby community center. With the help of the center's manager and another police officer, he quickly determines that the center's security cameras couldn't have caught anything that took place in the park; they aren't aimed at the right places. Flores gets in his Impala and cruises up and down Oxon Run Drive, which borders the park, hoping to find a house with security cameras aimed toward the street. On his third pass, he spots a camera under the awning of a house; in front of it is parked a colorfully decorated light blue van advertising a clown business.

The detective knocks on the door, which is answered by a cheerful black woman with blond highlights in her hair. "How can I help you?" she asks, tugging at the hem of her thick black-and-white striped sweater.

Flores explains his interest in her video footage. The woman says she installed the security system to ward off vandals targeting her van, which she uses in her work as a clown. A minute later, Flores follows her into a bedroom that is littered with piles of clothes and clown costumes.

As the woman clicks a computer keyboard and presses buttons on a remote control while trying to access the video monitor atop a dresser, Flores's eyes begin to water. A tear streaks down his left cheek. At first, he thinks fatigue has caught up to him. Then he feels something brush against his left leg. Looking down, he spots a large cat. It's an allergy attack.

*I can't catch a break,* he thinks.

"We'll have a crime-scene technician come pull the video," says Flores, fleeing the room and heading off to regroup with Eckrich and his squad's other investigators.

By 2:30 that afternoon, Flores, Eckrich, and Detective D. J. Windsor, a squad mate, are at the evidence lab, inspecting the piece of paper found in the dead man's pocket. It's a day-old receipt for a bus ticket from Raleigh, North Carolina, to Washington, DC. Windsor plugs the reservation number into the carrier's website, which he has loaded on his smartphone, but no personal information appears.

Flores and Eckrich yawn—they need rest before returning for the midnight shift, which starts at 11:00 p.m. But Flores insists they don't have time to sleep.

"It's going to be a marathon, Eddie, not a sprint," Eckrich says. "Remember, things will kick off tomorrow. You'll be begging for five minutes to do nothing. Cancel any plans you have for your private life for the rest of the week."

PG COUNTY'S HOMICIDE Unit is broken into five squads, each comprised of a sergeant and five detectives, and further into pairs of detectives. Though mathematics dictates that each squad has one loner—which can be an advantage, given the idiosyncratic personalities of some detectives—most investigators believe that it's better to be assigned a partner. Pairs of detectives can share duties, divide work by skill set, and cover for each other when one has to spend all day in court or take an hour's break to attend to some personal business. Over time, partners develop a keen sense for how their counterpart handles everything from interrogating a suspect to consoling a grieving mother.

Pairing detectives is particularly helpful when one is more experienced than the other, as in the case of Flores and Eckrich. A rookie detective can attend every training session offered by the department, but he will never understand the job until he shadows a veteran. Flores is thankful that he's been assigned such a good partner, someone truly interested in the craft of police work, an investigator who cares about getting things right and is willing to offer guidance and advice. After less than a month in homicide, Flores has already learned that not all detectives in the unit are so friendly or helpful.

The real test for any rookie comes when he catches his first murder. In other police departments, homicide detectives handle whatever murders happen to fall on their shifts, but some years ago PG County adopted a system to ensure that murders were evenly—and randomly—distributed among the investigators. It works just like a baseball batting lineup and cycles through all twenty-five detectives in the unit. At any one time, the officer due to take the next homicide is "at bat," the investigator behind him in line is "on deck," and the third on the list is "in the hole," their last names written on a dry-erase board next to the door to the unit's office. The next murder might be a smoker or a red ball; most detectives simply accept the unpredictable nature of their work and attribute the sequence of cases to fate, the homicide gods, or the random nature of life and death in a violent place like PG County.

Flores had been at bat for seven days when the call came and he learned that his first murder victim had fallen. Now, fifteen hours later, with the clock approaching midnight, he sits at his desk, facing Eckrich in the squad room's first row of workstations. Except for the two detectives, the room is empty; the evening shift has long since departed. Surprisingly, Flores and Eckrich feel somewhat rested. Flores went home, took a nap, had a shower, put on a new suit, and stuck his omnipresent Bluetooth headset into his right ear. Upon returning to work, he decided that he needed another nap and grabbed one in the driver's seat of his Impala in the headquarters's most remote parking lot. He tried to sleep longer, but his eager mind refused to relax.

The details of the case are still whirling in his head. He's trying to turn nothing into something, but he has no witnesses, no shell casings, no security video (the clown's feed proved useless), and no clues. He doesn't even have the victim's name. The one good piece of news is that he has been able to obtain an approximate time of the killing: two residents near the park reported hearing a single gunshot between 11:00 p.m. and midnight. They hadn't bothered to call 911, they told the police, because gunshots are so common in the neighborhood that they've become background noise.

Despite catching the new case, Flores and Eckrich get no respite from midnight duty. The unit's workload is too heavy. PG County's homicide detectives do much more than investigate murders: each year they respond to scores of suspicious deaths, suicides, and police shootings. Not infrequently, they have to waste valuable time investigating hoaxes involving text messages sent to strangers suggesting that someone has just buried a body. Up to a dozen of the unit's detectives work during the day and evening, but the midnight shift is handled by either a single detective or a pair of them.

While awaiting the shift's inevitable callout, Flores assembles his thin case file and inserts a few pages of notes into the left flap of the file's jacket. He types a "continuation report," a short synopsis that updates his progress on the case, and places that, as well as the 911 call logs, in another part of the file. When finished, he looks across the row of desks and spies Eckrich chugging a Coke.

"Jeff," Flores says. "What do I do now?"

"Nothing, brother." Until they pick up the victim's fingerprints from his corpse during the autopsy and run them through the FBI database, Eckrich says, they'll have to spin their wheels. Once they get a name, they'll have a place to start.

"Think about it this way," Eckrich says. "You only have to wait twenty-four more murders until you get one you can solve."

"Fuck you," Flores says. "I have to solve his murder. I gotta solve this case."

Flores cannot sit still. Even at this late hour, he yearns to get back to work: more than anything, he wants to make a name for himself as a detective. His zeal stems from his upbringing as the child of hardworking Salvadoran immigrants in Montgomery County, another Maryland suburb adjacent to Washington, DC. His parents, who operated a janitorial company, made no secret of their wish for their son to prosper, an ambition that in their minds would be fulfilled when he took a job that required him to wear a suit. Growing up, Flores had watched lots of crime shows on television; early on, he'd decided that becoming a police detective would not only satisfy his parents' aspirations but also be fun and interesting.

At twenty-one, he applied to the PG force and was soon patrolling the county's streets. Four years later, he was promoted to district-level detective and began handling everything from assaults to burglaries. Fourteen months after that, he was assigned to a centralized robbery squad; only two years later, he was tapped to join homicide.

Some homicide detectives grumbled that Flores's rapid ascent was the result of affirmative action. It was true that to keep pace with the county's changing demographics, the department had been making a concerted effort to boost the number of Hispanic officers. When Eckrich joined the force, in 1994, about 3 percent of the police department's officers were Hispanic, which was in line with the county's relatively small Hispanic population. Nearly two decades later, PG's Hispanic population has surged to more than 16 percent of the county's nearly 900,000 residents. And while the department has done its best to be more reflective of PG's changing demographics, its 142 Hispanic officers account for just 8.6 percent of the force.

Creating a police department that mirrors its community is a familiar challenge in Prince George's, which has long struggled to keep pace with societal changes. In the 1970s, as African Americans began moving from the District to the county to take advantage of its affordable housing while remaining in close proximity to Washington and its jobs, the department was 95 percent white and had a reputation for relying on brutal forms of street justice far too often. In the early 1990s, thanks in part to the leadership of then-chief David B. Mitchell, the county police force became increasingly diversified. Today, its ranks are evenly divided between whites and blacks—45 percent to 43 percent—and minorities account for 55 percent of its 1,645 officers, though the department still falls short of mirroring the county's overall minority population, which comprises 81 percent of its residents.

Over the years, the Homicide Unit's makeup has fluctuated. Currently, of thirty detectives and sergeants, eight are black, two are Hispanic, and the rest are white. Though commanders insisted that ethnicity played no role in Flores's assignment to homicide, the fact was that a Spanish-speaking detective had just been promoted out of the unit. And with so few Spanish speakers in the five squads, the supervisors obviously felt pressure to find someone who could handle murder investigations and also help interrogate Latino gang members, interpret for witnesses, listen to Spanish speakers on jail calls, and translate social-media postings and text messages. They quickly settled on Flores, who had a solid reputation for solving robberies. Though he's been on the job for only three weeks, so far he has impressed his colleagues with his eagerness to work.

WITH HIS FIRST case at a standstill, Flores gets up, walks around the row of desks, and takes a seat next to Eckrich. "I have to solve this murder," Flores says again.

Eckrich studies his young charge and chuckles. He has cautioned Flores that many first murders never go down. In fact, Eckrich's own first murder remains wide open. In January 2008, a drug dealer was shot at 2:00 a.m. on a deserted street; recently, Eckrich showed Flores the thick case file that documented five years of fruitless work.

"It's all in what case is given to you," Eckrich says. "What's more important is that you *try* to solve it. Either way, you will always remember the one that popped your cherry."

Indeed, that is how the unit's clerk tagged Flores's first homicide: following long-standing tradition, she drew two cherries on a stem next to his name in the logbook. The unit had recently added an unprecedented five newcomers, and it was the fourth time in less than four weeks that she had drawn a pair of cherries. And the murders caught by the four rookies had so far proved the validity of Eckrich's observation: only one had been solved. A bizarre slaying that included the abduction of an alcoholic liver-transplant recipient, it was deemed a "fair catch" by veterans. The case had been easy to crack because the identity of the killer was known before detectives even arrived on the scene.

The remaining three, including Flores's, are far more challenging. In one, a Jamaican drug dealer was executed in a garage in an industrial park. Members of Jamaican criminal gangs have a reputation for being ruthless and efficient killers who rarely leave behind evidence or witnesses; the rookie working the case had no clues and had been told by veterans to hope that a gang member would be eager to trade information for a more lenient sentence. The second, caught by Jamie Boulden, in the M-40 squad, is equally arduous, in part because his victim was widely despised. The dead man, who was shot to death in his town house complex's parking lot late one night, was a twenty-three-year-old drug dealer who had intimidated his neighbors by brandishing an AK-47 and burglarizing their homes. Boulden clearly stood little chance of finding a witness who would risk his or her life to help solve the murder of such a frightening figure. "Thank God he was killed," one male neighbor told a detective. "Karma's a bitch, right?"

Eddie Flores knew all about the other two unsolved cases. He had spoken with Jamie Boulden about the drug dealer's murder, and he agreed that it would be difficult to solve. But at least Boulden had the one crucial piece of information that every homicide detective relies on at the beginning of a case. He knew his victim's name.

**4:00 p.m., Monday, February 4**

Sean Deere and Mike Crowell fall into rolling chairs in the homicide office's conference room and drop their notebooks on its large wooden table. It's their first day of a week on the evening shift, which runs from 3:00 to 11:00 p.m., and they are meeting to discuss their next steps in the Amber Stanley investigation. They also want to sort through the information that came out of their extended interrogation of Jeff Buck on Friday and review the details provided by another witness they interviewed into the early hours of Saturday.

"Every time we bring someone in here, we get five or six more names to dig into," Deere complains, frustration lacing his voice as he looks over the new people on his list of witnesses and potential suspects. The detective unconsciously rubs his hands, as if he were outside in the cold. He may as well be: the room is frigid due to an engineering snafu involving the air-conditioning in a neighboring office and its computer servers.

"No kidding," says Crowell.

Deere looks up at Crowell and grins. "You get any?" he asks. He's been wondering whether Crowell managed to patch things up with his wife over the weekend after botching their scheduled liaison on Friday.

"You know it!" Crowell says, smiling broadly.

The two detectives have been fast friends since Crowell joined the Homicide Unit two years ago. Like Deere, Crowell grew up in Prince George's County; for a few years after high school he worked as a utility marker, making sure construction crews knew precisely where power and water lines were buried. But the job was dull, and he yearned for excitement. At one point he considered joining the PG police force, but he had heard it was in the midst of a hiring freeze. Then, one afternoon in 1993, Crowell and two friends were pounding Coors Lights and flipping through a newspaper when they spotted an advertisement for the Baltimore police force. Crowell challenged his friends to see which of them could pass the Baltimore PD's fitness test the next day. Crowell made the cut—his buddies did not—and he was soon patrolling what some called Charm City.

In 1996, when the chance came to transfer to his home turf and join the PG force, Crowell took it and quickly earned a reputation as an aggressive patrolman. Mere months after joining, he got into a shootout with a suspect and was wounded in the left shoulder. At the hospital, he refused to be taken to surgery until he could call his wife: he had warned her to expect the worst if a bunch of "white shirts"—commanders—appeared at her door, and he didn't want her to suffer such a shock.

A five-foot-seven dynamo with a penetrating gaze, a beer belly, and a hankering for cheeseburgers, Crowell loves the challenge of working murders. He also runs a fifty-employee private-security business on the side and is the father of two teenagers who cause him never-ending angst. He talks about sex constantly, rarely misses a Washington Redskins game, and parties hard. Nearly obsessed with playing practical jokes, he recently signed up squad mate Joe Bunce for tryouts with the Washington Redskins' cheerleading squad, and for several weeks he has been waiting for the right opportunity to superglue a bumper sticker to his Bunce's wife's car that says, I LOVE TO MASTURBATE.

Crowell has been working with Deere on the Amber Stanley case for the past two months. Just before the murder, Deere's partner learned that he was being promoted to sergeant, so for the first three months Deere largely worked the case alone. Ever since the night of the murder, in fact, Deere has focused exclusively on this investigation—he was banned from homicide scenes and removed from the rotation for catching new cases. But the investigation soon became stalled; worried that Deere needed help, in November commanders assigned the hard-charging Crowell to join Deere as a temporary partner, providing the case with an immediate jolt. When Crowell's stint with Deere is finished, he will return to working with Bunce, his regular partner.

Deere has also regularly received help from other detectives in the M-40 squad. At the beginning of most homicide investigations, several members of the squad will either visit the scene or assist the lead detective by conducting interviews, serving search warrants, and writing reports. But after a few days or a week, the other detectives peel off to handle their own cases, leaving the lead investigator and his partner to work the murder. The Amber Stanley investigation is different: the stakes are so high that the usual approach has been jettisoned and Deere's squad mates, particularly Crowell, have continued to assist him.

After chatting about their weekends and the Super Bowl, Deere and Crowell rehash what Jeff Buck told them during the interrogation on Friday and what they now know about the man. Buck said he had heard a rumor that his own enforcer had been involved in the murder; he knew Amber had been shot in the face; his cell phone had pinged a tower in the vicinity of the murder scene at the time of the killing. Although he denied having raped Denise, Amber's troubled foster sister, Buck clearly knew her well.

They also discuss another interview, one that started just before midnight on Friday. After letting Buck go, Deere and Crowell had picked up another potential suspect: David Norris, the grocery clerk who was a close friend of Denise's. The foster sister had reported being raped while walking home from Norris's house, and comments she made later that night suggest that she no longer trusted him. Because Buck admitted during his interrogation that he knew Norris and helped supply him with drugs, the detectives felt they couldn't afford to wait to question the clerk—there was a good chance that Buck would call Norris soon after being released. Within an hour of driving Buck home, they tracked Norris to his workplace and hauled him into homicide. Crowell and Bunce took the first shot at the twitchy young man, but they made little progress beyond causing him to sob uncontrollably for a good ten minutes.

When Deere took Bunce's place in the box, he initially handled Norris gently. But he grew frustrated when Norris claimed to have barely known Denise. Finally Deere jumped up from his plastic chair, sending it crashing into the wall. "You guys were best friends!" he shouted. "Every swinging dick in Mitchellville knows that!"

Norris froze, his face a mask of fear. Mitchellville is just north of Amber Stanley's neighborhood; Deere was making it very clear that he knew a lot about his witness's life. But Norris still wouldn't admit to being friendly with Denise.

"Get the fuck up!" the detective said. Pointing to the comfortable rolling chair in which Norris was sitting, he screamed, *"Get out of my fucking chair!"*

Norris stood up, and Deere smashed the rolling chair into the wall.

"You must just think this is going to go away," Deere sneered, his face an inch from Norris's, his spittle spraying the suspect's forehead.

Norris quivered, slumped his shoulders, and again convulsed into tears. He finally admitted that he had been tight with Denise and that she had even confided in him about the rape. He agreed to undergo voice stress analysis, and he failed just one question: his denial that he suspected anyone in the sexual assault appeared to be false, which Deere took as an effort to protect Jeff Buck. Norris also told them that Denise was being pimped out by two of his friends, the twenty-one-year-old driver of an illegal taxicab and the cab driver's high-school-aged girlfriend.

In addition to those two new suspects, Norris gave Deere yet another: Gerry Gordon,* a friend who was caught spying on a young woman through her bedroom window. Norris told Deere that Gordon also had a crush on Denise and was upset that she had spurned him.

Now, after concluding the review of the interrogations of both Buck and Norris, Deere maps out their next steps. He tells Crowell he would like to scoop up Jeff Buck's potential alibi witness, the

---

*Not his real name.

man Buck said he might have been hanging with on the night of the murder. The detective wants to track down as many of Buck's friends as possible, and he's especially eager to talk with this witness. He would also like to interview Gerry Gordon, the Peeping Tom.

But first, Deere says, he wants to find the unlicensed taxi driver and his girlfriend. They have firsthand knowledge of Denise's prostitution clients, and Deere has a hunch that the foster sister spoke to them about the rape. Besides, Deere points out, taxi drivers see and hear everything.

Crowell needs no persuading. Smiling, he looks at his partner and says, "We'll grab them tomorrow, first thing."


AT 2:50 P.M. THE next day, Mike Crowell and Jamie Boulden take seats across the table from Jason Murray,* the twenty-one-year-old taxi driver. Murray has a diamond-like stud in each ear and is clad in a bright orange T-shirt and grubby blue jeans.

Crowell removes a pen from his shirt pocket, clicks it furiously, and eyes Murray for a moment before introducing Boulden and himself.

Murray smiles, saying nothing. His eyelids are droopy, and he seems completely at ease, as if sitting in the box across from two homicide detectives is the least worrisome thing in the world.

*Is this guy retarded or just high?* wonders Crowell.

Crowell and several other members of the M-40 squad had started their shifts early and spent the morning looking for Murray and his girlfriend. They had finally located the taxi driver about twenty minutes earlier in the parking lot of his girlfriend's high school. Murray didn't protest when Crowell told him to get in his Impala and then drove him to homicide; he also gave them permission

---

*Not his real name.

to inspect the contents of his phone. Deere, who had been reviewing his case notes in the office while the others hit the streets, decided to look through Murray's phone rather than interview the taxi
driver, so Boulden joined Crowell in Interview Room 1.

The girlfriend, whom detectives picked up as she left her school,
was anything but cooperative. Since being brought in and deposited
in another interview room, she has been protesting her detention
so loudly that she has drawn the attention of officers and detectives
passing through the outer hallway.

Crowell starts the interview with Murray by asking for his
biographical information, including his date of birth and family
history. Soon Murray is providing details of his interactions with
key players in the neighborhoods near Amber Stanley's home. Surprisingly, he is completely forthcoming: he readily acknowledges
that he's an unlicensed taxi driver, known in Maryland as a "hack,"
and he admits that his girlfriend pimped for Amber Stanley's foster sister, Denise.

A few minutes into the interview, Murray leans back in his chair,
lifts his hands and folds them atop his head. An acrid stench fills
the room—the man has perhaps the worst body odor the two detectives have ever encountered. The smell prompts Crowell to ask
Murray about his living arrangements; Murray says he resides in his
beat-up Honda. He then says he spends his days shuttling friends
and others around the county and the District to earn money for gas,
as well as for marijuana and synthetic marijuana, a relatively new
product marketed as incense and sold at gas stations and convenience stores. His needs are simple, he tells the detectives: keeping
up his car, smoking pot, and having sex with his girlfriend.

"How do you sleep, especially now, in the cold?" asks Crowell.

"I just turn the heat on for fifteen minutes, cover up with blan-
kets, push back the seat, and sleep. Not a problem."

After gathering a bit more background, Crowell questions Murray
about his relationship with Denise. The man says his eighteen-year-

old girlfriend is a friend of hers and began arranging sex clients for her shortly after they met, the previous spring. Their deal was simple: the girlfriend collected three dollars from every fifteen-dollar blow job Denise performed. Crowell asks Murray whether he has ever seen Denise with clients or lovers and under what circumstances. Without hesitation, Murray provides the names of five men who have slept with the foster sister. When Crowell asks whether Jeff Buck has had sex with her, Murray says he's not sure.

The taxi driver also tells Crowell that a twenty-year-old friend of his was "burned" by Denise, meaning that he caught a sexually transmitted disease from her. Murray provides the name of this man as well.

Crowell then asks what Murray knows of Amber Stanley's murder, and the hack says that all he's heard is that the high school senior was shot and killed in her house. He learned about it, he says, after seeing reward flyers posted all over the neighborhood.

"Who do you think did it?" Crowell asks.

The taxi driver goes quiet and taps the table with his fingers. His eyes drift to the ceiling.

"You know," Murray says, "it could have been Crazy K." He stares ever more intently at the ceiling tiles, as if concentrating in an effort to retrieve a distant thought. "Yeah, Crazy K!"

"Crazy K, as in the letter *K*?" Crowell asks.

Murray nods.

Crowell asks Murray if he knows Crazy K's real name.

"No idea."

"Why is he called Crazy K?"

"Why do you think?"

Crowell tilts his head and purses his lips, signaling Murray to answer the question.

"Because I saw him once at the gas station stabbing at the gas pumps with a knife. He even serves himself at KFC—just hops over the counter, fills up a bucket, and runs out."

"That's crazy," Crowell says.

"Yeah, he's Crazy K!"

But Murray's description of Crazy K doesn't match the one of the killer provided by Amber Stanley's sister. Besides, Crowell thinks, Crazy K seems too erratic to be the calm and collected gunman.

The witness's next tidbit, however, seems more promising. According to Murray, Denise and her sex clients sometimes visited a huge house in Woodmore, a well-to-do neighborhood about a mile north of Amber's house. The home was abandoned, Murray tells the detectives; as far as he could determine, nobody had been in the place for months. Strangely, though, it was still furnished— big-screen televisions, chairs, sofas, closets full of clothes. "There was all kinds of sports stuff—signed helmets, signed pennants, jerseys on the walls," Murray says.

Crowell is intrigued, but he has never heard of a wealthy person vanishing and leaving those kinds of possessions behind. *Sure,* he thinks, *poor people get evicted all the time. But rich guys?*

Although Crowell presses Murray, the details do not change, and the driver goes on to claim that he watched two of his friends have sex with Denise in the back of a silver sports car in the home's garage. Crowell jots down the names of Murray's two friends. One is the man Murray mentioned earlier, the twenty-year-old who caught the STD from Denise. The other is a teenager who is familiar to Crowell: his name had come up earlier in the investigation, but he has been ruled out as a suspect because he was in jail at the time of the rape and the murder.

Crowell's mind goes into overdrive as he considers Murray's story about the mansion. If it's true, Crowell thinks, the house has potential evidentiary value—two men, one of them a possible suspect, had sex with Denise in that house. Maybe the mansion was the site of Denise's rape; if they get really lucky, they might even recover some physical evidence, like a spent condom or a weapon. And if Murray is fibbing and there is no rich man's house, the detectives will have caught him in a lie, a mistake they might be able to exploit.

Crowell stands up and stares down at Murray. "Okay," he says, "we're going to find this place—now."

SEAN DEERE IS working at his desk, typing on his keyboard and clicking his mouse as he navigates through the information he downloaded from Murray's phone—a call log and a few texts. So far he has found nothing incriminating or particularly revealing, just some calls between Murray and Jeff Buck and some texts to arrange rides and marijuana purchases. When Deere gets to the folder containing forty-three photos and videos, he feels mildly optimistic, allowing himself to believe that the folder could yield a trove of potential documentary evidence. The photos and videos might show Murray's girlfriend and Denise, or Denise and Jeff Buck—or maybe even Amber Stanley. But his hopes dim the moment he opens the first file, a shaky video of Murray and his girlfriend having sex in the front passenger seat of Murray's car.

Deere clicks on the next file: same thing. And the next, and the next. The first thirty of the forty-three videos and photos depict sex acts by Murray and his girlfriend, all of them apparently taken by Murray himself. Deere is tempted to stop, but he has to open each file on the slight chance that Murray used his phone to capture something pertinent to the investigation. As he clicks on the thirty-first file, he senses a presence off his left shoulder. Turning, he sees Crowell, whose eyes are glued to the screen.

"Porn! Come on, Sean," Crowell says.

Deere laughs. "Nah—this guy has a shit-ton of homemade stuff in his car, with his girlfriend. I still have more to go through."

Crowell stifles a laugh. The file's video has just finished loading, and an enormous erect penis fills the monitor. "Well," Crowell says, jerking his thumb in the direction of the interview room in which the girlfriend is being held. She is from a well-off family, and the detectives have been wondering why she would want to date a homeless taxi driver. "Now we know what she sees in him."

Crowell briefs Deere on what Murray has told them—about Crazy K, the guy who caught the STD, his girlfriend pimping out Denise, and the abandoned mansion.

With one eye on the video running in the background on his monitor, Deere listens to Crowell and wonders whether the new details will help him build a case against Jeff Buck.

"Field trip?" Crowell asks, eager to check out Murray's story about the house. "It helps us either way—he's lying or he's telling the truth. Maybe that's where she was raped, maybe there's something there."

Deere turns his attention back to the computer and sees that the sex video has finished. He hovers the mouse over a folder and confirms that he has a dozen more videos and photos to review. The choice is easy.

"Let's go," he says.

FORTY MINUTES LATER, Deere, Crowell, and Boulden pull their Impalas to the curb in front of a large brick colonial on a street of similar houses with manicured lawns in a neighborhood about six miles east of the homicide office. Deere strides to the front door, where he studies a vacancy notice that has been posted on behalf of the owner's mortgage company. He returns to the driveway and addresses Murray, who is sitting in Crowell's car. "It's vacant," Deere says.

Nodding, Murray steps out of the car. "We can get in around back," he says, leading the trio of investigators around the side of the house to a rear door. But when Murray tries the handle, it won't budge. Crowell shakes his head, skeptical that the guy really knows how to get into the house.

"I can climb through the window," Murray says. "It will open. Watch."

Before Deere or Crowell can stop him, Murray pushes on one of the windows. After its top half slides down, he scrambles awkwardly through the opening and crashes into the house. Deere grimaces, thinking about the mounds of paperwork required to explain how a witness fractured his neck while breaking into a house. A minute later they hear more banging; a lock flicks and the back door swings open, revealing a beaming Murray, who steps aside and dramatically ushers the three detectives into a messy kitchen.

Papers are strewn everywhere, and drawers and cabinets yawn open. There's an unopened FedEx package dated two years earlier, as well as utility bills and bank statements. The contents of the shelves and cabinets litter every surface—broken dishes, bowls, cereal boxes. A pile of clothes sits in a far corner. The refrigerator's doors are open, revealing a dark, empty space.

Crowell instinctively tries a light switch, but there is no power. He pulls a flashlight out of his pocket and shines the beam around the kitchen. "Which way to the garage?" he asks.

Murray points to his right, through the kitchen, and starts in that direction, the detectives in tow. A few moments later, the investigators are studying a silver Nissan 300ZX sports car with flat tires. They are somewhat surprised at the accuracy of Murray's memory, considering his heavy drug use and poor sleeping habits.

Crowell approaches the passenger window and aims his flashlight into the dusty interior.

"In the back seat?" he asks.

"Yes," says Murray. "She was in the back seat."

"And he was, you know, fucking her in the back seat?" Crowell says, referring to the twenty-year-old who caught the STD. "There is room for that?"

"The passenger seat was pushed all the way forward," Murray says.

"And your man was standing half in and half out of the car?" Crowell asks. "And he was buck naked?"

"Yeah."

Crowell tilts his head to the left, staring into the back seat.

"Two guys?" Crowell asks, remembering that Murray said the twenty-year-old had been joined by his teenage friend. "One at a time, obviously—right?"

Murray nods, and Crowell tilts his head to the other side, trying to figure out the mechanics of the act.

Crowell casts a glance over his left shoulder at Murray. "What was he, King Dingaling?"

Deere stifles a chuckle, thinking, *Only Crowell. He's probably already fantasizing about doing the same thing with his wife in his BMW.*

Pacing around the car, Deere shines his flashlight beam on the floor, looking for a discarded condom or a cigarette butt, anything that might have DNA. But there is only dust. After five minutes of scouring the garage, the detectives head back to the kitchen, where Deere picks up some of the mail and tax documents and pops the name he presumes to be the owner's into his smartphone's Web browser. The owner is not dead or missing or in hiding—in fact, he had been active on social media as recently as a few months ago.

Deere shrugs and follows the crowd into the living room, which is arranged just as Murray had described it. A half dozen swanky swivel chairs face a television screen the size of a compact car. On the wall is a signed professional athlete's jersey.

On the second floor Deere and the others find two bedrooms, each with a bare mattress on the floor. One bedroom is mostly empty; in the other, clothes, toys, and board games are scattered across the plush beige carpet.

"Why did they have sex in that little car if they have mattresses up here?" Crowell asks.

"No idea," Murray says.

"I like this layout," says Boulden, standing on a balcony and looking down into the living room. "It's nice."

"Probably cost him four hundred and fifty thousand," says Deere.

"Depends when he bought it," says Crowell. "I wonder if he bought it before the height of the market."

Since the onset of the Great Recession, the detectives have been inside plenty of abandoned homes; as in many suburbs, those in PG County were hit hard by the financial crash and the foreclosure crisis. The detectives have a rule when entering such houses: Never lean against a wall. A stain might ruin a perfectly good suit, or you could find a cockroach crawling across your arm. But this place is different. Though cluttered and moldy, the house feels relatively clean.

On a hallway wall, Deere spots a pennant signed by what must be a professional sports team's entire roster. "You didn't take anything?" he asks Murray. "Not a Redskins helmet or a jersey or something?"

"What would I do with that? Where would I keep it?"

*Makes sense if you live in your Honda,* thinks Deere.

He trails Crowell and Boulden into the mostly barren master bedroom and stands next to them as they stoop to study deep impressions in the carpet.

"Those are from a water bed," Crowell says. "I had one of those once. It was fun."

While Crowell and Boulden debate the merits of waterbeds, Deere heads into the master bathroom. He checks the toilet; it's dry, the water obviously having been shut off long ago. He steps over to a square window and looks out at a nearly identical mansion across the street. Then he turns and catches himself in a large mirror. *Fuck,* he thinks, *I look old and tired.*

Dropping his eyes to the sink, he spots a toothbrush and a hairbrush on the edge of the basin. To his right, a towel has been flipped casually over the shower stall. If the water hasn't been working, Deere thinks, that means the towel and brushes weren't left by vagrants—the owner must have departed his house rather suddenly after taking a shower and brushing his teeth and hair. Maybe he expected to return, maybe he didn't. It's impossible to know.

After frowning once more at his face in the mirror, Deere rejoins Crowell, Boulden, and Murray, who are still gabbing about the benefits and disadvantages of waterbeds. Deere gestures for the group to head downstairs, and they retrace their steps out the back door and around the house to their cars. There they stand in the driveway, all staring at the beautiful house and its immaculate lawn, pondering the incongruity of what they've seen.

"Will we be finished soon?" Murray asks the detectives.

"No," says Deere. "No, we have more to do."

9:50 a.m., Wednesday, February 6

Detective Eddie Flores's eyes are burning. He hasn't slept more than eight hours since he stood over his corpse two days earlier, and he has enjoyed only two power naps in his cruiser and a brief visit home for a shower and a short snooze. Even so, he has no desire to sleep. The first crucial piece of his puzzle has fallen into place: he's put a name to his victim.

Flores learned the identity of the corpse the previous day, thanks to some flirting by Detective D. J. Windsor with a female customer-service representative for the bus company that transported the man from Raleigh, North Carolina, to Washington. After complimenting the call taker's southern accent, Windsor charmed her into violating company policy and providing him with the phone number of the person who had purchased the one-way ticket. Jeff Eckrich then called the number and asked the woman who answered about the ticket's provenance. She said her mother had purchased the ticket for a cousin and gave Eckrich his name: Salaam Adams.

A search of databases revealed that the twenty-year-old Adams had a lengthy criminal history, including arrests for auto theft, robbery, and possession with intent to distribute cocaine. As Flores and Eckrich reviewed Adams's eleven-page rap sheet, Eckrich recalled the murder scene and the angel wings in the dirt. "Well," he said to Flores, "he certainly was no angel."

This assessment was confirmed by one of Adams's aunts, who told Flores that her nephew lived in Durham, North Carolina, and had been a cocaine dealer. Adams's criminal history and his out-of-state residence ensure that there will be no pastor-led candlelight vigils, no calls from county council members demanding an arrest, no coverage by the media. For better or worse, Salaam Adams's murder will now be recorded as a statistic: the county's eighth homicide of 2013, the first in the month of February.

The killing will also be added to the numerator in a quotient that drives homicide detectives to distraction: solved murders divided by total murders produces their clearance rate. If there is any pressure on Flores to solve this case, it will stem from that simple statistic, which is tracked daily by the detectives' supervisors, the assistant chief, and even the chief. Yes, the captains and lieutenants care about a victim's family, and they take seriously their responsibility to speak for the dead. But they also like their jobs, and the clearance rate is the measure by which their work is judged. On this account, the PG police department does a good job of solving homicides: in 2012, for example, the unit mustered a 73 percent clearance rate, significantly better than the 62 percent national average. The commanders and chief would dearly like to keep the rate where it is, if not improve it.

Since learning his victim's identity, Flores has been trying to reach Adams's mother. She was informed of the death in person by a North Carolina police officer, so Flores doesn't have to take care of that sad task, one of the worst parts of the job. But the detective would still like to express his condolences and try to build a bond—he knows mothers are often amazing conduits of intelligence. He has traded two messages with his victim's mother already, and he decides it might be time to try again. After checking the clock on the wall between Interview Rooms 2 and 3 and deciding that it's not too early to call, he punches in the mother's number.

This time he gets through; when she answers, the detective introduces himself and says he is sorry for her loss. After promising to do his best to arrest her son's killer, Flores gets down to business. Why, he asks, was her son coming to Washington?

"He was visiting a friend to watch the Super Bowl," she says.

"Do you know who that is?" Flores asks, pulling out a pen and flipping to a new page of his steno pad.

"No, but I might have the man's phone number," she says. Flores hears fumbling, as the mother presumably consults her phone's memory. Twenty seconds later, she's back on the line. "My son called this number from my house, and it called back," she says. She gives Flores the phone number, repeats it, and then says, "I think this is who he went to see." She says the call was made on Friday, two days before her son left town.

Flores smiles. With today's advanced tracking capabilities and call registers, a phone number is often as valuable to an investigator as a name.

The detective thanks Adams's mother for her help, hangs up, and walks around the row of workstations to Eckrich's desk. Flores tells his partner that Adams called a friend before coming to Washington and asks Eckrich who he thinks his victim was calling.

Eckrich ticks off the possibilities: a drug connection, a fellow gang member, a friend, or maybe all of the above. The detectives simultaneously raise their eyebrows as they both come to a realization: if Adams called a friend or business partner, the person who received that call might be at risk, since presumably the man who shot Adams would have no qualms about hurting one of his friends.

Back at his desk, Flores queries a commercial database and determines which cell-phone carrier owns the number he's been given. After filling out a request for subscriber information, recent call data, and updates on the phone's location, he faxes it to the company. As soon as the carrier replies, he will give the information to the police department's fugitive squad, a sergeant and five detectives who spend their days rounding up witnesses and suspects. With a little luck, they'll be able to track the phone and grab its owner.

After his fax goes through, Flores wanders back to Eckrich's desk. "I hope he's alive," the rookie says.

Eckrich smiles sympathetically. "Me, too, Eddie."


THE GREENHORN GODS are generous: five hours later, Flores and Eckrich enter the box to question the cell phone's owner. He was tracked to a classroom at Bowie State University, which is not far from the homicide office, and grabbed by the fugitive squad. As the two detectives take their seats across the table from the student, they try to assess him, but his head is buried in his arms and covered by the hood of a blue-and-green striped Polo sweatshirt.

Flores nudges the student's arm; the man slowly lifts his head, his eyes barely rising to meet the detectives'. Flores introduces himself and Eckrich and asks for the spelling of the man's name and his date of birth. The man mumbles that his name is Robert Ofoeme; he is twenty-nine, and he lives in the DC suburb of Silver Spring, Maryland. He is an African immigrant, a citizen of Sierra Leone, he says, and he's taking classes at Bowie State in information technology.

Ofoeme's response is indifferent, if not disrespectful. His attitude strikes Eckrich as cocky.

"Hey, buddy man," Eckrich says, "we brought you in here because of a phone call you may have made to somebody."

No response. The man's eyes drop to the table, and his head descends back into his arms.

"Look, man, sit up," Eckrich says, his voice hardening. He taps the man on the left shoulder.

Again there is no reaction.

"We don't know if you have any involvement in this," Eckrich says, "but you are making me really suspicious."

Ofoeme remains silent.

Eckrich puts his hand on the man's left forearm. "Come on, man, look up," he says sharply.

"Stop it!" Ofoeme shouts, sitting bolt upright. "Don't beat me! Don't beat me!"

Eckrich recoils. Shaking his head, he says, "I'm not going to beat you."

"That nigga is going to beat me!" Ofoeme wails, his eyes wild.

"Ain't nobody going to beat you, man," Flores says.

"If I called you that word, you'd be calling the newspaper, hiring a lawyer," Eckrich snaps.

Ofoeme immediately calms down. "I'm sorry," he mumbles, his face disappearing into his arms on the table, his head again hidden by the hood of his sweatshirt.

Eckrich sighs, then exchanges looks with Flores. It's time for the tried-and-true good cop, bad cop routine. The veteran leans back, folds his hands across his stomach, and glares at Ofoeme. After fifteen seconds of eye-fucking the witness, he slams his hands on the table and stands up.

"You can have him," Eckrich sneers. He walks out of the box and loudly bangs the door shut.

Flores allows silence to hang in the room for a few moments. Then he leans forward and places both elbows on the table.

"I don't know what his problem is today," Flores says. "But whatever you've got against him, leave it. I've treated you with respect, and I expect you to treat me with respect."

Ofoeme acknowledges nothing; his head remains buried in his arms.

"Just look at me while I'm talking," Flores says gently. "You are a grown man."

Ofoeme lifts his head two inches and studies Flores from under heavy eyelids.

"Now take off the hood."

Ofoeme pulls off his hood.

"Good. The faster we can get this going, the faster you get out of here."

Ofoeme jerks up straight and smacks the table. "Let's do this!"

Flores suppresses his shock at the instantaneous change in attitude. *This dude is either schizophrenic or nervous as shit and having trouble masking it,* he thinks.

Before questioning Ofoeme, Flores takes stock of the room, and he doesn't like what he sees. The student is not handcuffed, and the way the table is arranged, Ofoeme is closer to the door than he is. Flores doesn't feel secure in the box unless he is between the door and the witness. He prefers this arrangement partly for security reasons—if he had to, he could prevent a suspect from dashing out the door. But he also believes that it provides him with a psychological advantage. When a detective sits between a man and his freedom, the investigator cannot be ignored.

Flores motions for Ofoeme to stand up and then rearranges the table and chairs. Once they've resettled in their new spots, Flores asks, "Did you have a friend, someone who was supposed to come see you from North Carolina?"

For just a moment, Ofoeme looks Flores in the eyes. But he soon drops his gaze to the table and yanks his hood on again.

*Jesus,* Flores thinks, *this is going to take forever.*

"Look at me," the detective says quietly, as if addressing a five-year-old. When Ofoeme raises his eyes again, Flores asks, "Did anyone come to visit you from North Carolina?"

"I don't know what you are talking about," Ofoeme says.

"Did you exchange calls with someone in North Carolina on Friday?"

"Yeah."

"Who?"

"Slug."

"Who is Slug?"

"I only know him as Slug."

The detective presumes that Slug is Salaam Adams and presses Ofoeme to describe their relationship.

Gradually Ofoeme becomes more talkative. He tells Flores that he and Adams became friends the previous year, and whenever Slug was in town they hung out and smoked weed. Flores asks Ofoeme whether he slings drugs—before Ofoeme arrived in the homicide office, Flores learned that he drives a flashy Mercedes, and he's also wearing a sweatshirt that would be too expensive for many college students. After several minutes of back-and-forth, Ofoeme admits that he deals.

"The ladies love the Polo," he says, smiling and tugging at the logo of his sweatshirt. "I sell enough to get by."

Flores asks Ofoeme whether he met Slug when he was in town over Super Bowl weekend. No, Ofoeme says; he knew Slug was coming to town but hadn't been interested in hanging out with him, so he'd turned off his phone.

"You had a falling-out?"

"Just didn't want to see him."

Flores goes silent for a few moments. Ofoeme is difficult to read, and the detective cannot decide whether the man is telling the truth, lying, or playing a mix-and-match game. But even if Ofoeme didn't see Adams around the time of his murder, he ought to be able to confirm whether his friend Slug is in fact the dead man.

Flores leaves the box and soon returns with Adams's mug shot.

"Is that Slug?"

Ofoeme lifts his head from his arms, glances at the photo, reburies his head, and mutters, "Yeah, that's him."

"He's dead," Flores says, watching Ofoeme carefully. The man doesn't move; he seems to have no reaction at all. After a while, Flores asks, "Do you know what happened?"

Ofoeme raises his eyes long enough to say no before putting his head back in his arms.

Flores picks up the photo and walks out the door. He sits at his desk, closes his eyes, and thinks for a minute. He decides to leave Ofoeme alone for a bit; checking his to-do list, he sees that he has yet to make contact with Adams's girlfriend in North Carolina. When Flores calls her number, she answers, and he then guides her through a ten-minute conversation focused on her boyfriend's final days. Late Sunday, she says, Adams texted that he was driving around the Washington area with a friend she knows only as B-Gutter.

After hanging up with the girlfriend, Flores heads back to the box. He doesn't bother to sit down.

"Know someone named B-Gutter?" he asks.

Again Ofoeme lifts his head just high enough to eye Flores. He grunts, which Flores takes as a yes.

"Did Slug know B-Gutter?" Flores asks.

"I think so," Ofoeme answers.

"Do you know B-Gutter's name?" Flores asks.

"Maybe Wayne," Ofoeme says.

"You have B-Gutter's phone number?"

9:05 p.m., Wednesday, February 6

Jamie Boulden and Joe Bunce enter the hospital's antiseptic-smelling emergency department and ask a nurse where they can find their dead man. She points to a door to their right, and the two detectives head into a cramped examination room, where they see a corpse on a gurney. A sheet shrouds the body from feet to neck. An uneven gray beard covers the man's pale, craggy face, which is streaked with dried blood. An intubation tube protrudes from his mouth.

Almost no one looks good after leaving this life, but it's obvious to Boulden that the man on the gurney has spent decades abusing drugs and alcohol. Those punishing vices have ground him to dust: he looks eighty, more than twenty years older than his actual age. Clutching his legal-sized notebook against his belly to keep his thick overcoat and bright green tie from touching the corpse, Boulden bends over the man's face. His eyes are closed, and to Boulden they look peaceful, as if the man is taking a much-needed nap after an exhausting life.

Boulden steps back from the body and glances at Bunce, who is leaning against a wall, staring into space. It has been another long day for the detectives. Boulden spent the last few hours futilely pursuing leads in his first homicide, the fatal shooting on January 18 of a twenty-three-year-old drug dealer. The rookie has managed to pin down some likely culprits, members of a violent gang of car thieves in northeast Washington, but he doesn't have enough information to charge anyone in the killing. Nobody is talking, not even the victim's relatives. Like Flores, Boulden wants desperately to solve his first case, but that's beginning to seem unlikely.

Bunce, meanwhile, spent the early part of the evening shift helping Mike Crowell hunt for Gerry Gordon and other potential witnesses and suspects in the Amber Stanley murder. After striking out at six residences and businesses, Bunce and Crowell drove to the PG jail, where they questioned a cousin of Jeff Buck's enforcer, the alleged triggerman. The inmate had been detained since September on serious robbery charges, and the detectives hoped this might give them some leverage. But despite an intense interrogation followed by direct pleas for his help, the cousin provided little information and ended the session with a comment that hinted at the possibility that he knew something more: "I have too much on my plate right now."

Back at the office, Bunce and Crowell briefed Deere on their interrogation of the inmate. As they were finishing, Sergeant Joe Bergstrom strode to the last row of desks and reported that the squad was being summoned to a local hospital to investigate the death of a fifty-eight-year-old man from a suspected heroin overdose. Though speaking to the entire row of investigators, Bergstrom kept his eyes locked on Bunce. His look said everything the detective needed to know: this was his case, and Bergstrom was penalizing him because recently he had cut out of work early a few times, irritating his squad mates.

After Bergstrom finished, Bunce tilted his head so he could see past his computer monitor and look directly at Jamie Boulden.

"Let's go," he told Boulden. As always, shit rolls downhill, which is how the addict's death became the rookie's problem.

Each week, PG homicide detectives investigate several deaths that aren't murders. Most often, the person has died from natural causes—a fall, a stroke, a heart attack—while not under the care of a physician. Others succumb to drug overdoses. The purpose of such investigations is relatively straightforward: they are meant to ensure that the person wasn't murdered. But sometimes they can be tricky, even for a rookie with as much police experience as Boulden.

An eight-year veteran of the force, the balding and beefy thirty-four-year-old Boulden had dreamed of becoming a homicide detective for as long as he can remember. After high school in

Delaware, he worked at a bank and served as a volunteer firefighter. At twenty-one, he moved to Ventura County, California, to become a police dispatcher; within a year, he returned to the East Coast after landing a job as an officer with the U.S. Capitol Police. In 2005, after three years of guard duty, he joined the PG police force. Working his way up, he became a robbery detective and earned a reputation for being both earnest and dogged. Finally, five weeks ago, he attained his dream job. But Boulden understands that he can't take anything for granted: if he wants to remain in homicide, he'll have to learn a number of new skills, including the art and science of documenting a human being's demise.

Boulden is about to ask Bunce what to do next when a red-haired woman clad in blue surgical scrubs steps into the room. Boulden recognizes her as Trasee Cosby, a forensic investigator for the state medical examiner. They have crossed paths at a few scenes but have not formally met, so Bunce makes the introduction official.

Cosby smiles, and so does Boulden. There is no shaking of hands: a few minutes earlier, Cosby finished inspecting the body and assessing whether it should be sent to Baltimore for an autopsy. The general rule is that if a death is suspicious, the deceased is relatively young (under fifty), or he or she was a drug or alcohol abuser, there will be an autopsy. In this case, there is no question: the corpse is going to Baltimore.

Cosby, her hair gathered in a blue scrunchie, shifts her reading glasses to her forehead so she can better eye the investigators. She looks around and frowns.

"Where's Crowell?" she asks.

"We couldn't find a car seat for him," Bunce says, never missing a chance to poke fun at his partner's short stature.

Cosby snickers and then tells the detectives that she has already interviewed the dead man's relatives elsewhere in the hospital. Looking down at the man's weathered face, Cosby says he was a recovering heroin addict who had probably started using again. A resident of western Maryland, he was visiting his ex-wife and daughter when he left their house the previous day to see an old friend, a known heroin user. When he returned to his ex-wife's place, he fell asleep on the couch. "That was the last time she saw him up and moving," Cosby says. "By late morning, he was in distress. They called 911, and an ambulance took him here, where he died."

Cosby glances at Boulden, who is eyeing the dead man. The rookie looks a bit at sea, so she puts her reading glasses back on, which allows her to better see tiny details such as puncture marks. Then she begins an in-depth explanation of how she conducted her exam.

First she raises the man's right forearm. "He has no track marks on his arms or anywhere else, nothing between his toes. But that doesn't really matter." Cosby walks around the table and lifts up the left forearm. Track marks are not a guaranteed indicator of heroin use, she says, because the drug has become so pure that many addicts are snorting it.

Cosby removes the sheet. She lifts the man's right foot to eye level and then does the same with his right hand.

"See how the skin under the fingers and fingernails is purple, and how the ankle was swollen?" she says. "That is indicative of someone suffering from a cardiac condition. So it could be heart-related, too. Maybe he took heroin and it was too much for him. Everything being equal, and taking into account what his family said, it looks like a heroin overdose. But we won't know that for sure until toxicology comes back, maybe in a month or so."

Sighing, she sits heavily on a stool and props her glasses on her head again.

"No trauma?" Boulden asks.

"No trauma," echoes Cosby.

"No trauma, no foul play," Boulden says, jotting a note.

"Exactly."

Boulden hears the flat tone in Cosby's voice and says, "You look beat."

"It's been a long two days," Cosby says, explaining that this is her eleventh corpse over the past forty-eight hours, a particularly rough stretch.

"You too tired to strip for us?" Bunce asks.

Boulden narrows his eyes. Bunce must be putting him on. *Stripping? In a hospital?*

Bunce chuckles. "She was a pole dancer in her previous life—I swear," he says, explaining that so many detectives know about her first profession that one of them once dared Cosby to perform after noticing a bronze pole at a crime scene. To everyone's surprise, Bunce tells Boulden, she put on quite a show.

Boulden studies Cosby, who is fifty-three. Carrying more than a few extra pounds, she's not built like any stripper he's ever seen.

"Be careful, or I might even give you a golden shower," she tells Boulden.

"What the fuck?" Boulden says.

"Wish I hadn't worn underwear," says Bunce.

"I've even taken a diuretic," Cosby says, cocking her eyebrows at the rookie. "So be ready!"

"Oh, shit," says Bunce.

Cosby looks at Boulden's worried face and finally breaks into a smile. "I wasn't really a stripper," she says.

"No, that was just a joke," Bunce says. "Jamie, seriously. A joke."

Boulden isn't so sure. He's still trying to find his feet in the Homicide Unit, but everyone he works with seems like a lunatic—Crowell, Deere, Bunce, now Cosby. Yet it's moments like these when he loves this job: these people may be nuts, but they're a lot of fun. He also appreciates the way his colleagues cope with the horror of their work, making light of even the ghastliest situation. How else could Cosby's psyche survive eleven corpses in just two days?

The trio cracks a few more jokes before returning to the task at hand. Boulden realizes he has forgotten something important: how is he supposed to handle the death notification?

"So who is his next of kin?" he asks Bunce. "Who do I notify? I can't notify the ex-wife, right? A brother or sister? Shit. How do I put that in the report?"

"No, it's already done," says Bunce. "Remember, the ex-wife and his daughter were here. His daughter is the death notification. You don't even have to do it, but you should follow up with them tomorrow."

"Anything else I need to know?"

Cosby doesn't answer; she's too tired. With her elbows on her thighs, she stares vacantly at the dead man's scalp.

Boulden checks his notebook to be sure he has all the facts he'll need for his report: the man's name, age, circumstances of death, ailments, potential recent drug use, and a summary of Cosby's observations.

Satisfied, he closes the notebook and winks a thank-you to Cosby, who returns the gesture with a slight smile. Then he glances at Bunce, who says they can go.

As the detectives move toward the open door, Boulden turns and pauses for a moment. He is sure he is forgetting something. When nothing comes to mind, he eyes the dead man a final time and gives him a wink, too.

2:00 a.m., Thursday, February 7

Before he even enters the box, Eddie Flores knows that his witness, Harvey Brandon "B-Gutter" Gunter, is a lying piece of shit. It's that simple, and now Flores must decide how to proceed. Does he press hard right off the bat, or does he go nice and slow, allowing the man to build a matchstick house of lies that Flores can then smash to bits?

Finding Gunter hadn't been difficult. Eight hours ago, after Robert Ofoeme gave him Gunter's phone number, Flores queried a couple of databases and soon came up with Gunter's home address, in the Maryland suburb of Silver Spring. Flores's next stop was Gunter's town house, where he and other detectives scooped up their witness. One of Flores's squad mates, Detective Mike Ebaugh, questioned Gunter on the car ride to homicide and then spent a few minutes with him in the box.

Predictably, the witness's story was pure fiction. Gunter told Ebaugh that he hadn't spoken to Slug—a.k.a. Salaam Adams, the victim—in days. He also said he'd spent Sunday night at a bar in College Park, sixteen miles from the murder scene. But once again, Flores had sent off a fax to the appropriate cell-phone carrier, and its records had revealed that not only had Gunter exchanged texts with Adams on the day of his death but his phone had pinged a tower in the vicinity of the murder scene at the time Adams was killed.

Flores enters Interview Room 1 and takes a seat next to Gunter at the table, hoping his proximity to the witness will help him get a better read on the man. A moment later, as Jeff Eckrich slips into a rolling chair across the table, Flores inventories the witness. A slim man clad in a gray sweater, Gunter has a slight mustache, tightly cropped hair, and a flat nose. Flores remains unsure how to proceed until he focuses on the witness's eyes: they are wide open, as if dilated, and they are darting all around the room.

*He's nervous,* thinks Flores. *He's mine.*

Flores begins by gathering some basic information: Gunter is twenty-six, and he lives with his sister. Next Flores turns to his left, puts his right arm firmly on the table, and looks Gunter in the eye. After a brief pause, he goes in for the kill.

"We know you are lying to us," Flores says.

His eyes whirling, Gunter bites his lower lip as the detective retrieves two pieces of paper from his steno pad. Flores unfolds the two documents, smooths them out, and places them on the table. One contains information about Gunter's calls and texts, as well as the locations of nearby cell-towers; the other is a map depicting the murder scene and the surrounding neighborhood.

"See this?" Flores says, pointing to a spot on the map. "This is where you placed the text from." The detective is fudging—the cell tower is close to but not at the murder scene.

"We know you were here," Eckrich says, jumping in. "These records are precise. This is where you were standing."

Gunter picks up the papers, which rattle in his hands.

"I know you're scared, but this is your time," says Flores. "If you don't come clean, the next time I will have done more homework and you won't be given this opportunity. You will be in handcuffs."

For a long minute, Gunter's eyes remain glued to the list of calls. Finally he says, "Okay, you got me." He reaches across the table for a bottle of water and slowly unscrews the lid. He takes a tiny sip, then another, then a third. His eyes open and close with each swallow.

"Come on," Flores says.

When Gunter looks up, his expression is slack and defeated.

Goose bumps ripple up Flores's arms. *Holy shit,* he thinks, *this case is about to break wide open.*

Gunter clears his throat and says yes, he knows Salaam Adams— in fact, he had been a witness to his murder. With only a bit more prodding from Flores, Gunter provides a detailed account of how it happened.

The night started when he got a call from a friend named Brandon Battle, who said Gunter should come into DC to hang out with him and their mutual friend Slug Adams. Gunter tells Flores he hopped on the Metro and got off at Gallery Place, a hip area of town that includes the Verizon Center sports arena, Chinatown, and dozens of bars and restaurants. Not long after he settled into a seat at a bar, Battle and Adams picked him up in Battle's Ford Mustang, Gunter says.

With Gunter sitting in the middle of the back seat, they drove randomly around town until Battle and Adams began arguing about a $2,000 drug debt. Battle asked if Adams had a gun, Gunter says, and Adams lifted up his shirt, revealing the butt of a pistol poking from his jeans. The three men drove for a while longer, finally pulling up to the Oxon Run park, at which point Battle asked Adams to get out of the car.

Gunter says he watched and listened—a window was cracked open enough for him to catch some of the conversation—as Battle told Adams, "It's fucked up. I looked at you like a brother."

"I agree, it's fucked up," said Adams.

Next Battle threw an arm over Adams's shoulders, and they headed down a hill. A minute or two later, Gunter says, he heard a gunshot and saw Battle running back to the car, holding a gun in each hand.

"What's going on?" Gunter asked.

"I was tired of that shit," Battle replied.

His story complete, Gunter slumps in his chair. "I nearly shit my pants," he tells the detectives.

Throughout Gunter's narrative, Flores has been carefully taking notes, but he's also been hearing the blood pulsing in his ears. Now, as he looks up at Gunter, an electrifying thought races through his mind: *My first murder is going down.*

Flores has Gunter repeat the story a second time and a third. The detective asks questions and looks for inconsistencies, but the witness's account seems solid. Flores learns more about Brandon Battle, a drug dealer who had been a friend and associate of both Gunter's and Adams's. Gunter tells the detective that after the shooting, after he and Battle left Adams to die in the park, they drove to Battle's apartment, where the dealer stashed the two guns in a safe above his refrigerator. Hungry, they went in search of food; Battle devoured a Philly cheesesteak, Gunter a tuna sandwich.

A half hour after hearing Gunter's account of Adams's murder, Flores is sitting with another detective in an Impala in the parking lot of a PG apartment complex; Gunter is scrunched in the back seat. The witness nervously points to a door on the second floor of a six-story building and identifies it as the entrance to Brandon Battle's place. With that, Flores has enough to obtain an arrest warrant for Battle and another warrant that will allow the police to search his apartment in an effort to find the two guns the drug dealer had in his hands after killing Adams.

It's now past 4:00 a.m.; the long night is almost over. After dropping the other detective off at the office, Flores drives Gunter home to Silver Spring and admonishes him to lie low until they catch Battle; he also tells his witness to call him if he needs anything. Gunter mumbles, "Sure," shuffles to the front door of his sister's town house, and slips inside.

For a moment, Flores sits in his car, staring at the town house and then at the dark and cloudy predawn horizon. He is bone-tired: he's been running on adrenaline for hours, and this is the first chance he's had to be alone with his thoughts. He envisions the speechless body of his victim, Salaam Adams; he turns over the stories he has heard from Gunther and Robert Ofoeme. He wonders what he missed during their interrogations and what he is still missing.

A notion, absurd to anyone but a homicide detective, passes through Flores's mind: *This has been too easy.*

Gunter has been too helpful and too consistent, especially for a witness in PG County. As Flores knows, this is a world in which people lie, and then lie about their lies. It usually takes far longer to dig out something approximating the truth; yet with little more than a nudge, Gunter rolled over like a cocker spaniel.

*There's got to be more to this,* Flores thinks. *How did this murder really go down?*

———

A COLD DRIZZLE prickles Eddie Flores's face as he and Jeff Eckrich stride up the short walkway to Gunter's sister's front door and ring the bell. It is just before noon on Friday, February 8, about thirty-two hours after Flores dropped Gunter off at this very spot. Flores is smiling and happy, perhaps as much for having slept twelve straight hours as for having officially closed his first murder.

But this is no courtesy call. Since the strength of Flores's case largely depends on this one witness, the detective knows he must thoroughly vet the man's story. Today he and Eckrich want to search his room and ask him a few more questions.

The two investigators would have visited Gunter sooner, but they had been busy the previous day arresting twenty-six-year-old Brandon Battle on first-degree murder charges. Flores had been told by his evidence technicians that the bullet fragments in Adams's head were likely too mangled to compare to a potential murder weapon, perhaps even to definitively determine its caliber, so he knew that to build an airtight case he would need Battle to confess. But the alleged killer said little during his brief interrogation beyond casually answering yes or no and providing some basic information. Within minutes, he clammed up.

Shortly after interrogating his suspect, Flores combed Battle's apartment and discovered a sizable stash of marijuana but only one handgun. This presented a problem, especially for Gunter, who had reported that Battle had deposited two guns in the safe above his refrigerator. That fact, and Gunter's willingness to betray his friend, have led Flores to feel somewhat skeptical about the account provided by his star witness.

The rookie rings the doorbell a second, third, and fourth time. Finally, the door opens, revealing a young woman with frazzled hair wearing a tan bathrobe.

"Is Harvey around?" Flores asks, using Gunter's first name.

"No," the sister says, rubbing her face. "He's in North Carolina."

"North Carolina?" Flores feels a flash of panic. It is never good when your key witness skips town.

"He's scared," she says.

That makes sense to Flores—after snitching, Gunter has every right to be frightened. Even so, the unexpected departure is cause for concern. *He shouldn't have left town,* the detective thinks, *not without first alerting us.*

"You need to get him on the phone," Flores says firmly. He would call Gunter himself, but he's concerned that his witness might not answer if he sees an unfamiliar number pop up on his phone's screen. The sister disappears and returns with her cell. She dials, and Gunter is soon on the line. She hands the phone to Flores.

"B-Gutter, what the hell?" Flores says. *"North Carolina?"*

The witness explains that he left the city because he was scared for his life. Flores tells Gunter that it was wrong to leave town without notifying him; Gunter promises to do better and says he plans to return to the DC area in three days. Flores hears something in Gunter's voice that suggests there is more to this story, but the detective cannot afford to scare his witness into fleeing more permanently; he also needs Gunter's permission to search his room. After getting it, Flores hangs up and has the sister sign a consent form to make sure everything is nice and tight.

With that, Flores and Eckrich step inside the gloomy town house. No lights are on and every curtain is drawn, making it difficult even to discern the color of the living room carpet or the furniture. The detectives head upstairs and find Gunter's room. It's a mess—papers and dirty clothes on the floor, the bed unmade, the white walls bare. Both men snap on latex gloves and dig through a mostly empty closet that contains three black plastic trash bags stuffed with dirty clothes.

"This is disgusting," Eckrich says, picking up a stiff white T-shirt and tossing it back on the floor.

After rooting through scraps of paper and food wrappers, they become satisfied that the room holds no evidence pertaining to the killing. Soon they're back in Flores's Impala, parked across from the sister's town house. Gunter's flight is still on the detective's mind; he decides to call his witness again so he can reiterate the importance of returning to PG County.

Gunter answers on the first ring. Flores calmly informs him that he and Eckrich have not trashed his room but left it just the way they found it. After delivering a stern warning about the importance of returning as soon as possible and informing him of any future trips, Flores goes silent for a moment. He can't decide whether to press Gunter for more information now or wait until he returns. But Flores can't help himself; he's too curious.

"Is there anything else you need to tell me?" Flores asks Gunter as gently as possible. "Don't lie, don't hide anything. Why did you run?"

The line goes so quiet that Flores checks his phone to make sure he is still connected.

A second later, Gunter clears his throat. "There is something," he says.

*Shit,* the detective thinks. *I knew it.*

"Robert is the one who set all of this up."

"What?" Flores asks. "Wait—Robert?"

For a moment Flores is confused, his mind spinning through the case file, but then he realizes Gunter is referring to Robert Ofoeme, the witness they brought into homicide just two days earlier.

"A couple of weeks ago," Gunter says, his words coming in a rush, "Robert called me to say he wanted Slug dead. But I was too scared to do it, so he told me he would get me in touch with Brandon."

*Fuck,* Flores thinks, *no wonder he ran to North Carolina.*

Gunter hesitates, clearly worried that he has said too much. Flores assures him that's it safe to continue.

Gunter explains that he and Robert Ofoeme are friends and

partners in the drug trade. Slug Adams owed money to Ofoeme, who was Adams's supplier. Adams was a difficult person, Gunter says, and Ofoeme had grown tired of him. The plan was simple: Ofoeme would lure Adams to Maryland on the pretense of a "leak"—an armed robbery—that would net them $10,000. Gunter tells Flores that Ofoeme was confident Adams would travel north because he knew Adams had committed robberies and had even shot a man during a holdup. After talking with Adams on the phone and persuading him to come to Washington, Ofoeme instructed Gunter to coordinate the hit.

When Gunter expressed reservations about killing Adams, Ofoeme enlisted Battle, his enforcer. Gunter says that Ofoeme's plan took shape over the next few days and was executed with precision. Gunter met Adams after he got off the bus near Union Station. They walked a short distance to Battle's Mustang—which was parked in an area where there were no surveillance cameras—piled into the car, and drove around looking for a quiet place to kill Adams. But the streets were teeming with Super Bowl fans, so they continued on, finally coming upon the deserted park in Prince George's County. Then, Gunter tells Flores, Battle walked Slug Adams deeper into the park and shot him dead.

After finishing his story, Gunter says, "I should have told you that earlier, I know."

"Jesus," Flores says. "You definitely need to come back on Monday. Everything will be fine. But you have to come back."

"Okay," says Gunter.

Flores hangs up the phone. Frowning, he ponders how his once straightforward investigation has suddenly become so complicated. One thing is clear: Gunter played a direct role in the murder of Salaam Adams, so Flores's star witness is actually an accomplice. The man may not have pulled the trigger, but Gunter lured Adams to his death and was in the car during his final hours, fully knowing what would transpire.

With his eyes focused on the town house in front of them, Flores grips the wheel and recounts his conversation with Gunter for Eckrich. The investigators agree that they need to speak to a prosecutor and strategize about whether to handle Gunter as a witness or a suspect. Most likely it will be the latter.

"He fucking lied," Flores says.

"They all lie, Eddie," Eckrich replies.

Flores puts the Impala in gear and stamps hard on the accelerator. Within seconds, the county is blurring past his window. He can't get to his desk soon enough—he has notes to write, prosecutors to brief, decisions to make.

Back in the office, the word CLOSED is emblazoned in red next to Flores's two cherries in the homicide log book. But the label means nothing now, and the rookie knows that his work is far from done.

## · CHAPTER 3 ·

11:05 a.m., Friday, February 8

Mike Crowell sits at his desk, thinking about how best to shake Jeff Buck's tree. He and Sean Deere now have the names of several associates of Buck and his crew, but Crowell is particularly interested in one of these men: Gerry Gordon, the Peeping Tom. At age thirty, Gordon is older than most of the people around Buck; perhaps, Crowell thinks, Gordon is mature enough to realize that it's better to help the police than to lie to protect his buddies.

But Gordon is intriguing for other reasons, too. For one, Amber Stanley's foster sister refused to have anything to do with him; as far as Crowell and Deere can determine, Gordon is the only man who has ever been rejected by Denise, the kind of slight that might spark a killer's rage. For another, the detectives recently determined that Gordon rented a room in a house that has been mentioned more than once during their investigation. Located in Mitchellville, it's one of several party houses frequented by Buck, a place where he and his crew hung out with women, drank liquor, and smoked weed. The fact that Gordon lived in the house means that he must have been trusted by those close to Buck; he also might have overheard loose talk.

Crowell looks around the office. The only member of his squad at a desk is Allyson Hamlin. He and Hamlin are the day's early birds: M-40 is on the evening shift this week, so its detectives are not scheduled to start until 3:00 p.m. Investigators usually begin taking cases an hour before the official start of their shift, and they often arrive at the office a bit early to get a jump on their day. But Crowell's motive for coming in today before noon is more pragmatic: he wants the overtime pay.

Crowell picks up the phone and calls Deere to let him know what he has in mind. Deere agrees with the plan but says he's tied up at the moment—he has some personal business to take care of, as well as a meeting about another case. He expects to arrive in the office at about the time their shift begins.

After texting Joe Bunce and suggesting that they meet at the house in Mitchellville, Crowell turns to Hamlin and asks if she is working on anything pressing. When she shakes her head, Crowell tells her that he wants to go find the Peeping Tom.

Thirty minutes later, the two detectives park their cars in front of the party house. But as Crowell is marching up to the front door, something strikes him as off. Slowing his pace, he carefully surveys the home and yard: the yellow siding and red shutters are unblemished, and the lawn is tidy and dotted with trimmed bushes. There are no crushed beer cans or shattered bottles in the grass, no glassine drug bags in the driveway. Crowell stops, puts his finger on the address in his notepad, and then cross-checks it against the metal numbers above the front door. *No*, he thinks, *this is the right one.*

Taking his final two steps to the door, Crowell glances over his right shoulder and spots Hamlin, who is standing about five feet away, her right hand resting on the butt of her gun. Beyond Hamlin he sees a leafless tree, the quiet street, and low, scudding clouds in all directions. Crowell turns back to the house, presses the bell, and hears a chime.

A moment later, the door opens, revealing a young woman in a neat white blouse and red skirt. Having expected a street thug or a drug addict, Crowell feels whiplashed: instead he's looking at a smiling June Cleaver.

"Hello, ma'am, I'm Detective Crowell with the county police, and this is Detective Hamlin," he says, nodding toward his fellow investigator.

The woman scrutinizes the detective at her door. Crowell looks ultraserious in his fugitive-hunting best: gray sweatshirt, bullet-resistant vest, blue jeans, and running shoes. He's also got a gun on his right hip. Stepping aside, she bids the detectives to enter.

Crowell is immediately overwhelmed by the delicious smell of freshly baked cookies. Or at least that's what he thinks he's smelling; for a moment, he wonders if his new diet pills are playing tricks on him. Two days earlier, he visited a doctor and asked for help losing weight. He was given an injection of vitamin B12 and a prescription for phentermine, a hunger suppressant that other detectives had taken with some success. The drug has side effects the chronically hyperactive detective doesn't need—an increase in energy, euphoria, and restlessness—but Crowell is already swearing by the pills, saying they've helped him drop several pounds even though he's continued eating his longtime staple: fast-food cheese-burgers.

Pausing in the foyer to get his bearings, Crowell tries hard not to betray his befuddlement. He looks around and sees hardwood floors, new bookshelves, and clean furniture in the living room. This is not at all what he was expecting.

"Cookies?" he asks, inhaling deeply. "Chocolate chip?"

The woman beams, and Crowell and Hamlin smile in return as they walk into the kitchen, which in addition to the scent of cookies has the new-appliance smell of steel and plastic. Crowell is now certain they have the wrong house—there is no way this is the neigh-borhood drug den where Jeff Buck and his crew hung out.

In the kitchen, Crowell is mesmerized by the spotless cabinets. "Cherry?" he asks, rubbing his hand along one.

"They're beautiful," says Hamlin. She points to the stove. "Stain-less steel? Nice."

"Thank you," says the woman as a girl and a pair of little boys scamper into the kitchen, two of the children nearly plowing into Hamlin's legs before veering into the living room and vanishing down a hallway.

Hoping to clear up the confusion, Crowell asks the woman if she knows Gerry Gordon. When she says no, Crowell gives her a descrip-tion of the man, but that doesn't register, either.

"He doesn't sound familiar," she says. "No."

Crowell asks how she came to live in the house, and the woman says she bought it a few months ago. The previous owners had fallen behind on their payments, she explains, and she and her hus-band were able to purchase the house at such a steep discount that they still had enough money to renovate. Crowell nods, thinking back over various interviews and realizing that witnesses had mostly talked about spending time in this house during the past summer, before Amber Stanley was killed.

"Good thing, too," she says. "It was a disaster—a real mess."

She can't remember the previous owners' names, but her descrip-tion confirms Crowell's suspicion that they must have owned the party house.

Crowell closes his pad, shakes the woman's hand, and thanks her for her time. She politely leads the detectives to the front door, where she takes Crowell's outstretched business card and promises to call if she hears anything about Gerry Gordon.

As the door closes behind him, Crowell wishes more witnesses were like this woman. Regretting not having grabbed a cookie—on these diet pills, he is convinced he can eat anything and still lose weight—he rolls his eyes at Hamlin and trudges down the walkway toward his Impala.


WAITING FOR CROWELL and Hamlin is Joe Bunce, leaning against the passenger door of his cruiser. After kidding Bunce about his late arrival, Crowell explains that Gerry Gordon and Jeff Buck's associates haven't lived here in months. Bunce smacks the door of his car: while digging out the information that the Peeping Tom had been renting a room here, he'd taken the trouble to search computerized land records to verify the address and the owners. The county clerk's office, he gripes, must be behind in processing deeds.

Bunce looks around. "Where's Detective En Route?" he asks.

Crowell tells Bunce that Deere is busy with other stuff and that he didn't feel like waiting for him. Then he eyes the double row of single-family homes stretching away from what he now thinks of as the cookie house. The street and its sidewalks are empty; he doesn't even see a dog walker.

Turning back to Bunce, he says, "Remember the Crown Vic?"

Bunce nods. Two days earlier, the two detectives were standing on a curb in this very neighborhood when a dark blue battle wagon passed them. Jacked up on struts and with speakers pounding out rap music, the car trailed a plume of marijuana smoke from a rear window, as if powered by a steam engine. Through the thinly tinted glass, Crowell saw a young man looking straight at him, delivering a blatant eye-fuck. He and Bunce hopped in their cars and gave chase, crisscrossing the area for a good fifteen minutes without finding the Ford Crown Victoria.

"Well, I want that car," Crowell says. "It had drugs and a gun in it—I know it did."

Bunce rolls his eyes. On the diet pills, his partner is even more intense than usual. For two days, he's been talking nonstop about the Crown Vic. Bunce decides to move on. "What's next?" he says.

Checking his notebook, Crowell recommends that they visit the home of the twenty-year-old who caught the STD from Denise. Bunce and Hamlin agree it's a good idea—the man lives fairly close by—so they climb into their Impalas and head out.

Not forty-five seconds later, Crowell is approaching a major thoroughfare when he spots a pedestrian in a thick black peacoat walking toward him on the opposite side of the street. Crowell draws closer; the man abruptly stops and spins around, then speed-walks in the opposite direction. As Crowell drives by, he glimpses the man's face.

*There's something about that guy,* thinks Crowell. *What? What?*

The investigator's mind races but comes up empty; he can't figure out why the man looks familiar. Instinct takes over: Crowell whips the car around and guns the engine. The car lunges forward and then halts with a screech, not ten yards from the startled man, who stares open-mouthed at the detective.

"Hey, buddy, buddy," Crowell says, leaping from the car. "Can I talk to you? I want to talk to you."

The man turns and quickly scans his surroundings, clearly calculating his chances for escape.

"Don't do it, buddy!" Crowell yells. "If you run, it will change your fucking life!"

The man blinks and says nothing, his focus entirely on Crowell now.

"Get your fucking hands on my fucking car!" Crowell yells, pointing to the trunk of the Impala with his left hand while letting his right drop to the butt of the gun on his hip.

The man shrugs, shuffles to the car, and places his hands on the trunk. Crowell keys his radio and lets Bunce and Hamlin know that he's just grabbed someone. They respond that they're on their way.

"What's your name?" Crowell asks. He frisks the man for weapons; finding none, he spins him around.

When the man tells Crowell his name, Crowell asks him to repeat it. He does.

*No way,* thinks Crowell. It's Jeff Buck's alibi witness, Scott Allen,* the friend the dealer said he was probably hanging out with on the night of Amber Stanley's murder. Allen is on their list of witnesses to interview, because he could help undermine at least one of Buck's potential alibis; he's also a close friend of the dealer and knows the players in the crew. Crowell has seen his photograph a couple of times. Perhaps the detective somehow recognized the man, or maybe he just got lucky. Either way, he feels charmed—he and Deere and the others could have spent weeks trying to find Allen and come up dry.

Crowell looks down at Allen's right hand and notices that it's not lying flat on the trunk of his car; it's half open, as if the guy can't quite make a fist. A scar runs across the thumb, near the wrist. It looks like a fairly recent knife wound. *Maybe he cut his hand while raping Denise,* Crowell thinks. *Maybe the blood on her shirt is his.*

"What happened to your hand?" Crowell asks casually. "You cut it?"

"I lacerated my tendon," Allen says. "I lost the nerve. I can't feel anything."

"How did you do it? That is what I asked."

"Car accident in Texas," says Allen, his voice carrying a slight quiver.

Crowell is certain the man is lying.

An hour later, Crowell and Bunce are devouring Big Macs at their desks while Allen is stewing in Interview Room 1. Crowell finishes his cheeseburger, a Coca-Cola, and a large container of fries. "I feel like I have nitrous in my system," he says, meaning the fuel additive for racing cars.

---

*Not his real name.

"How much have you lost?" Bunce asks.

"Eight pounds," says Crowell.

"That's good."

"This shit is like gold," Crowell says. "My wife called me, asking where I had left the pills. I told her on the counter. She wants to use 'em. She says she just needed one. I told her not to take another until tomorrow."

"Why?"

"Because then there won't be any left for me! I told her, 'Get your own shit—stop stealing mine.'"

Ten minutes later, the two detectives take their seats across the table from Scott Allen in the box. Allen's coat is slung over the back of his chair, and he is wearing a plain gray long-sleeved T-shirt. The room isn't particularly warm, but sweat is dripping down the man's forehead. He's also wringing his hands.

Though Crowell can see that his witness is nervous, he's not sure how to play this. He needs Allen's consent to obtain his DNA, but if he asks for it without explanation, Allen might shut down and refuse. The detective doesn't want to mention the murder yet; he'd like to find another way to persuade the man that he has good reason to ask for his consent, something serious but absurd enough to prevent the guy from freaking out.

Crowell begins the interview in the manner of a dull bureaucrat and learns that Allen graduated from a PG high school a few years ago. He's twenty-one, has a girlfriend, and still lives with his parents. As he listens to the man answer his questions, the detective twirls his pen in his fingers, and looks at the ceiling.

"Listen," Crowell says abruptly, "I know this is going to sound far-fetched, but did you have sex with a twelve-year-old girl?"

Allen's eyes grow wide with incomprehension. "Wha-wha-what?"

"It's just, just—that's what somebody told us," Crowell says, his tone offhand. "We have an individual alleging something. Look,

I don't think you're having sex with twelve-year-olds, but I am wondering if we can get your DNA sample. It will prove you didn't."

"Sure," Allen says, rubbing a sweaty cheek. "Sure."

"Sign here," says Crowell, passing the required form across the
table. "It's really no big deal. Just have to check this out, a twelve-
year-old girl and all."

As soon as Allen affixes his signature, Crowell summons an evidence technician into the box to swab the man's cheeks. After she
has finished and shut the door behind herself, Crowell scrutinizes
the sweaty man in front of him. *No better time than now,* he thinks.

"So, you know anything about a girl getting killed?"

The man is obviously puzzled, his mind desperately churning.
His eyes dart between Crowell and Bunce, and his shoulders slump
as he realizes that this is no pro forma interview to clear up ridicu-
lous allegations involving a sexual assault.

When Allen doesn't answer, Crowell gets more specific. They are
investigating the murder of Amber Stanley back in August, the
detective says. Does he know anything about it?

"I—I don't."

Bunce opens a folder and slaps color mug shots of Jeff Buck and
his associates on the table, one after another.

"Know him?" Bunce asks, tapping the photo of Jeff Buck.

Allen shakes his head.

"How about him?" Bunce asks, pointing to a picture of someone else.

Again and again, no. Six times, no.

"Bullshit!" Bunce says. "We know you know these guys. Why
lie to us? You hang out with them!"

"You lie about the little shit, you make us question what you say
about the big shit," says Crowell, drumming the table with the fingers
of his left hand.

Allen says nothing.

"You look nervous," Crowell says.

"I am nervous. Your questions—"

"You're sweating," Crowell says.

"I sweat a lot."

"You sweat a lot?" asks Crowell, shaking his head, looking at his partner. "Joe, there's a medical condition like that. What is it?"

Bunce doesn't reply. He stares at Allen and watches a drop of the man's sweat hit the table. Allen swipes his damp cheek with a forearm.

"We know you're tight with Jeff Buck," says Bunce.

"I don't—"

Crowell slams the table with both palms so suddenly that both Allen and Bunce sit bolt upright.

"I'm out of patience! I don't want this to be a long fucking day!"

Allen's eyes grow wide again.

"Come on!" Crowell yells. "This is bullshit! Tell me why you're so nervous!"

"I'm—I'm worried about myself."

"You're worried about going home tonight?" Crowell asks.

"No," Allen says, his eyes now glued to one of the mug shots on the table. He nods toward the photo, the one closest to Bunce. "I'm scared *of him*."

Crowell and Bunce eye the picture—it's the one of Jeff Buck.

"I lied earlier," Allen says. "I know him."

It takes the detectives a half hour more to peel away silly lies—Allen gives two fake names for his girlfriend, another for his baby's mother, a bad phone number for his girlfriend in Texas. They learn that he cut his thumb in a fight with his girl, not in a car accident. Most important, by checking airline records and speaking to Allen's mother, the investigators confirm that Allen was in Texas from at least August 13—four days before Denise's rape and nine days before Amber's murder—through the end of December.

At first, Crowell and Bunce are disappointed: they had almost believed that they'd stumbled across the man who had raped Denise. But there's some good news, too, because what Allen has told them appears to have eviscerated the best of Jeff Buck's alibis. If Allen was in Texas on August 22, Buck wasn't hanging out with him on the night of the murder.

As the interrogation wears on, Crowell and Bunce probe deeper into Allen's friendships with Buck and his associates. Allen claims he doesn't know much about Amber Stanley's murder beyond some neighborhood gossip and what he read on a flyer posted at a gas station. When Crowell asks him whether he's ever seen Jeff Buck with a gun, Allen says he once saw Buck and his enforcer brandishing pistols at a party held in the house Crowell had visited that very morning.

Crowell asks Allen where Buck keeps his guns.

"I honestly don't know," Allen says, "but I know he doesn't trust nobody, not after some shit got lost."

"Shit got lost?" asks Bunce.

"A gun."

"Who lost it?" asks Crowell.

Allen provides the name of one of Buck's friends and says Buck told him that this man had "misplaced" the pistol.

"When did he lose the gun?" asks Bunce.

"During the summer," Allen says. "When I was in Texas."

"When did you hear he lost it?"

"Jeff told me about it when I got back."

"Why did he let his friend have the gun?" Crowell asks.

The friend "had to take care of something," Allen says, shrugging.

*Maybe Buck lent the gun to his friend to kill Denise,* Crowell thinks.

"What happened to the gun?"

"I don't know. It just got lost."

"What kind of gun?" asks Bunce.

Allen tells them its precise caliber.

"Are you sure?" asks Crowell.

"Yes, positive."

It's the same caliber as the pistol used to kill Amber Stanley.


AN HOUR LATER, Crowell escorts Allen to the men's room. As he steers the witness through the bathroom door, Crowell spots Sean Deere sauntering down the hallway. "Solving your case for you, Sean," Crowell jokes.

Deere chuckles, acknowledging the dig. After taking care of his personal business, Deere had met with a prosecutor about another case. The appointment had gone longer than expected, and he is only now settling in for the evening shift. Deere stands by the open restroom door while Allen uses the urinal. When Crowell and his witness emerge, Crowell motions for Deere to follow them into the old evidence bay.

"Let's all smoke," Crowell says.

Allen takes a seat, and Crowell hands him a cigarette. The two detectives stand over him as Crowell tells Deere what they've learned from Allen. After finishing his summary, Crowell turns to Allen.

"Did I get all of that right?"

"Yes, sir, you did."

"How did he lose the gun?" asks Deere.

"I don't think he actually lost it," Allen says. "I think he threw it."

"Why?"

"Because he got scared, or he did something with it that he didn't want traced back to him."

Deere and Crowell exchange a glance. This could be very good news.

"Where do you think he tossed the gun?" asks Deere.

"I don't know," Allen says. "But I can help you."

"How?"

Allen offers to work as an informant. "I can ask what happened to it, what they know about the murder, and get back to you. It would be natural for me to ask about it."

Deere nods encouragingly but doubts he will ever hear from Allen again. He has the sense that the man will say anything to persuade the detectives to ease up on him.

At Crowell's prompting, Allen provides numerous details about Jeff Buck's drug dealing and how other local gangs sling narcotics. He tells them about another party house that belongs to a friend of Buck's, where they record music and hang out. It's the same one Buck had mentioned during his interrogation a week ago. Deere makes a mental note to ask the drug unit to conduct "trash rips" on the house so he can gather evidence of narcotics dealing and get a warrant to raid the place.

Deere asks how everyone gets around town, and Allen says that whereas Buck often pays Jason Murray for rides, he himself tends to get lifts from a friend who owns a blue Crown Victoria.

"No shit. Was that you in it the other day?" asks Crowell, naming the street where he spotted the same type of car.

Allen smirks. "I saw you," he says. "That was us."

"Gun in the car?"

"No."

"Drugs?"

"Yeah."

Crowell slaps his hands together. "I knew it," he says.

As they take their final puffs, Deere notices that Allen is gripping his cigarette in a strange way in his right hand. The detective looks closer and spies the scar on his right thumb and wrist.

"How did you get that?" Deere asks.

"Punched plate glass in a fight with my baby's momma," Allen says. "It was a self-afflicted wound."

"No," corrects Deere. "A self-*inflicted* wound."

Sitting with his chin in his left palm, Detective Mike Ebaugh leans forward, squints, and concentrates on the final moments of his victim's life—for at least the fiftieth time. The video playing on the computer monitor at his desk is time-lapsed and grainy, which is why the investigator has watched and rewatched it, then watched it again, even projecting it onto a floor-to-ceiling video screen at the department's training academy in an unsuccessful attempt to catch a previously missed detail. Each time, he sees nothing new or unusual—beyond the cold-blooded execution of a father in the presence of his two-year-old boy.

Ebaugh again replays the silent clip, which begins at 9:51 a.m. on a bright December Wednesday. His twenty-five-year-old victim, Nicoh Mayhew, pulls his white Kia Optima sedan into the parking lot of a nondescript apartment complex in Seat Pleasant, a town of 4,600 not far from the DC line. The security camera recording the video, affixed to the roof of a nearby leasing office, is aimed at the parking lot and shows Mayhew backing his car into a spot in front of the three-story building. The car vanishes behind a sport-utility vehicle, but the video captures Mayhew's head above the SUV as he walks around the Kia. Mayhew ducks near the right rear door, and a moment later his two-year-old son can be seen walking from the back of the Kia across a short bridge to the apartment complex's stairs, which are hidden from view.

As Mayhew retrieves a bag from the trunk, the video shows two men in dark clothing strolling into the lot. They crouch behind a row of cars as Mayhew shuts the trunk and crosses the bridge, bag in hand. Just as Mayhew vanishes into the stairwell, the men bolt after him. Ten seconds later, the men reappear, sprinting toward the street and a dark BMW that has pulled to the curb. They jump inside, and the car speeds away.

Left behind—out of camera range—was Mayhew, shot dead. He was struck by four bullets, including one to the head. His son, clad in Elmo pajamas and sipping apple juice from a McDonald's juice box, was wounded in the right arm.

Ebaugh rewinds the footage and studies it again, starting and stopping, starting and stopping. With his eyes only inches from the screen, he thinks he recognizes the brand of sneakers worn by one of the gunmen—popular Nike Foamposites.

Removing his wire-rimmed glasses, the detective pinches the bridge of his nose with one hand and rubs his crew cut with the other. Then he puts his glasses back on and clicks Play. He badly wants to solve this homicide, and not just because Mayhew was slain in the presence of his toddler, which unnerves Ebaugh, the father of two young children. No, he is convinced that because this case is so difficult to crack, it will prove his worth as an investigator.

Mayhew, a marijuana dealer, had been a key prosecution witness in a looming trial involving the execution-style killings of two fellow dealers, one of whom had been a close friend of Mayhew's. As Ebaugh and all detectives know, murders of witnesses are notoriously hard to investigate. Who would ever agree to serve as a witness in a case where another witness was slain? Nobody in the Homicide Unit—not even Ebaugh's partner, D. J. Windsor, or his sergeant— thinks he stands much chance of winning investigative glory this time at bat. On the night of the murder, a top supervisor gave the detective a sympathetic pat on the back and said, "Good luck solving this shit sandwich."

It would be a tough case for any detective, but it's especially challenging for a new one. Ebaugh, thirty-one, is still considered a rookie despite having joined homicide two years earlier. And although he attacks the job as if born to it, he wound up in the department quite by chance. A native of Michigan, Ebaugh joined the army after high school, fulfilling his dream of being a soldier. But one day, while pushing hard during a forced march, he wrecked an already battered right knee. After a medical discharge, he became an airplane mechanic, married, and moved with his wife, Krystel, to Prince George's County, where she was entering the PG police academy. To save money, they lived in a room behind the small office of Freeway Airport, a general aviation airfield where Ebaugh fixed Cessnas and Pipers for $11.50 an hour.

One night in 2004, while he was having a few drinks with Krystel and her fellow cadets, his wife and the others urged him to join the force. Ebaugh's stepfather had been a criminal psychologist, and he had long been intrigued by the shrink's stories of cops and felons. After injuring his knee, Ebaugh hadn't given law enforcement much thought; now, with his knee fully healed, he decided to apply. He joined the force later that year; ironically, his wife dropped out of the academy, in part because they agreed that one cop in the family was enough.

A hard and frenetic worker, Ebaugh drew the attention of commanders early on and won promotion to specialized units and a robbery squad. In 2011, he was tapped to join homicide and soon solved his first murder, a cold case that another detective had been unable to crack. Even those who sometimes find Ebaugh's personality grating agree that he's remarkably dogged. As D. J. Windsor puts it, "Ebaugh may not know precisely what he is doing, because—let's be honest—he is kind of nuts. But he will work it and work it and work it, and just by doing that, he will solve it."

The gangly, six-foot-two Ebaugh knows he's a strange duck. He obsessively reads self-help books and policing manuals. He downs fifty protein pills a day, which gives his sweat a musty odor. He sprays himself and his car with cologne to mask the scent of the occasional cigarette, telling his fellow officers that Krystel will kill him if she catches him smoking.

To say he lacks a verbal filter is an understatement—a torrent of words and stories streams from his mouth. He once admitted that he was late for an assignment because a jellyfish had stung his testicles while he was skinny-dipping. He divulged that he euthanized his own dog with a snub-nosed .38 after it had broken its back and because it was a pain in the ass. He brags about having killed a bear so he could obtain a fur rug on which to have sex. When encountering the police department's psychologist in the hallway, he will sometimes say, "Joe, why do I still cry when I masturbate?" A devotee of herbal erection enhancers, he provides a full-throated endorsement of one he nicknamed the Diamond Cutter.

His endless chattering can annoy his colleagues, who occasionally accuse him of grandstanding. Particularly galling was an incident that occurred one Saturday night the previous December, when Ebaugh was leaving the homicide office for his long commute home to the Eastern Shore. Hearing a man screaming nearby, Ebaugh pointed his Impala in the direction of the noise. A few seconds later, he came upon an enraged man clubbing another man with a shovel. Ebaugh jumped from the car, stopped the assault, and made an arrest, preventing what surely would have been a homicide a mere block from police headquarters.

The following Monday, Ebaugh stood next to the clerk's station in the homicide office and regaled a dozen of his colleagues scattered about the room with the story of his life-saving deed. He complained about having to give an interview to a reporter on television and then read a passage from a congratulatory e-mail sent to him by the major: "Thank you for preventing a murder in these final days of 2012. You have no idea what it means to the Homicide Command Staff."

Ebaugh's braggadocio was met with a chorus of grousing: cops are supposed to grumble about accolades, not revel in them. From the far side of the room, Detective Billy Watts piped up: "Ebaugh did what a normal police officer does every day. Come on!"

From the opposite corner came the voice of Ebaugh's squad mate Jeff Eckrich: "I can't believe the department is risking its image by putting you on television!"

"Wait until the reporter finds out you murdered your Chihuahua," said Detective David Gurry, standing to Ebaugh's left at the fax machine.

Ebaugh glared at Gurry. "He wasn't a Chihuahua—he was a Chihuahua mutt! He weighed twenty-five pounds. He had a broken back and a thyroid problem. And he was a real asshole!"

"Yeah," Eckrich said, "he was an asshole, but that doesn't mean he deserved to die."

Where another detective might have retreated under this verbal onslaught, Ebaugh doubled down. Smiling broadly, he said, "Fuck you, guys! This is going to get me laid for a week!"

The background chatter ceased. You could hear the unit's collective thought: *Did he really just say that? Of course he did—it's Ebaugh!*

Sergeant Tony Schartner, who had so far ignored the bullshitting as he worked on a report at his desk, turned around and stared at Ebaugh. He started to speak, stopped himself, and then went ahead anyway.

"He thinks he's S-s-super Cop," Schartner stammered.

"Poor Krystel," said Eckrich.

His face growing red as he stuttered, Schartner said, "I can see it n-n-now. 'C-c-c-all me a hero, K-k-krystel! C-c-c-call me a hero!' "

The room exploded in laughter. Detectives launched more zingers. They drummed on their desks with their fists, and a blushing Ebaugh finally held up his hands in surrender.


NICOH MAYHEW WAS killed on the morning of December 19, 2012, just as Police Chief Mark Magaw was about to begin a press conference hailing the year's substantial drop in homicides. That's invariably how it goes in PG County: a police official opens his mouth about good numbers and somebody dies. A week earlier, Kevin Davis, the assistant chief, had boasted to an auditorium packed with detectives about their soon-to-be-record-setting year, during which the county experienced the lowest homicide total since 1986. As investigators left the meeting, Detective Mike Barnhardt turned to Dave Gurry, the detective then on deck, and said, "Better be ready to catch your case." Not three hours later, Gurry was standing in a blood-smeared foyer.

While Chief Magaw was speaking to the press the following week, Mike Ebaugh and D. J. Windsor were at the PG County jail, interviewing a witness in one of Windsor's cases. Because cell phones are not permitted in the jail, Ebaugh did not receive word of Mayhew's murder until more than an hour after it had occurred, causing the superstitious detective to question his decision to interview an inmate during the chief's media appearance. When Ebaugh finally pulled into the parking lot of the apartment complex, at 11:20 a.m., he was confronted by a swarm of detectives, officers, TV trucks, and reporters, most of whom had raced to the scene directly from the press conference.

Ebaugh and Windsor—a stocky thirty-four-year-old with a crew cut and rosy cheeks—navigated the chaos until they found the investigators holding down the scene. Huddling with the four other detectives in the parking lot, the two homicide cops learned that Mayhew had been shot and killed outside his mother's door, where his body remained. His mother, Cynthia Mayhew, and his youngest brother, a nineteen-year-old, had been in the apartment at the time of the shooting, but the brother had apparently fled the scene after an ambulance took Mayhew's wounded toddler to the hospital. The mom was still inside, where she was being interviewed by detectives; she had already told them that she was certain her son had been killed in retaliation for being a witness against his own nephew and a friend in a 2011 double homicide. Ebaugh had heard about the case: two men were found shot dead in a silver Lexus, and the car had been doused with bleach and gasoline.

Detectives had solved the homicides thanks to an astute

observation by Sean Deere: he spotted a unique price tag on a bleach bottle left in the car's trunk. Deere tracked the tag to a convenience store, and investigators watched hours of security video until they spotted the man who'd purchased the bottle. After more solid police work, the buyer was identified as Nicoh Mayhew.

Under intense questioning, Mayhew eventually flipped on the killers, telling detectives and, later, a grand jury that a friend, Kenan Myers, had told him to buy some gas and bleach and then head to a meet-up in an out-of-the-way location, the driveway of a closed quarry. When Mayhew arrived at the quarry, he spotted Myers and Brian "Block" Mayhew, his nephew, sitting with two other men in a silver Lexus. As Mayhew pulled up next to the Lexus, he heard four or five gunshots. Moments later, he recognized the two dead men in the car—Sean Ellis, twenty-four, and Anthony McKelvin, twenty-eight. One of the men, Ellis, was Mayhew's best friend, and both were friends of the two killers.

Mayhew watched as Myers and his nephew grabbed the gas and the bleach from his car and doused the Lexus; their plan was to destroy forensic evidence and set the vehicle ablaze. But no one had remembered matches, so the two men climbed into Mayhew's car and all three of them took off. Mayhew said he had feared for his life, telling the grand jury that "they would have shot me" if he had refused to help.

Such is life in the drug trade—sometimes you have to kill your friends. Thanks to Mayhew's information, the police charged his nephew Brian Mayhew, twenty-one, and his friend Kenan Myers, twenty-five, with first-degree murder. But life as a homicide witness can be perilous. Police and state prosecutors urged Mayhew to move to another jurisdiction. Mayhew refused, telling the police he didn't want to leave his friends, his girlfriend, or his young son. He also preferred to stay close to his customers: he sold a pound or two of marijuana a week.

After being briefed by the on-scene detectives, Ebaugh and

Windsor headed for the mother's apartment. They crossed the short bridge, passed under the green awning above the entrance to 6812 Seat Pleasant Drive, and climbed six steps to the second-floor landing. Mayhew's body lay sprawled in front of an open door. Brain matter and blood were splattered against the door jamb, and the floor was covered in blood. Clad in a green windbreaker, black sweatpants, and black high-top basketball shoes, Mayhew lay facedown on the concrete landing.

As Ebaugh studied the body, he heard a woman wailing inside the apartment. He turned to the female evidence tech cataloging the scene and pointed his chin toward the interior. "Mom," the tech said. Ebaugh nodded and got down on his haunches to better examine the spatter, which was about three feet above the floor.

"I don't get why it's all down there," the tech said, pointing to the blood and the brain bits. "Shouldn't there be some higher, where he would have been standing?"

"What do you think?" Ebaugh asked.

The tech hypothesized that the gunmen had started shooting as they were running up the stairs, perhaps striking Mayhew in the lower body. When he fell to the ground, they shot him in the head. A preliminary assessment of the scene, she said, supported that theory: Mayhew had a bullet wound to his right leg, another to his back, and what appeared to be two entrance wounds at the back of his head.

Ebaugh liked her theory, but he had his own: "Maybe he squatted to protect his kid. He went down like this"—Ebaugh crouched carefully so as not to touch any blood—"and that's why it's so low? Or maybe they made him kneel."

Windsor, removing his wraparound sunglasses, studied the pool of blood on the concrete landing and some streaks of blood across the threshold on the apartment's carpet. "What happened to the boy?"

"Mom or her son dragged him inside after," the tech said.

Ebaugh asked Windsor to monitor the rolling of the body by the forensic examiner. "I'm going to talk to Mom," he said, stepping over the corpse and walking through the open door, into the apartment.

To his right, Ebaugh spotted Cynthia Mayhew sitting at a circular dining room table. The detective introduced himself, sat down, and told the victim's mother that he would do everything he could to solve the case. But Mrs. Mayhew clearly wasn't listening. She stared vacantly over Ebaugh's shoulder at her dead son's right arm, which was splayed across the apartment's threshold.

"You pulled the grandson inside?" Ebaugh asked.

She nodded.

"Is that how he was lying?" Ebaugh asked, motioning with his head toward her son's body.

"Yes," Mrs. Mayhew said, her eyes still locked on the arm. "I heard my [youngest] son come out of the bathroom. Then I heard the shots—*pow, pow, pow, pow*—and I started screaming and running toward the door. And my son grabbed me, pulled me back. 'Don't go out there, Mom—be quiet,' he told me."

She paused, composing herself. "We didn't know what was going on out there. And I heard the baby crying, and I figured out what was going on." She said her younger son "opened the door, and I reached out and snatched the baby and brought him inside."

"I'm sorry," Ebaugh said.

For the first time, Mrs. Mayhew turned her tear-soaked eyes on the detective. Her face was ravaged with overwhelming pain.

Before Ebaugh could ask another question, Mrs. Mayhew launched into the sad tale of her family's history. She pointed to a laminated newspaper clipping, partly hidden behind two rows of framed family photographs; it was an article about how her eldest son had died in a car crash back in 1992. She said her next oldest was in jail on a murder charge—he had, in fact, been arrested by Mike Crowell, who had cracked a cold case—and that her youngest, the nineteen-year-old who had been inside the apartment with her at the time of Nicoh's murder, had been shot in the buttocks in May. She also talked about how Nicoh, her second youngest, had been a reluctant witness. He knew the risks but felt he didn't have a choice. If he testified, he'd be a target for having snitched. If he didn't, he would be charged as a co-conspirator. The dilemma had weighed on him, she said.

"Ever since, he's been looking over his back, knowing somebody would come do this bullshit to him," she told Ebaugh. "Since the murders, it was just him and his girlfriend and his baby. While she worked, he watched him every day right here."

She pointed to a pile of toys against the wall—an Elmo doll, a small chair, a Thomas the Tank Engine table, a tricycle. "He was a wonderful father. He loved that boy."

Mrs. Mayhew stood and took three quick strides toward her son's body. She could see him fully now, lying there, and she watched as a forensic investigator rummaged through his pockets. Standing over the investigator was D. J. Windsor; the detective looked up from the body and briefly made eye contact with the mother before returning his gaze to the corpse.

Ebaugh gently cupped Mrs. Mayhew's shoulder and directed her back to the table, putting her in a chair facing away from the door.

"I'm really sorry about all of this," Ebaugh said, wondering why he hadn't moved her away from the door earlier. "I should have—"

"It's all right," she interrupted. "I kissed him and told him good-bye. I told him I loved him. He knows I loved him. I kissed my boy. God will take care of this."

"I'm very sorry," Ebaugh said again. Remembering what he'd read in a manual about the importance of directing relatives' desire for retribution toward helping an investigator solve the case, he told her, "I will do my very best to ensure that these men all rot in jail for having done this. I will work very hard to catch them. I will catch them. And they will rot in jail."

Mrs. Mayhew wiped tears from her cheek and started to speak, but her voice cracked. Staring at her family photographs, she stiffened. "I hope they rot in *hell*," she said, her voice suddenly sharp with anger. "I knew my son was dead when I kissed him. I could see his brains."

IT HAS NOW been nearly two months since Nicoh Mayhew was killed, and Ebaugh is still watching and rewatching the security video. After ten more minutes of fruitless viewing, he calls it quits, deciding that he isn't going to see anything new. Yet the video is all he really has, and time is running out—the trials of Kenan Myers and Brian Mayhew in the double homicide are scheduled to start in July. The cases were originally slated to begin today, but the prosecutors had recently won a delay, in part to give Ebaugh more time to work. Prosecutors can rarely introduce information provided by a murdered witness, but if Ebaugh can prove that Nicoh Mayhew's killing was ordered by Kenan Myers or his nephew Brian Mayhew or both, the prosecutors might be allowed to read Nicoh Mayhew's damning grand jury testimony into the record.

Ebaugh is not 100 percent certain that Mayhew was slain to prevent his testimony. He was a drug dealer, after all, and not long after his murder, the detective learned that Mayhew had shot and wounded a notorious PG thug back in 2010, meaning he had a wide assortment of potential enemies. But with the trial looming, Ebaugh and his sergeant, Kerry Jernigan, have decided to focus on the witness angle. It's the most obvious motive, and it came with a deadline.

Ebaugh shuts down the video clip and drums his fingers on his desk. He flips through his notes, back and forth, back and forth, and finally closes the case file. He's about to head home when he thinks back to the murder scene and Mayhew's mother. Since that sad day in her apartment, Ebaugh has spoken to her more than a dozen times, hoping that she might pick up some information on the street and pass it along. He reopens his case file, turns to a page of phone numbers, and dials. She doesn't answer; Ebaugh hangs up.

Not five seconds later, the phone rings. Cynthia Mayhew is on the line.

"How are you doing, Cynthia?" he asks.

He keeps the conversation light, treating her as if she's an old friend. He asks about her apartment complex, when she'll be moving, how her youngest son is doing. After a few minutes, Ebaugh asks if she has come across anything new about the murder. "It might be completely insignificant to you," he says, "but it might help me."

Mayhew's mother says she has heard something and launches into a complicated tale about a man who owns a BMW and was seen in the neighborhood the day of the murder. The story makes little sense. Before asking her to repeat the tip so he can understand it well enough to get it down on paper, Ebaugh says, "Anything else?"

The line goes quiet, and Ebaugh guesses that Mrs. Mayhew is either thinking hard about something or weighing whether to fully trust him. As the silence drags on, Ebaugh figures it must be the latter. He is about to let her off the hook and return to the improbable BMW story when she says, "There is something else." Again, there is a pregnant pause, and now Ebaugh is sure she's deciding whether to confide in him.

Finally she speaks: "I hear that two guys did it. They are brothers."

Ebaugh writes down the information and gently asks again if there is anything else.

After another pause, she says, "Their names are John and Stan."

The detective frowns; he has already ruled out one John who had been in jail on federal gun charges at the time of the murder. Now he has another. *Or maybe it's the same guy and the streets are just recycling old rumors,* he thinks.

"Thanks, Cynthia, I'll run this down. That all?"

This time she doesn't hesitate. "I think one got locked up in some armored-car robberies."

Ebaugh writes that down, too. He stays in close contact with the Robbery Unit, which works right next door to homicide. But he hasn't heard of any big arrests involving armored-car robberies committed by someone named John or Stan.

After getting Mayhew's mother to repeat her tip about the mysterious BMW and writing it down, Ebaugh hangs up, grabs his notebook, and heads down a narrow back hallway into the Robbery Unit room, which looks almost identical to homicide's. He spots a lone detective at his desk and asks about recent arrests of a John or Stan in armored-car robberies. The investigator isn't certain he's heard of any but recommends that Ebaugh check back on Monday, when more detectives will be around, or call the FBI, which handles such crimes.

Ebaugh thanks the investigator and looks at his watch. It's nearly 5:00 p.m.—he's got to leave if he wants to get home in time for dinner with his family. He heads out to his car. Slipping behind the wheel, he pulls away from the building and begins to let his mind wander. He does some of his best thinking during his commute; this trip is no different.

As Ebaugh mulls over his phone conversation with Cynthia Mayhew, he isn't sure what to make of her tip about the two guys. It could be nothing; it could be everything. Two first names. Armored-car robberies. Brothers.

*John and Stan, John and Stan. Who are you?*

**12:35 a.m., Saturday, February 9**

Detective Billy Watts pulls his Impala to a stop in front of the apartment building and surveys the scene: a dozen police cars and vans parked at various angles, officers and detectives and evidence techs racing about, their shoulders tilted into a bitter wind. Watts peers into the darkness and scans each face until he finds his rookie, Detective Jonathan Hill, who is standing on a curb near the entrance to the building where a woman has been shot to death by one or more police officers.

Hill, the lead investigator on the case, is bundled in a thick tan overcoat, its lapels flipped up to protect his ears; his hands are jammed in its pockets. As Watts watches, Hill steps toward a white police car and knocks on the driver's window; it cracks a few inches and Hill says something, his breath creating a cloud of condensation. Inside the cruiser, illuminated by the pale yellow glow of a dome light, a female officer nods, eyes Hill, and then looks down as the window rolls shut. Watts imagines Hill offering words of reassurance while explaining to the officer that she will soon be heading to homicide for questioning.

Watts grabs a letter-sized notepad from the passenger seat and steps from the car, his ears immediately stung by the cold. He walks across the parking lot to Hill's side and surveys the scene once again. It is clear from the way officers and techs are scurrying around that they want to finish their work as quickly as possible, but Watts is not the sort to rush things. A perfectionist, he is methodical and relentless, and his primary job at this scene is to ensure that his rookie doesn't screw anything up.

"Whatcha got?" he asks Hill, who is blowing into his gloved hands.

Hill tells Watts what he has learned in twenty minutes at the scene. They are here to investigate the fatal shooting of a woman who lived on the first floor of the squat, red-brick building over his right shoulder, one of more than a dozen such buildings located just off bustling Annapolis Road in the heart of Bladensburg. A scrappy working-class town of 9,400 residents, shaped a bit like a foot kicking the northeast edge of Washington, Bladensburg is best known as the site of a battle in the War of 1812 during which President

James Madison rode onto the field. Today, like much of PG County, the town struggles with crime and difficult economic challenges. Nearly 20 percent of its residents live below the poverty line, and over the past few decades the town has witnessed the flight of its wealthier white residents to more distant suburbs.

Hill explains that tonight's incident started when an older female living in apartment 1 began screaming and yelling in the building's stairwell, threatening two women living in apartment 4, on the second floor. Apparently the woman had been involved in other such incidents, but this situation was more serious. When a resident in apartment 4 looked out her peephole, she saw the woman brandishing a knife above her head and screaming, "I know what you did with the little girl!"

After more yelling, the woman went back downstairs and returned to her apartment. Someone called 911, Bladensburg police were dispatched, and three officers and their sergeant soon arrived. They knocked on the woman's door, and when she opened it she was holding a six-inch blade above her head. The officers identified themselves and told her to drop the knife, but she refused and lunged. Three officers opened fire, striking the woman multiple times; she died later at Prince George's County Hospital Center. The woman—whom Hill presumes to be the apartment's leaseholder—didn't have any identification on her. Moreover, the detectives discovered no ID in her apartment, and no residents got a look at her before she was carried away in an ambulance.

Hill reports that evidence techs have thus far collected ten shell casings from the stairs and landing, and he tells Watts that all four of the Bladensburg cops—including the female officer in the car and her sergeant, who did not fire his weapon—are being sent to homicide for questioning. As is typical in such cases, the three officers will likely decline to speak until they consult lawyers. Like any potential suspect, they can invoke their right to remain silent when being interviewed by homicide detectives, though later they will be compelled to speak with internal affairs investigators. The sergeant, however, has to provide a detailed account of the shooting because he is considered a witness.

Hill and Watts are managing the criminal investigation into the death and the circumstances surrounding it. The Bladensburg Police Department, meanwhile, will conduct an administrative review to determine whether its officers acted in accordance with its rules and regulations. In that sense, the homicide detectives are likely to have an easy job of it—from what Hill has gathered, the Bladensburg police officers appear not to have broken any laws because they can show that they used lethal force to defend themselves against an armed and dangerous assailant.

Watts doesn't like investigating police shootings—it's too much like being an internal affairs investigator, and he has no interest in that type of work. He also can't abide the way officers involved in such incidents are portrayed in the media. He is already envisioning citizens and TV news reporters raising questions, second-guessing one of the most difficult decisions a police officer ever makes. Why not shoot her in the leg? Why not shoot the knife out of her hand? Why were four cops afraid of a little woman with a knife—weren't they wearing bulletproof vests?

Watts has heard it all before, and he has never been shy about providing the answer: Life isn't a video game, and you can't risk missing someone's arm or leg in a confrontation that could lead to your own death. Besides, what if you aimed for a leg and missed and the bullet zipped through a wall and struck an innocent five-year-old? That is why police officers are trained to shoot center mass: to incapacitate, to stop the threat, to kill. As for the vests, they are great at stopping bullets, but knives go through them with relative ease. That means that an older woman with a knife can be just as dangerous as a big guy with a knife.

Watts—a nineteen-year veteran of the force—has pulled his gun while on duty, but he has never fired it, in self-defense or otherwise.

He's met a number of officers who have pulled the trigger, though, and the vast majority are good cops who feel horrible, confused, upset, and sad about killing another person. Moreover, he has never met an officer whose own life hasn't been wholly altered by taking another's. After a shooting, an officer's actions are scrutinized by grand jurors, prosecutors, internal affairs investigators, homicide detectives, and the media. The officer is placed on administrative duty, often behind a desk. He or she gets some counseling and is usually put back on the street. Yet for years, many relive a split-second decision that can never be undone.

Watts looks up from his notes and notices that the squad car carrying the female police officer is gone; he assumes she's on her way to homicide. Turning, he sees Hill staring into space, and he wonders if his rookie is pondering his own shooting. Hill's story is so outlandish that his fellow detectives joke that it could have occurred only in PG County. One night in October 2009, Hill was off duty and in his police uniform while working as a security guard in a mall when he spotted two women stuffing clothes into a bag and then leaving a store. After they walked through the parking lot and hopped into a Chevy sedan, he confronted them. When the women refused to get out of the car, he reached through an open window and attempted to grab their bag.

The driver raised the window, clamping Hill's arm in place. She gunned the accelerator and the car peeled out of the lot, dragging Hill with it. Somehow Hill pulled his gun from his holster and fired five rounds, shattering the driver's window and sending him cartwheeling across the pavement as the Chevy crashed into a parked car. Only later did he learn that the thieves—both of whom were seriously wounded by Hill's bullets—were not women but cross-dressers. Forever after, Hill was the butt of juvenile cop humor.

Though Hill takes the jokes in stride, the memory of that traumatic day haunts him. When speaking with colleagues about the incident, he claims he has never second-guessed pulling the trigger because he was faced with a simple choice: shoot or die. But some-times, when talking with close friends, he admits to doubts, to wondering whether and how he could have handled the situation differently. He will live with those questions for the rest of his life.

Watts motions for Hill to follow him into the apartment build-ing. They push through the front door, which opens with a squeak. In the vestibule, the detectives are greeted by the hunger-inducing smell of a Latin American dinner, perhaps a chicken-and-rice dish. To their right, taped to a white wall, is a poster seeking information about a difficult-to-crack December homicide that occurred in this same complex.

Watts and Hill climb the five wooden stairs leading to the build-ing's first-floor landing. Ahead of them is the door to the dead woman's apartment; it's open, so Watts peeks inside and sees that an evi-dence tech is taking photographs of the interior of the place. Not wanting to disturb the tech's work, he steps to his left and knocks on the neighbor's door. When it opens, Watts sees a teenage girl standing in a dark hallway. Watts introduces himself, and the girl motions for him to come inside.

Trailed by Hill, Watts walks into a dimly lit living room where ten or so Hispanic men and women are sitting and standing around a card table. When the detective asks if anyone speaks English, the teenage girl raises her hand.

Watts asks what she and her family witnessed, and the teen says that earlier that night they heard their neighbor screaming at the people upstairs. "She was yelling really loud, bad words, names, calling them lesbians," the girl says. "She has done this before. She talks to herself a lot in the middle of the night, yelling. I guess she was yelling at herself—we never hear anyone yell back. We've never had a problem with her."

"How did you know the police came?" Watts asks.

"They started knocking on the door and saying, 'Police!' and 'Put your hands up!'"

"They were saying, 'Police'?"

"Yes."

"How long were they saying, 'Put your hands up'?" asks Watts.

"A lot of times."

"Did she say anything?" Hill asks.

"No, she was quiet."

"How many gunshots do you think you heard?" asks Watts.

"Five or six."

Watts asks the girl if she or others in her family knew the dead woman. The girl replies that although they occasionally saw her, they weren't friends and rarely said more than hello.

After thanking the teen and the family for their time, Watts explains that he and Hill will be back the next day to take a formal statement. "It will only take a few minutes—okay?"

The detective gives the girl his card. As the two investigators turn to leave, she touches Watts's sleeve. "What happened to the woman?"

Watts considers holding back some details but decides that the neighbors deserve to know. "She was shot," he says. "Ultimately, she was taken to the hospital, and she didn't make it."

The girl frowns, turns to the others in the room, and translates Watts's reply into Spanish. They all frown and shake their heads. "That is very sad," the teen says.

Watts and Hill leave the apartment and return to the dead woman's front door, which is still open. Just beyond the threshold, the floor is smeared with blood. Watts pokes his head inside and determines that the place is empty—the evidence techs are gone.

"Let's see if we can find any medications, anything that might point to a mental illness," Watts tells Hill. "If she has any, we can call the doctor listed on the prescriptions. We should also try to find an ID, something with her photo and information."

A more experienced detective than Hill would probably have been annoyed to have the mission spelled out so explicitly for him. But Hill is a rookie and has yet to prove his worth. Watts and his partner, Ben Brown, have been training Hill for the better part of a month, and the veteran investigators are not yet convinced that he will make a good homicide detective. Though Hill is extremely intelligent and has an excellent pedigree—he is the son of one of the first black officers in the DC police department—the thirty-four-year-old has spent the last six years in the Sexual Assault Unit, where detectives are known for working their shifts and going home; there are few nine-to-five days in homicide. Hill's quirky personality also hasn't helped his cause: he's a bit of a goofball and such an obsessive fan of *Star Wars* that his computer screen saver is the face of Darth Vader and his phone's ringtone is "The Imperial March." In sum, he could not be more different than the ultraserious detectives training him.

Short and stubby, Watts is a gruff forty-year-old with a generous belly who wears department-store suits and has his blond hair cut long. Married, with two teenage children, he suffers from high blood pressure and possesses so much nervous energy that his leg often pumps like a jackhammer under his desk. Watts is intense about everything, whether it is interrogating a suspect or drinking beer. A fan of the NFL's Baltimore Ravens, Watts wears a purple shirt and tie on the Friday before every football game, and on fall Sundays he relaxes in the parking lot at his "command post," a pop-up trailer he has transformed into a tailgater's dream, complete with a big-screen TV, a grill, and other essential supplies. On the job, Watts does not suffer fools gladly and expects a lot from those around him—even rookies.

Watts and Hill enter the dead woman's living room, which is furnished with a dresser, a tall cabinet, a green throw rug over brown wall-to-wall carpet, and a pullout bed. Watts finds an address book on the dresser and then turns to a small stack of books lying on the bed. He picks the books up and flips through them; one is a Bible and two are diaries. He hands them to Hill, who examines a few of the diaries' pages.

"Writing is very cramped," Hill says. "Just gibberish—run-on sentences."

"That's a sign of mental illness, maybe schizophrenia," Watts says. Thus far, the case has all the hallmarks of someone struggling with a serious mental disorder.

Watts and Hill next visit a study just down the hall, where the shelves are lined with books and magazines, most with Christian themes. The magazines are carefully filed in boxes labeled by publication and year.

Hill glances at several newsletters and pulls a book of scripture from a shelf. After telling Watts that the woman seems to have been a Jehovah's Witness, he cracks, "She should have been used to people knocking on her door."

Watts is too focused to laugh, but he gives Hill a thin smile. *Maybe there's hope for the rookie after all*, he thinks. *Only a homicide detective could come up with a joke like that.*

The investigators turn down a short hallway and enter the kitchen, where Watts opens the fridge. It's empty except for a bowl of rice on the middle shelf. He inspects the sink: not a dirty dish in sight.

Watts pivots and walks to the bathroom. He checks the medicine cabinet and finds it empty—not even a bottle of aspirin. With that, they are done. Having turned up no medications and no ID, they head into the living room, where Watts collects the address book and Hill the journals.

Holding up the address book, Watts says, "I'll use this to see if we can find next of kin. And you should go to the hospital to confirm the ID."

"Got it. I'll get her MVA photo," Hill says, referring to the leaseholder's driver's-license picture.

As they head toward the door, Watts notices two photographs on top of the tall cabinet. One is of a large family dressed in Sunday finery. The other appears to be of a mother and daughter, both smiling for the camera. Watts feels Hill at his side.

"Shame," says Hill, breaking the silence. "Real shame."

Watts thinks he hears genuine sorrow in his rookie's voice. By contrast, Watts feels no emotional distress of any sort. It's not that he is coldhearted, although he is unquestionably jaded from having seen so many corpses and speaking to so many grieving mothers. But, in truth, his detachment runs deeper: it's about the job itself. Watts works so hard and so doggedly that he leaves no room for sentiment. It would just get in his way.

Saying nothing, Watts leads Hill to the entryway. Stepping over the chips of plaster and wood left by the evidence techs—they had cut bullets out of the walls—and then over the dead woman's blood, Watts motions for Hill to go on ahead. Then he fiddles with the door's lock, steps into the hallway, and shuts the door hard behind himself.

THIRTY MINUTES LATER, Jonathan Hill arrives at Prince George's County Hospital Center. On his smartphone he has the leaseholder's driver's-license photograph, which he will compare to the dead woman in the morgue. So far, Watts and Hill have no reason to doubt that their victim is the leaseholder—the woman clearly lived in the apartment, and the detectives have learned from an apartment manager that the leaseholder was the only occupant listed in the manager's records. But if there is a cardinal rule in homicide, it is that a detective must never make a mistake when identifying the dead.

Hill enters a hallway just off the trauma bay and finds detectives Mike Delaney and Mike Barnhardt, as well as Trasee Cosby, the forensic investigator. Cosby asks if they're ready to head down to the hospital's basement to visit the morgue. Hill nods and mentions that he and Watts found no ID or medications in the apartment.

"That's probably why she was acting all crazy," quips Barnhardt, a tall detective with the face of a bulldog and the unit's driest sense of humor.

"It sounds like it went down crazy," says Delaney, who responded to the shooting and took statements from several witnesses, including the two women living upstairs in apartment 4. The residents all reported that the older woman living in apartment 1 was a loner, that they didn't know her very well, and that she had been acting strangely for a long time.

Joined by two evidence techs, the three detectives and Cosby walk down a hallway to a bank of three elevators. They file into the middle one and descend a level. When the doors open, they walk straight toward a doorway with a faded blue sign: MORGUE. They enter a short hallway, make a left, and stop at a wooden door with a piece of paper taped to it: PLEASE MAKE SURE DOOR IS CLOSED. To the right is a red phone for calling an attendant to open the locked door.

"Anyone have a knife?" Cosby asks.

One of the techs hands one over. Cosby opens the blade, jams it between the door handle and the jamb, and jiggles it. The door pops open. She smiles. "That did not happen," she says, handing the knife back.

Cosby strides to a large refrigerator door, opens it, vanishes, and returns pushing a gurney with a body bag on top. Once the detectives have gathered around, she unzips the bag about halfway, revealing a small black woman whose body is covered by medical tape and electrodes. She has what appear to be several bullet holes in her left arm and abdomen.

Moving to the head of the corpse, Hill pulls out his phone and holds it next to the woman's face. The photo on the phone looks similar to the dead woman's, but it's not a perfect match.

The detective frowns. The woman on the table seems younger and thinner than the woman in the photo. And her hair isn't right—it's too stringy. "Shit," says Hill.

Delaney, clad in a black jacket with the word HOMICIDE emblazoned on the back, leans over and looks back and forth between the photo and the woman. By now all three detectives are frowning.

"Does she have a wig on in the photo?" asks Hill. "Is that a Jheri curl wig?"

"That's no wig," says Barnhardt, his eyes glancing from the photo to the face.

"Yes? No? Maybe so?" asks Cosby. "Guys?"

The three detectives bend farther over the corpse. They agree that the woman in the photo looks heavier and older than the woman on the table. The leaseholder is sixty-three. The dead woman on the slab appears to be in her mid-forties. But everyone looks different after death.

"This is a tough one," Delaney says, pushing his wire-rimmed glasses up his nose. "Jonathan, pick her up and stand her against the wall."

Hill may be a rookie, but he's experienced enough to know that Delaney is joking.

"Does she look five-six?" Hill asks, referring to information on the leaseholder's driver's license.

"No," say Barnhardt and Delaney.

"She seems five-two," says Barnhardt.

To this point neither of the two techs has participated in the discussion about the woman's identity. But now one of them moves closer to the table and grabs Hill's phone. Holding it a few inches from his eyes, he peers closely at the photo.

"There's a distinct mark, a freckle, in the photograph," he says. Then he turns to the dead woman and studies her face. "But this one doesn't have any such mark."

The room grows quiet.

"Well, it goes up as an unknown," says Cosby. "It goes up as a Doe."

Hill hates the idea of sending the body to Baltimore for an

autopsy as a Jane Doe, especially on his first case. He wants to help the woman's family and conduct a proper death notification. He also realizes that he will now have to figure out why this Jane Doe isn't the leaseholder on her apartment.

Hill sighs and looks at the body again. "Must be a sister or a daughter or something," he says. "They look alike."

The other detectives nod in agreement.

"Damn it," Hill says, scowling in frustration. "A Jane Doe."

The room grows quiet as Cosby rezips the bag and wheels the gurney into the morgue. A moment later, she emerges and shuts the cooler's steel door.

As the detectives turn to leave, Hill hears the sound of someone crooning. The voice is Delaney's:

*Doe, a deer, a female deer . . .*

"That's a musical," Barnhardt says helpfully.

"You know it?" Hill asks Delaney.

"I'm a Renaissance man," says Delaney, smiling and continuing to sing:

*Ray, a drop of golden sun . . .*

As they head for the elevator, Hill, Barnhardt, and Cosby cannot resist. They join in, becoming a motley choir:

*Me, a name I call myself*
*Far, a long long way to run.*

# · CHAPTER 4 ·

Detective Andre Brooks walks into the living room and halts at the blood-smeared hardwood floor. Tapping his left leg with his notepad, he stares at the crimson smudge for a full minute before shifting his gaze to the sun setting behind patterned window shades. He blinks to clear his vision of the golden glare and steps back to better scan the cluttered room. Against the far wall is a leather couch with a split seam; on the opposite wall is a twin-sized bed. The room is littered with open boxes, food containers, a portable toilet, a tilting bookcase. *Jesus,* thinks Brooks. *Figuring out if anything was stolen from this place is going to be a bitch.*

Returning his attention to the floor, Brooks wonders how such a violent death spilled so little blood. He feels a surge of anger over the slaying of his victim, an innocent seventy-one-year-old homebody named Geraldine McIntyre, whose corpse is already on its way to the morgue. Two hours earlier, a visiting relative had found the woman bleeding and unconscious in this very spot, not three steps from the front door. Stabbed numerous times in her torso, she was rushed to the hospital, where she died in the emergency room.

Brooks scowls. He cannot understand why someone would kill an elderly lady, let alone in such a horrible way. McIntyre wasn't just old, Brooks has learned—she was defenseless. Partly paralyzed from a stroke, McIntyre somehow had been caring for her disabled forty-six-year-old daughter, who slept on the bed in the living room. Fortunately, the daughter wasn't home today; she was at a nearby hospital being treated for bedsores.

After walking through a small hallway, Brooks enters McIntyre's bedroom, where evidence technicians are taking photographs. On the unmade bed are a TV remote, a plastic bag filled with prescription bottles, a stack of mail, and a DVD case; next to the bed is a small table covered with personal items. In the left corner of the room is an overstuffed white armoire. Clothes are scattered across the floor, and a woman's brown hat rests on a plastic fan.

Brooks's attention turns to an upside-down black milk crate on a knee-high white stand. Pressed against the far wall, the crate is perfectly positioned for someone watching television in bed, but there is no TV. The detective steps closer, and an evidence technician points to the floor. Brooks dips his head and sees a severed coaxial cable.

Brooks has no doubt about what happened here: McIntyre's television has been stolen.

Pivoting, the detective finds his partner, Mike Delaney, standing behind him. "You know what kind of set she had?"

Delaney has just finished speaking to McIntyre's relatives; following his earlier survey of the scene, he had asked them this very question. "Flat-screen GPX," Delaney says, referring to an inexpensive brand sold at local convenience and discount stores. The relatives, Delaney adds, are certain it must have been stolen, because McIntyre would not have sold or given away the thirty-two-inch set without mentioning it to them.

"Fucking crackheads," Brooks mutters, using his preferred street term for anyone addicted to cocaine, heroin, or some other drug.

Within minutes of getting the call about the murder, Brooks figured that McIntyre was killed in a robbery gone bad. The detective knows the dead woman's neighborhood well: Capitol Heights has a plethora of addicts—both of crack and heroin—who mow lawns, paint houses, and practice minor carpentry to earn money to finance their habit. Many of them are notorious hustlers and thieves, willing to do or steal anything to get their next fix.

Shortly after arriving at the scene, Brooks learned that investigators had already interviewed a neighborhood boy who'd spotted someone who might well be a neighborhood handyman outside McIntyre's house earlier that day. The youth reported seeing a grubby older man wearing a black cap and dark clothes; carrying a black bag and a hammer, the man entered the house about 9:30 a.m.

Brooks guesses that the killer stopped by McIntyre's house and offered to perform an odd job. The handyman likely knew McIntyre, and either he was allowed inside after knocking or he simply walked right in—Brooks has been told that McIntyre often left her front door unlocked to facilitate food deliveries. As Brooks imagines it, once the intruder got into the house, he went straight for the bedroom and snatched the television. On his way out, the thief encountered McIntyre in the living room; when she put up a struggle, he pushed her to the ground, jumped on top of her, and stabbed her several times with a small knife. Or maybe, Brooks thinks, the murder was even more cold-blooded than that. It's entirely possible that the thief killed McIntyre after taking her television simply because she knew him from around the neighborhood and would be able to identify him.

"Fucking crackheads," Brooks says again, attempting to leave the bedroom but finding the hallway too crowded with police officers to squeeze through. Tall and broad-jawed, the forty-five-year-old detective is so rotound that his shirttails constantly pop from his pants. Waiting impatiently for the traffic to clear, he is oblivious to the fact that his salmon-striped white shirt hangs below the bottom of his suit jacket.

Once the crowd thins out, Brooks moves into a chilly bathroom, where he watches a technician apply black fingerprint dust to a window jamb. The tech tells Brooks that the window was found open, unusual for February. Brooks steps forward, leans over a big bathtub, and sticks his head out the window. Directly below him, after a drop of five or six feet, is a patch of bare earth.

*Maybe he threw the television outside or jumped from the window,* Brooks thinks.

He turns and sees Delaney standing in the doorway. "Why not just carry the TV out the front door?" Brooks asks, as much of himself as Delaney.

"He was trying to be careful," Delaney says.

"But he could have broken it tossing it out the window," Brooks replies. "That doesn't make a lot of sense."

Brooks fixes his eyes on the evidence tech, who is dressed in a black jacket and black fatigues.

"Get any?" Brooks asks.

"We might have one," the tech says. "Good but not great."

"I don't care if you have to cut out the window to get it," Brooks says, leaving the bathroom and returning to the living room. A moment later, he spots a tan leather purse under the daughter's bed. Kicking it into the room with his left foot, he bends and dips a pen between its folds, prying it open. The purse is empty except for a pile of mice droppings. Brooks looks up, sees a laptop computer sitting on an overturned wastebasket, near the couch, and briefly wonders why the killer didn't steal that, too. *No,* he thinks, *the guy was too busy with the TV.*

The detective walks back out the open front door and onto a wooden porch that extends into a wheelchair ramp. He grips the railing, squints against the dying sun, and studies three houses across curving Chapel Oaks Drive: one is blue, another is red brick, and the third is white. It's a working-class block in a rough neighborhood, and Brooks hopes it's the kind of street where people keep an eye on one another and are not afraid to call the police.

The detective trudges down the ramp, turns left, rounds the corner of the house, and heads into a backyard darkened by the home's long shadow. He stops below the open window, where he is joined by Delaney, their sergeant, Trevel Watson, and Lieutenant Brian Reilly. The four men study the window and the patch of earth below the window; they also look over a nearby pile of dirt and a small trench at the base of the foundation. The mound of dirt isn't fresh—it has sprouted weeds and moss and is layered in decaying foliage—suggesting that the job being done here was abandoned long ago.

Brooks scans the ground beneath the window once more. "I don't see any shoe prints," he says, "but we need to come back in the daylight and see if there are any. Cigarette butts, too."

"No cameras?" asks Reilly, wondering if a nearby house has a surveillance system that might have captured the burglar coming or going.

"Not yet," says Brooks. He checks his watch: 5:15 p.m. It will be dark soon.

Watson asks if the killer would have thrown the TV out the window, given the risk of breaking it.

"Maybe he dangles it out the window by the cord and just lets it fall," says Delaney.

"Could be," says Reilly.

They walk back to the front of the building. After Watson and Reilly head for the warmth of the house, Delaney tells Brooks that he will dispatch their rookie, Paul Mazzei, to conduct a quick canvas of neighbors.

"Let's make Mazzei get the pizza tonight," Delaney adds.

Brooks likes this idea—it is always best to make the rookie

pay—but he suggests that they avoid a certain restaurant. "It gave me the shits last time."

Delaney mentions another pizza place.

"Didn't that give Mazzei the shits last time?" Brooks asks.

"Mazzei gets the shits from everything," Delaney says.

The two chuckle. They have an easy rapport that goes back two decades, to when Brooks trained the rookie Delaney on the streets; Delaney returned the favor by training Brooks when he joined homicide, in 2005. They are so close that they act like a married couple, sharing everything and sparing nothing, not even their mothers. At a recent crime scene, the whine of an electric saw sparked Delaney to quip to a dozen detectives, techs, and officers, "That sounds just like Andre's mother's love call!"

Delaney slaps Brooks on the back and says he is going to find Mazzei. Brooks turns and looks back at Geraldine McIntyre's house. Jamming his left hand into his pants pocket, he jiggles a fistful of change.

*He's got to be from around here,* the detective thinks. *Someone knows this guy.*

A FEW MINUTES later, Brooks is looking up and down the block when his gaze settles on a woman bundled in a gray winter coat who is standing in front of a bright green house a few doors away. Peering through the twilight, he sees that the woman is glaring at him.

Brooks walks toward the woman's house but stops before passing through the gate in her chain-link fence. Standing five feet apart, they eye each other for a few seconds.

The woman, her curly hair protruding from under a thick winter cap, breaks the silence.

"What happened?" she asks.

"She was murdered," Brooks says.

"She was handicapped," the woman says.

"I know," Brooks answers sadly.

The woman says nothing and shoves her hands into her coat pockets, obviously wary of engaging with a homicide detective.

"Do you know if there were any handymen who went over there? To do chores, cut grass?"

"I cut my own grass."

"No, over there," Brooks says, jerking his right thumb toward the McIntyre house.

"I cut my own grass."

"As you say, ma'am, she was handicapped—did anyone help her?" Brooks asks, trying not to let his frustration show.

"No. Sometimes people would deliver stuff to her."

"Who?"

"I never looked that closely."

"Any crackheads? Crackheads doing handiwork in the area?"

"Not that I know of."

Clearly the woman is not eager to be helpful. Such intransigence is common, and Brooks no longer finds it frustrating or insulting. It's just part of the job.

He thanks the woman for her time and heads back up the street. As he nears McIntyre's home, he spots another woman, this one entering a squat house a few doors down in the other direction. Brooks walks quickly to the woman's front door and knocks. A skinny cat with mangy gray fur brushes against the detective's right leg, then purrs and opens its eyes. The left socket is empty; in the porch light, the right one glows gold.

"Ghetto tabby," Brooks says softly. "Nice ghetto tabby."

The woman answers the door. She hasn't yet taken off her coat, but as soon as she sees the detective, she grins. Brooks returns the gesture, his first smile of the day.

"I'm Detective Brooks, with the county police," he says. "You knew I wouldn't be talking to all the other neighbors and not to you."

She smiles again and steps aside to let him enter. Brooks settles into a chair at the kitchen table, and she takes one across from him. The room is quiet and dimly lit—Brooks still cannot tell if her coat is dark blue or black.

The woman clasps her hands together on the table. "How can I help you?" she asks.

"Did you know Ms. McIntyre?" Brooks asks.

"I saw her a few times. She was very quiet."

"Any problems with burglars?"

"Last year—last summer—I left a window open and someone stole a computer and a television."

She cranes her neck to see what Brooks is writing in his notepad, then returns her eyes to the detective's face.

"Was that a break-in?" she asks, pointing in the direction of McIntyre's house.

"Yes, and it turned violent. She's dead."

"Oh, no," the woman says, gasping and putting a hand to her mouth. "How did they get in?"

"We think she might have left the front door unlocked."

"Oh, my. The reason I ask is because I sleep in my basement, and last night somebody was at my back door trying it, pulling it," she says, banging the table to re-create the racket.

Brooks asks to see the door; they step outside and walk around to the side of the house. A large tree blocks the view of the door from the street. *Perfect door for a burglar,* Brooks thinks.

He makes a note to have evidence techs dust the door for prints, thanks the neighbor for her time, and heads back up the street.

Delaney and Mazzei are standing on the sidewalk in front of McIntyre's house, and Brooks can tell by the smiles on their faces that they have good news. Delaney reports that they just interviewed a neighbor who lives behind McIntyre. The neighbor told them that he heard rustling in McIntyre's backyard between 9:30 and 10:00 that morning. When he looked out his rear window, he saw a man, clad all in black, carrying what looked like a large board toward the front of McIntyre's house.

"He just assumed the rectangular item was wood," Mazzei says.

Mazzei, a stocky investigator with an oval face who doubles as the goaltender on the police union's hockey team, looks to his right; Brooks and Delaney do likewise. Down the street, a man is shuffling away from them into the gathering dusk. To the three detectives, he appears to be a drug addict.

"Nobody eats until this is solved," says Brooks. His meaning is plain. The police will crack down on this neighborhood so hard that drug dealers will not make a penny and their clients will not get their fixes—not until Geraldine McIntyre's killer is in handcuffs.


BROOKS DROPS INTO the chair at his desk and dumps his notebook on top of the computer keyboard. Over the past few hours, he recanvassed the neighborhood and supervised the collection of evidence; he also fruitlessly chased a police bloodhound as it investigated the surrounding blocks. The dog eventually led him and other detectives to a tightly boarded-up house that clearly hadn't been occupied in months.

He checks his watch: it's just after 9:20 p.m. He realizes that he won't get any sleep for at least another eight hours; as happens all too often, he has caught a murder while working the midnight shift. Because PG police use a rotation system to assign murders, detectives don't get to choose the timing of their cases. Whenever your murder falls, whether you're in the middle of a shift, eating dinner at home, or dead asleep, you go to work. If necessary, you investigate your homicide all day and straight into the evening, and then you still show up at 11:00 p.m. for graveyard duty.

Brooks exhales, squints, and rubs his weary eyes. The new case is the least of his reasons for feeling so exhausted. After twenty-three years on the job, he is eligible to retire, but he has a son in college and another in preschool, so he needs a steady paycheck. But it's not enough: to make ends meet, he moonlights as a security guard at a cemetery. Sometimes he finds himself mulling a life without callouts and corpses, but in truth he still loves the job. It's in his blood.

The son of a DC police officer, Brooks was drawn to the notion of going into public safety from the time he was young. In the late 1980s, his father—who moved to a desk job after heroically taking a bullet for his partner in 1971—said he could help get Andre hired by the DC police. But he warned his son that "some of the same guys we locked up are getting hired here now." That was only a slight exaggeration: when the District was swamped by a wave of crime in those years, the police department junked its hiring standards. The DC police classes of 1989 and 1990, for instance, became two of the most notoriously corrupt and troublesome in U.S. policing history.

Instead of working on his father's turf, Brooks joined the PG County police department. He'd always admired the way PG police officers carried themselves—they took no crap. In Brooks's youth, it was widely understood that if you were going to screw around, you didn't do it in PG; if you did, you were going to get your ass beaten by the cops, who ruled the streets. Brooks and many other African Americans believed that county officers were abusive and discriminated against minorities, a perception fueled by the department's lack of diversity and its racial insensitivity. Still, Brooks felt that the rewards of working as an officer would outweigh the department's legacy of intolerance, and he has never regretted the decision.

Brooks soon fell in love with the street and garnered a reputation for being tough. He built sources, made arrests, and earned the respect of criminals—he did not tolerate bad behavior on his beat. But the grueling nature of the work and his own impatience occasionally led him to be confrontational with suspects, some of whom complained. Particularly vocal were several johns he arrested. They weren't upset with Brooks for arresting them; they were angry that he called their wives to report that they'd had sexual contact with prostitutes who might have HIV or AIDS.

In time, Brooks was promoted to investigative assignments and, finally, to homicide, and if his aggressive approach sometimes landed him in trouble, it also often worked in his favor. A few months back, he'd grown so frustrated with the inability of the county's crime-scene technicians to find forensic evidence in one of his homicides that he'd insulted them by commandeering a key piece of evidence—a minivan in which he believed a woman had been strangled—and trucking it to a federal lab. The lab's investigators discovered the victim's blood in the back of the vehicle, ensuring the killer's conviction.

Now, as he sits at his desk and gathers his thoughts, Brooks feels Delaney brush behind him and take a seat at his workstation, two down the row. Delaney reports that their sergeant, Trevel Watson, has been promised help from patrol, the district-level detectives, and drug squads. Brooks frowns at his partner, and Delaney nods back with a knowing look.

Both detectives are skeptical that the aid will amount to much. In particular, they doubt the patrol officers can be counted on to dry up the drug market in Geraldine McIntyre's neighborhood. Brooks and Delaney often complain that today's officers are soft. They don't own the streets, they don't develop sources, and they don't view a murder on their beat as a personal affront. Sounding like the battle-hardened cops who trained them back in the 1990s, the two men say that the younger generation of officers lacks motivation. Today's cops don't see their work as a calling; to them, it's just a job. So once again the detectives will be shouldering the load.

It is nearly 10:00 p.m. when Sergeant Watson swings by and tells Brooks and Delaney that it's time to meet and review the case. After gathering their notebooks, the partners trail Watson to the freezing conference room, where Brooks slides behind a couple of chairs and takes his seat at the head of the table. Delaney and Watson sit next to him, and soon they are joined by the three other detectives from the M-20 squad: Paul Dougherty, Dave Gurry, and Paul Mazzei. The last to arrive are Lieutenant Brian Reilly and Captain George Nichols.

Ordinarily the unit's captain wouldn't attend this sort of post-scene meeting, particularly on a Saturday. But this is a high-profile case, and Nichols will soon have to brief the major, the assistant chief, and the chief. Having just appeared at a community event, the captain is in uniform, giving him an added aura of command. Easygoing and quick to laugh, at forty-two Nichols has a boyish manner that can cut against his authority, making it difficult for some detectives to take him seriously. But this is hardly a moment for levity, and tonight he is all business.

Brooks runs down what he knows, which isn't much. He reports that their current theory is that a local drug addict killed McIntyre, either after or while stealing her television. By tomorrow, Brooks says, he expects to receive a list of known burglars and thieves in the neighborhood; once he has that in hand, the squad will start shaking the trees. Next Brooks points to Gurry, who visited the hospital to check on the corpse.

"We stopped counting the stab wounds at eleven," Gurry says. "Left side, face, neck, arm."

The detectives shake their heads in disgust.

"What happened with the bloodhound?" asks Nichols, taking a sip of McDonald's coffee.

"It took a shit," says Brooks.

The detectives laugh, but no one is surprised. They rarely find bloodhounds to be helpful.

"The print?" Brooks asks Gurry. "The one on the sill?"

Gurry reports that he spoke to the fingerprint lab and learned that apparently the print isn't good enough to enter into a national database, though it may still be of some use, since examiners will be able to compare it to a suspect's print. "It looked good, I thought," Gurry says.

"I thought the same thing," says Brooks.

"So evidence-wise, we don't have anything—just the print?" asks Watson.

Brooks nods and then glances down at his notes. "Ms. McIntyre only had thirteen hundred dollars in her bank account. The way that house looked, I can't see she had a stash of cash somewhere. This is just senseless."

The room grows quiet, except for the humming of the always-running air conditioner.

Captain Nichols leans forward, elbows on the table, his smartphone clutched in both hands. "Just so you know, this case has the chief's attention." He holds up his phone, turning its screen toward Brooks and displaying an e-mail from Assistant Chief Kevin Davis to the top commanders in the department. The message from Davis says that he's looking forward to tomorrow morning's conference call about "this red ball murder."

"There is some good news and bad news," Nichols continues. "The good news is we will get a reprieve from Amber Stanley. The bad news is we have Ms. Geraldine McIntyre."

By invoking the case that hangs over the entire unit, Nichols has delivered a clear message that this murder of an elderly lady must be avenged. The department will spare no expense in seeking justice, the captain says, and every available resource will be at Brooks's disposal in the morning.

When Nichols finishes, he leans back in his chair. The room again goes silent, and the investigators return their attention to Brooks. This is his case, and he—not the sergeant, the lieutenant, or even the captain—will have the last word. Brooks shuffles his stack of notes and papers as his eyes bounce from his fellow detectives to the sergeant to the lieutenant and finally the captain.

"We are going old-school here," he says. "This is a red ball. An innocent old lady was killed. *An innocent lady.* If anybody has any problems with going old-school, it's time for you to step off the train."

Nobody says a word.

Sean Deere and Mike Crowell are beat. They haven't slept in at least thirty hours, the result of their squad's having caught a case the previous night at absolutely the worst time: 11:15 p.m., just as they were both getting ready for bed. Receiving the call at 3:00 a.m. would have been better—at least they would have snagged a few hours of shut-eye.

But the two detectives are more than tired; they're frustrated. The new case isn't even a murder. At the very least, a fresh homicide would have taken their minds off Amber Stanley while generating some decent overtime pay. Instead, their squad mate Joe Bunce was assigned a police-involved shooting that sounded about as justified as they come. An off-duty sheriff's deputy had returned to his home in Fort Washington just before 11:00 p.m. last night to find his front door busted open. He went inside to retrieve his service weapon, which he'd hidden under a pillow on his bed, but the room had been ransacked, and the gun was missing. After grabbing his backup weapon from a locked box stashed in a laundry basket, he saw a man in dark clothing emerge from his basement door and start walking toward him. Figuring the man was a burglar who now had his other loaded gun, the deputy opened fire. The burglar dove back into the basement. A minute later, the man reappeared and charged at him, and the deputy fired several more shots. The burglar managed to escape the deputy's house, but after running a little ways he collapsed, dead of gunshot wounds, in a nearby yard.

It was an open-and-shut case. Even so, Deere and Crowell spent the whole night working it—no matter how straightforward, a police shooting must be handled with the utmost care.

Just as the two detectives were about to pack up their papers and head home for a nap, however, they got an unexpected and unwanted gift: the delivery of three men they had been seeking in the Amber Stanley investigation. An hour or so earlier, the department's fugitive squad had captured the men and deposited them in the Homicide Unit's three interview rooms.

The previous week, when Deere and Crowell had failed to turn up Gerry Gordon and the twenty-year-old who had caught a sexually transmitted disease from Denise, Deere had turned to the fugitive squad for help. Two days ago, he'd given its members short dossiers on the two men; he'd also given them information about a third man, a twenty-three-year-old who was close friends with Jeff Buck. All three were wanted on warrants that charged them with crimes ranging from trespassing to failing to appear in court in a drug case.

Earlier this morning, realizing that he and his squad mates were too exhausted to conduct meaningful interrogations, Deere phoned the fugitive unit's sergeant and told him to call off the search, at least for a day. But his instruction was ignored, and now Gerry Gordon was in Interview Room 1 and the STD victim was in Interview Room 2. For good measure, the fugitive squad had also snatched the STD victim's twenty-six-year-old brother, and he was in Interview Room 3.

"Assholes—they fucked us," Crowell tells Deere as they stand by the clerk's station, munching on stale doughnuts.

Deere agrees. He would like to believe that this screwup is the result of a miscommunication, but he's more inclined to think that it's a genuine "fuck you" to M-40. In recent weeks, Crowell and

Bunce have been complaining vocally about the fugitive squad's abilities, particularly since its detectives have not arrested any of the five suspects that M-40 has recently charged in homicides.

A month or so ago, the ever-antagonistic Crowell printed out the definition of "fugitive" and made a point of handing it to a fugitive-squad detective who had stopped by the homicide office to say hello. "You aren't going to find anyone in here!" Crowell yelled. "Go catch our guys!"

Clearly irked by Crowell's abusive behavior, the detective left the room in a huff.

Now Deere and Crowell are paying the price for disrespecting their colleagues. "I'm dying, Sean," Crowell says. "How do we do this?"

Deere is not clearheaded enough to conduct intensive interviews, but he cannot let their witnesses—or suspects—go free. He has no idea when they'll be able to grab them again.

So Deere decides to perform triage: he and Crowell will do their best to take some basic information from the men and get their DNA. They will start with the twenty-six-year-old brother because he has no apparent connection to the murder investigation, though he might be able to provide some helpful intelligence about the neighborhood's workings. After that, they will hit the STD victim and the Peeping Tom, Gerry Gordon.

The detectives eye the clock on the wall—it's just after noon. Seeing the time makes them feel even wearier. "Let's get these done as quick as possible," Crowell says, grabbing his notebook.

DEERE AND CROWELL enter Interview Room 3 and find the twenty-six-year-old brother sitting at one end of the table, leaning back and completely relaxed. He hasn't bothered to take off his black hat with earflaps or his thick black coat. Crowell lets go of a yawn as he drops into a seat at the other end of the table, next to the wall, and Deere takes a spot just off the man's right knee.

The interview starts just fine, as Deere and Crowell pepper the man with questions about his associates, girlfriends, babies' mothers, and his brother and his brother's friends. The witness seems like a decent guy; he holds a steady job and asks the detectives politely if he may call his employer, because he will be late for work.

As Deere is pressing the brother about Jeff Buck and his crew, Crowell's eyes grow heavy and he gently rests his head against the wall. His eyes close, spring open, close again, and finally stay shut. He snorts and begins to snore.

The brother is in the middle of explaining that he hasn't seen Buck for months when he pauses and looks over at the slumbering investigator. Then he turns to Deere, who shrugs as if to say that detectives always catch a nap in the box.

"Any fights involving your brother?" Deere asks, refusing to be distracted by Crowell's snoring.

"No, no fights," the witness says.

"In the last few months?"

"No."

Deere asks the brother whether he has ever seen Jeff Buck with a gun; he also asks whether he has heard about the rape of Denise or anything about Amber Stanley's murder. The brother shakes his head.

Deere glances at Crowell, whose oversized head has drifted four inches down the wall and has halted on his propped right hand. Saliva bubbles on his lower lip; he is breathing deeply, and his bobblehead-like cranium is pressing awkwardly against his thumb.

The pain at last snaps Crowell awake. Shaking his head, he blinks wildly, thinking, *What did I miss? Was I really asleep?* He checks Deere, who hides a shit-eating grin behind his notepad. Crowell furiously clicks his ballpoint pen, trying to loosen his thumb as well as clear his foggy mind. *Christ, my thumb hurts,* he thinks. *Did I dislocate it?*

He squints, then opens his eyes as wide as he can. "So, how did you meet your girlfriend?" he asks the brother, returning to a question he posed earlier.

The witness seems perplexed. "Like I said before, through Facebook."

"Facebook?" Crowell repeats, trying to think of something to say. He eyes Deere, but his fellow investigator offers no help. Watching Crowell scramble is too enjoyable.

Crowell furrows his brow. He checks his notes but sees nothing that might get him back on track. *Well,* he thinks, *might as well have some fun.*

"What is this *Facebook*?" he deadpans in a sinister tone, emphasizing the word as if it were a heretofore unknown criminal enterprise.

The brother rubs his hands in his lap. "You know—it's social networking."

Crowell says nothing; Deere says nothing. They stare at the witness, now shifting uncomfortably in his chair. Ten seconds pass in utter silence.

"So, you read books on it?" Crowell asks.

"No."

"Oh."

"It's—you, you keep in touch with people," the man says.

"Ah, like e-mail," Crowell says. "I get it."

"No—"

"Ah, like text messages then," says Deere.

"No, it's Facebook," the brother says. "*Facebook!* It's social!"

"How do you know what people are talking about on this Facebook?" asks Deere.

The man sighs and drops his head into his hands.

Crowell decides it's as good a time as any to get the witness's consent for a DNA swab, but he doesn't want him to know the reason he is here—not yet.

"You spend much time in Laurel?" he asks.

The detective is referring to a city ten miles beyond the Beltway in a quieter section of PG County. Crowell guesses that his witness, who was picked up twenty miles away, in Mitchellville, has no connection to Laurel and might never even have set foot in it.

"Not really," the man says. "No."

Crowell pinches the bridge of his nose between his left index finger and unhurt thumb. "We are investigating the theft of twenty-seven cartons of Marlboro Red cigarettes from a gas station up there," he says, looking down at his pad, flipping a page forward and back as if checking his notes to make sure he has his facts right. Then he raises his head and stares hard at the man. "You didn't steal those cigarettes, did you? I don't think you were involved. But we got a tip, and we have to run it down. That's why you're here."

"No," the brother says, startled. "I don't smoke no Marlboros. I didn't steal no Marlboros."

Crowell knows that black guys generally don't smoke Marlboro Reds; Newports tend to be the preferred brand. But he hopes the witness will be rattled by his questions and, thus, more likely to cooperate.

"Anyway," Crowell continues, "we would like to clear you, and if you could give us your DNA, that would help. The guy who stole the cigarettes scraped his hand on the counter, and we are collecting DNA to match it. We just got a bunch of names, and we have to run it down."

The brother's eyes shift from Crowell to Deere and back again. Slowly, the tension in his face eases.

"Sure, that's fine," he says.

With that, Deere opens the door, signaling the evidence technician to come inside. While she takes photos of the witness and swabs his cheeks, the detectives leave the box and head to the clerk's counter, where they join detectives Joe Bunce and Allyson Hamlin, who are eyeing the stale doughnuts.

"I was worried you were going to keep sleeping," Deere jokes.

"I was pushing it," Crowell admits.

"It's a scary feeling," Deere says. There is no shame in falling asleep in the interrogation room. They have all done it. When you routinely work forty-eight hours straight, exhaustion is bound to catch up to you sooner or later—and it's far better to nod off in the box than while driving home, which has happened to more than one detective.

"You like the Marlboro Reds line?" Crowell asks.

Deere agrees that it was funny and then says, " 'Facebook? What is this *Facebook?*' "

"It's like e-mail," Crowell says, laughing loudly.

Bunce and Hamlin roll their eyes at their colleagues' nonsensical banter. But Bunce is too tired to join in, so he shrugs and walks to his desk to finish some paperwork. Hamlin picks up a doughnut, inspects it, and puts it back in the box. Yawning, she stretches her arms toward the ceiling and heads outside for some fresh air.

"Well, let's get this one," Crowell says to Deere, shaking his sore thumb and pointing to Interview Room 2, which houses the man who had sex with Denise in the empty mansion's garage.


When the detectives enter the box, they find a thin twenty-year-old who, like his brother, is open and friendly and answers their questions without hesitation. Yes, he says, he had sex with Denise in the sports car. But he claims he never paid for it and no longer hangs with Buck or his gang. For the second time, Crowell employs the Marlboro Red ruse and gets consent for the witness's DNA. Pretending to admire the man's tattoos, Crowell convinces him to partially disrobe so he can surreptitiously check the rest of his body for potential scars from a knife. There are none.

After obtaining the DNA in near-record time and taking a smoke break, Deere and Crowell enter Interview Room 1, where they find Gerry Gordon. A scrawny thirty-year-old who looks twenty, he is clad in a tight-fitting blue shirt, pajama-style pants, and flip-flops.

Crowell runs the cigarette ruse again, and Gordon consents to give them his DNA. When the female evidence tech finishes swabbing Gordon's cheeks, Deere and Crowell press their witness about everything from his sexual habits to his rejection by Denise.

"She didn't like me," Gordon says simply.

"How did that make you feel?" asks Deere.

"Bad—mad," he answers.

"So how many times did you have sex with her?" Deere asks. "Come on, we know you did."

"I never had sex with her."

"Bullshit!" Crowell shouts. "I'm calling bullshit!"

Under pressure, Gordon finally admits that he was approached by Denise's pimp, the girlfriend of Jason Murray, the illegal taxi driver. The girlfriend proposed a sex act for forty dollars A bit of haggling got the price down to twenty dollars, but then Gordon changed his mind and backed out. Besides, he says, he didn't have the money.

Neither detective believes this. Who negotiates a twenty-dollar deal if he doesn't have the cash? During a break, Deere comes up with a cunning sleight of hand, a fake DNA report that links Gordon to the blood found on Denise's shirt. They show him the report, and Gordon becomes a sobbing, snot-bubbling mess.

Returning to the box from a second break, Deere and Crowell find Gordon crying in the corner. After another hour or so of tough questioning, he nearly confesses to Denise's rape, but he puts the crime in the wrong place at the wrong time. The detectives decide that he is trying to please them with his answers and that, in fact, he had nothing to do with the sexual assault.

As they leave the box, Crowell is surprisingly hyper for a guy who fell asleep in mid-interrogation a couple of hours ago. He jokes with Allyson Hamlin that he could get Gerry Gordon to confess to anything. "Have any open murders that need to be closed?" he asks.

When the squad's rookie, Jamie Boulden, quips that it would be great if Crowell could get Gordon to confess to his tough-to-solve homicide of a despised drug dealer, the detective throws his right arm over Boulden's shoulders. "We'll solve that one next, buddy, no worries," Crowell says. "Once we get this one done, I'll do everything I can to help you."

Deere, meanwhile, heads to his desk and stares vacantly at his notes, pondering the weeks ahead and his race on a human hamster wheel. He's keeping busy but getting nowhere, and at this point his best hope for solving Amber Stanley's murder is that Jeff Buck's DNA comes back as a match with the spot of blood on Denise's shirt. He checks his calendar—he guesses he has at least another ten days, maybe two weeks, before he gets the results.

His head is throbbing, but Deere knows that he and Crowell will have to take another crack at Gerry Gordon to gather more intelligence about Jeff Buck's crew. It's important work, and they can afford to let Gordon calm down a bit. The greater priority, Deere decides, is to grab a nap.

Without consulting Crowell or his sergeant, Deere takes his coat from a nearby rack, trudges to his Impala, and drives to the lower parking lot. He backs into a space, turns the heat up, leans his seat all the way back, and sets the alarm on his phone to wake him in twenty minutes. He puts the phone on his chest and closes his eyes. He is instantly lost in sleep.

4:00 p.m., Wednesday, February 13

Detective Mike Ebaugh sits at his desk, waiting. He knows he has done everything in his power to solve his shit sandwich of a case. He has played and replayed the video of Nicoh Mayhew's murder, spent countless hours poring over his notes and the evidence reports, listened to dozens of jail calls, and exhaustively questioned members of Mayhew's family and his friends. Not long after receiving Cynthia Mayhew's tip about the brothers named John and Stan, he left messages with the FBI and with detectives in the county's Robbery Unit. But so far he has come up with nothing.

For the past three days Ebaugh has been so busy on other matters that he has barely thought about the case. He spent Monday working with county prosecutors who were gearing up for a trial in an unrelated murder, while also lending a hand to Eddie Flores on the slaying of Salaam Adams. He devoted the previous day to helping his partner, D. J. Windsor, investigate a high-profile murder-suicide that occurred just after midnight on Monday. Even by PG standards, Windsor's case was tragic: a University of Maryland graduate student had fired on two roommates, a promising junior and a senior. After killing one and wounding the other, the grad student shot and killed himself. Though Windsor's investigation was mostly a mop-up operation, the case generated intense media interest, in part because the gunman had been found with a fully loaded Uzi in a large black bag strapped to his back, suggesting that he'd planned to go on an even more gruesome shooting spree.

Late yesterday, as Ebaugh and Windsor compiled reports and briefed supervisors on the murder-suicide, Ebaugh bumped into Sergeant Jeremy Bull. An investigator who specializes in targeting violent offenders, Bull has an encyclopedic knowledge of PG County criminals. Hoping Bull could help him develop some new leads in the Nicoh Mayhew case, Ebaugh peppered his thirty-five-year-old comrade with questions about players in Mayhew's neighborhood and asked whether he'd picked up any rumors about the murder. Bull said he hadn't heard anything, but he promised to swing by the office the next day at 4:00 p.m. to watch Ebaugh's security footage and see if he recognized anyone in the video.

So Ebaugh waits. For the second time in two minutes, he checks the wall clock: it's now 4:03 p.m. and Bull is still not here. Ebaugh opens his thick case file and flips through his notes and evidence reports, again running through his facts. Nicoh Mayhew—a key witness in the looming murder trial of his friend Kenan Myers and his nephew Brian "Block" Mayhew—was gunned down in the vestibule of his mother's apartment complex on December 19. Ebaugh strongly suspects that Myers and/or Mayhew ordered the hit on his victim, but he has been unable to find a link between either of them and the crime. He even paid a visit to the two men in jail and tossed their cells, hoping to intimidate them and perhaps prod them to talk about the murder over a recorded phone line. But neither of them mentioned the visit in subsequent phone conversations, or in letters that jail officers intercepted on Ebaugh's behalf.

Ebaugh hears a commotion to his left and looks over to see Jeremy Bull bullshitting with Joe Bunce by the interview rooms. Ebaugh signals Bull to come over, and the skinny sergeant rolls up a chair and sits down.

"Let me show you this," Ebaugh says. He clicks Play on his computer, and a video clip of the apartment complex where Nicoh Mayhew was killed fills the monitor. Ebaugh clicks and clicks—freezing the tape, allowing it to run, freezing it again. A small hourglass pops onto the screen as the computer seizes up, unable to keep pace with Ebaugh's frenetic commands.

"Jesus, Ebaugh, just let it play," says Bull, scratching the thin beard on his round, youthful face. Finally the clip continues; two minutes later, Bull shakes his clean-shaven head.

"Again," he says, leaning close to the monitor.

Ebaugh plays the clip twice more.

After the second replay, Bull shrugs and slaps Ebaugh on the left shoulder. "Sorry, man."

"Fuck a duck," says Ebaugh.

"What else you got?" Bull asks.

Ebaugh provides a brief update on his investigation and mentions the mother's recent tip about the two brothers, John and Stan, at least one of whom had supposedly committed armored-car robberies.

"I've reached out to robbery and the feds on it, but I haven't heard back yet," Ebaugh says. "It's probably nothing. Man, I have dick—just dick."

Bull purses his lips, rolls his eyes, and chuckles. "John and Stan? Armored-car robberies?"

"Yeah, John and Stan."

"Dude," Bull says, "come on. Really? Do some fucking police work, Ebaugh. John and Stan, as in Jonathan and Stanley Winston. Stanley Winston got locked up for some armored-car robberies—not that long ago, I think."

"Aw, shit," Ebaugh says, immediately grasping the significance of Bull's comment. He actually knows Jonathan Winston very well. Early in the investigation, a witness told Ebaugh that Mayhew had feared that Winston was going to kill him for cooperating with the authorities. Winston had a long rap sheet of arrests on charges ranging from gun possession to assault; he had even beaten a murder rap. But Jonathan Winston couldn't have killed Nicoh Mayhew—at the time of the murder, he had been in jail on federal firearms charges.

When Ebaugh mentions this to Bull, the sergeant isn't impressed.

"True," Bull says, "but his brother *Stan* only got locked up in December—I think not too long after your murder. He and some other dudes were robbing armored cars, really violent. So Mom might be right about that. It makes sense."

Ebaugh makes fists with both hands, wondering how he'd failed to put this together. *John and Stan, the brothers grim.*

"These guys are not afraid to kill," Bull says.

WITHIN MINUTES OF finishing his chat with Bull, Ebaugh races over to the Robbery Unit and pesters the investigators there until he confirms Bull's information about the armored-car robberies and gets a solid contact at the FBI, an agent by the name of Richard Fennern. Before he goes home that night, Ebaugh calls Fennern and sets up an appointment.

A few days later, Ebaugh is sitting at Fennern's desk in the FBI's PG County offices. A slim thirty-one-year-old former accountant who is an expert at analyzing databases and tracking cell phones, Fennern is the lead agent in the federal investigation into a string of violent robberies. After Ebaugh provides a quick summary of the Nicoh Mayhew case, Fennern gets on his computer, and five minutes later he determines that the phones belonging to two of his eight robbery suspects were hitting off a cell tower near Cynthia Mayhew's apartment at the time of Mayhew's murder—and that the suspects had been in that area only once before during the preceding three months. Ebaugh and Fennern know what this means: the two suspects almost certainly played a role in killing Mayhew.

Fennern also has access to Stan Winston's cell-phone records, so the detective and the agent scan Winston's text messages and discover several exchanges between Winston and a woman who uses Brian Mayhew's nickname, Block, when referring to someone in jail; at one point, she specifically asks Winston to put money in a jail-phone account so Block can call them. In another text, she tells Winston that "Block is going to call later—make sure you answer the phone 'cause he wants to talk to you." A further inspection of Winston's cell-phone records reveals dozens of calls received from the jail's outgoing number.

Block had not been using his own jailhouse account to call anyone except a relative. Ebaugh and Fennern are not surprised—inmates know that their calls are recorded, and the smart ones avoid talking about anything sensitive on their own accounts. To stymie investigators, they purchase other inmates' phone codes or swap codes.

The day after they first meet, Ebaugh and Fennern continue their digging, this time in the homicide office. The detective and the agent are sitting knee to knee at Ebaugh's desk when Ebaugh logs into a jail-call database. He enters Winston's cell number, clicks the Search button, and a moment later the program spits out the jail account that had been calling Winston's number. More sleuthing reveals that the account is assigned to a twenty-seven-year-old being held for violating his probation in a handgun and robbery conviction.

Ebaugh navigates to the account's list of calls, utters a silent prayer, and clicks on a call made to Stan Winston just after Nicoh Mayhew was killed on December 19. The detective clicks Play, leans close to the small speakers on his desk, and turns the volume up as loud as it will go.

"Hello?" asks an inmate in a nasal voice that Ebaugh recognizes as Brian Mayhew's from the mundane calls he has already reviewed.

Ebaugh hits Pause. "That's definitely Block," he tells Fennern before pressing Play to continue the call.

"Hello, my nigga," replies a voice that Ebaugh feels certain must belong to Stan Winston, a fact he will later confirm.

"What's happening with you?" asks Brian Mayhew.

"Enjoying this beautiful day. Wonderful morning. Hell of a morning."

"What part?"

"Your man lost his mind out of that bitch. He was going crazy—all over the place. Shot out the cannon."

Ebaugh hits Pause and eyes Fennern. They touch elbows. Both believe Stan Winston and Brian Mayhew are speaking in sloppy code about the slaying of Nicoh Mayhew, whose brains were literally blown out of his head. Not only that, but one of Stan Winston's armed robbery accomplices is a twenty-three-year-old named Anthony Cannon. Perhaps, Ebaugh thinks, Stan Winston is telling Brian Mayhew that Cannon was the gunman.

The detective clicks the mouse, and the recording continues. Winston begins to sing: "Six-four one." The first number—64—is the county police radio code for a homicide, and Ebaugh hears a revolver spin in the background.

"Maybe I'm coming home, man!" Brian Mayhew says.

Ebaugh is elated. He and Fennern have just discovered a link between one of Ebaugh's prime suspects and one of the two men who may be the actual killers of Nicoh Mayhew. Now the investigator just needs evidence that Brian Mayhew played a role in planning the murder and wasn't simply informed of it.

Ebaugh clicks on a second call, made the night before the homicide. It is clear from the conversation that Brian Mayhew is annoyed that his uncle wasn't killed that morning. He tells Winston that it's "showtime tomorrow."

Brian Mayhew asks to talk to Cannon. Winston adds Cannon into the call, and Mayhew provides the duo with details about his uncle's schedule and whereabouts the next morning.

"You have to get some sleep tonight," Mayhew says, reminding his hit men that the job is scheduled for between 9:30 and 10:00 a.m. He also mentions a "white girl named Kia," code for his uncle's car, a Kia.

"You have twenty-two hours to make sure what I want done, you hear me?" Mayhew tells Winston and Cannon.

Ebaugh leans back in his chair and for a moment tries to take in the importance of the trove of evidence he has just uncovered. But he's too excited to sit still, so he plunges back into the calls. After listening to a few other incriminating recordings, Ebaugh returns to the call made just hours before the homicide; he wants to catalog exactly what was said. He puts his ear next to his desktop speakers to better pick up the scratchy voices.

"Listen," Mayhew says to Winston and Cannon. "Remember that junk that you said got in the way? That might be with him."

The words swirl in Ebaugh's head. Clearly Mayhew appears to be discussing an earlier, aborted attempt to kill his uncle. But what does he mean by "junk"? And then it hits the detective. Mayhew is probably talking about his uncle's two-year-old son, who must have "got in the way" during the aborted attempt. Mayhew doesn't seem to care if the boy is there or not, Ebaugh thinks. He just wants the job done, no matter the collateral damage.

"What about it?" asks Cannon.

"Nothing," Mayhew says. "You just have to go all the way up in there."

And that's exactly what the killers had done.

### 7:55 p.m., Thursday, February 14

Andre Brooks navigates through the growing crowd, shaking hands, patting backs, caressing women's arms, until finally he reaches Geraldine McIntyre's front yard. Ascending the steps to her house, the detective turns and surveys the scene he helped orchestrate. It is a cold night, but the throng has grown to perhaps forty people, a sizable number given that it's Valentine's Day, and Brooks is especially pleased to see a television news crew and a radio reporter setting up. *Perfect,* he thinks.

Eyeing a makeshift memorial constructed by neighbors on McIntyre's front lawn—Christmas lights strung along a retaining wall, a rocking chair decorated with stuffed animals—Brooks wishes he had found a better photograph of his victim. Grim and unsmiling, her driver's-license visage adorns not only each of the fifty flyers in the stack tucked under his left arm but also the four-foot-tall poster board festooned with four red heart-shaped, helium-filled balloons to his left. But there is nothing he can do about the photo, certainly not now.

The detective checks his watch; the vigil is scheduled to start in five minutes, so he descends the steps and again joins the crowd, shaking more hands, touching more shoulders. He hands out a flyer here and there. Having somehow banished his gruffer, old-school self for the occasion, he is empathetic, flirtatious, kind, caring.

"I hear you have a lovely voice," he tells a neighbor who will sing soon after the vigil begins.

"You have a nice yard," he tells another.

"I hear you are quite the cook," he compliments a woman who made McIntyre Thanksgiving dinner a few years back.

The third neighbor grins ear to ear and blushes a bit. "Why, thank you, Detective."

Brooks asks her what she knows.

"Nothing," she answers, saying that she hasn't even heard rumors about who killed her neighbor or why.

"Nothing at all?" Brooks asks gently.

"Nope," she says, all smiles.

"You know who to call if you hear anything, anything at all," he says.

She grips his right biceps and winks. "Of course. I have your number in my phone."

It has been five days since Geraldine McIntyre's murder, and if Brooks is going to solve his case, he needs the help of these friends and neighbors. That is why he prodded McIntyre's family to hold this vigil. When friends gather to sing hymns and pray for a loved one, the shared experience can be cathartic. But vigils can also be a useful investigative tool. Brooks hopes the event will cement his bonds with McIntyre's relatives and friends by proving that he cares enough to pay his respects, even on Valentine's Day. The vigil also affords him the chance to catalog the face of every person in attendance. Brooks knows from experience that sometimes a killer or a witness wants to see the grief caused by the crime.

Brooks also needs help from reporters and the press. Even when working on a red ball, PG detectives can never count on media attention. The DC area serves up a steady diet of violent crime, and stories about a gruesome homicide often lead the evening news and fill the *Washington Post*'s Metro pages. But as the days pass, it gets increasingly difficult to persuade a reporter to run a follow-up article about the case, even a major one. That is why Brooks asked the police department's media-relations office to alert the press to the McIntyre vigil, and the detective even worked a few contacts of his own. Not only will coverage of the event remind potential witnesses that the case remains unsolved, it will inform the public that there's a sizable reward—up to $25,000—for information leading to an arrest.

The key to this case, Brooks knows, will be finding McIntyre's stolen television and tracking it back to the killer. The detective remains convinced that he's looking for a drug-addicted handyman, and he's spent the last five days interviewing such men. Most had alibis or didn't seem capable of such a brutal act. One appeared to be a plausible suspect, but Brooks and Delaney were not able to crack him. As Brooks's investigation continues, the detective is being careful not to focus too intently on any particular person. Tunnel vision is an occupational hazard, and it has ruined many an investigation.

Just as Brooks expected, the assistance provided by the police department had been lackluster. Extra patrol officers and detectives hit the streets for a few days, but they turned up no serious leads and quickly returned to their regular jobs, leaving Brooks and Delaney to spend a significant portion of each day sitting in parked cars in a nearby gas station lot to disrupt the neighborhood's open-air drug market.

As he makes his way through the crowd, which now numbers more than fifty and includes several pastors, Brooks approaches an older woman wearing a thick coat and a gray cap and gives her a big hug. She is sixty-seven-year-old Barbara Stewart, Geraldine McIntyre's youngest sister; when she asks Brooks about his progress on the case, he tells her he still doesn't have much.

Their conversation is interrupted by one of McIntyre's neighbors, who begins singing "I Won't Complain," a gospel song about God's healing power. The crowd goes quiet, mesmerized by the woman's beautiful and mournful voice.

*I've had some good days*
*I've had some hills to climb . . .*

As the song ends, the neighbor dips her head. The mourners clap and issue a chorus of heartfelt amens. Someone hands Brooks a lighted candle, and soon everyone has one.

Holding his candle in his left hand while protecting the flame with his right, Brooks maneuvers through the crowd, checking each face and occasionally scanning nearby yards and the street to see if anyone is watching the ceremony from a safe perch.

As he moves past a clutch of mourners, Brooks spots a man half-hidden by a parked SUV. The man, who is wearing a mangy dark coat and blue jeans, sees Brooks and scuttles into a nearby house. Brooks thinks he recognizes him, and he makes a mental note to return the next day to scoop him up.

Just as Brooks finishes circling the mourners, the pastors begin their preaching.

"Dear Lord, mend the hurt that is there," prays one. "Jesus, come in and help the family right now. Help them heal."

"The spirit of Geraldine McIntyre will live through each and every one of you," proclaims another.

"Dear Lord, we pray that the demonic person who decided to take vengeance into his own hands does not have a comfortable sleep," declares a third. "None of us feels safe tonight because we know a devil is amongst us, a thief is amongst us, there is a murderer amongst us. Dear Lord, we pray right now not to let them sleep peacefully. I want you to fix it so that everything they do is so uncomfortable, they might have to come tonight and no later than first thing in the morning, so that they come in and say, 'I am the guilty one! I did it!'"

*Amen,* thinks Brooks.

As the neighbor with the beautiful voice delivers another gospel ballad, Brooks is pleased to see a television cameraman and the radio reporter recording the singer. He hopes that after the vigil, McIntyre's family and friends will make a direct appeal to the public. Earlier that evening, he explained to two of McIntyre's sisters exactly what they needed to say to encourage witnesses to call the police.

As Brooks continues to scrutinize each face, he listens to McIntyre's friends and neighbors speak to the crowd, extolling her gentle and caring nature. A bus driver describes how McIntyre had become more than a rider. "She was my friend," she says. Another recalls McIntyre's "beautiful hair and smile." An older woman, holding her candle in trembling hands, notes simply, "She was a quiet woman killed in a horrible way."

Barbara Stewart, McIntyre's sister, steps forward and thanks everyone for being such good friends. She looks at Brooks and then turns to the television camera. "If anyone knows anything that can solve this heinous crime, please contact the Prince George's County police," she says.

*Excellent,* thinks Brooks.

Thirty minutes after it began, the vigil ends. The neighbors trudge back to their homes, the relatives and friends begin piling into their cars. Brooks approaches Stewart and gives her another hug.

When she steps back, Stewart smiles and scrutinizes Brooks from bottom to top, her eyes lingering on his haggard face.

"You work crazy hours," she says.

"I've been hitting the streets hard," Brooks replies.

She flashes him a look that asks, *Do you have anything?*

"If I lock someone up," he says, "I'll call you—even at three a.m."

"You better call," Stewart says.

"I'm still shaking the trees," he says.

She gives him another close look and smiles sadly. "I know you are."

# · CHAPTER 5 ·

5:35 p.m., Monday, February 18

In the fading light of a clear winter afternoon that feels as dry and cold as the inside of a freezer, Detective Spencer Harris walks up and down the sidewalk and across the dead grass, scouting for clues but finding nothing other than the foamy pool of blood where a fifteen-year-old shooting victim collapsed. The tall, well-dressed detective steps back and surveys the broader scene. A normally bustling street is empty of traffic, cordoned off for hundreds of yards in either direction. Five marked squad cars are parked inside the yellow police tape, and a half dozen detectives and officers are milling about, waiting for crime-scene techs to arrive. Detective Wayne Martin, one of Harris's squad mates, is standing in the middle of Twenty-Eighth Avenue, about sixty yards away.

Pulling his cap tight over his shaved head before jamming his hands into his coat pockets, Harris heads over to Martin. They nod hello and bitch about the cold, which is only going to get more intense after the sun sets, a few minutes from now. They stare into the distance, their gazes fixed on the nine or ten people from the neighborhood who are standing just beyond the tape and looking over the crime scene, or what remains of it.

Before Harris can ask Martin what he knows, the two detectives are joined by a robbery sergeant who responded quickly to the report of a shooting and watched paramedics treat the teenager before carting him away in an ambulance.

"I don't see how he's still alive," the sergeant says. "He looked really bad. I guess if they can bring that boy back, they can bring back anyone."

"Yeah, but they took him to Southern Maryland," says Martin.

The sergeant nods. "True."

The decision to take the teenager to MedStar Southern Maryland Hospital Center and not the better trauma centers at Prince George's Hospital Center or MedStar Washington Hospital Center, in DC, is a sure sign that he stands little chance of survival. Although the PG Homicide Unit rarely responds to a crime scene until a victim is officially pronounced dead, this is an unusual case for a host of reasons, which is why Harris, Martin, and their squad mates are either on the scene or are racing here, even though the boy may still be alive.

This isn't Harris's or Martin's case; it has been assigned to Marcos Rodriguez, one of their squad mates. But Rodriguez had taken the day off, and when the call came he was at his house, about thirty-five miles away. He is now on his way to homicide, where he will join Detective Kenny Doyle in interviewing witnesses. So that leaves the scene to Harris, Martin, and a third M-90 detective, which is fine with them. Even more than the other squads, M-90 investigates murders as a team. In some instances, squad mates do so much work—canvassing the neighborhood, questioning suspects, writing up warrants—that the lead investigator doesn't even have to testify at trial.

"Any word yet from the hospital?" asks Harris, who, at six foot three, towers over the slight Martin.

"No, not yet," says Martin.

Looking over at the bloody sidewalk, Harris asks Martin what he has learned since arriving at the scene, twenty minutes earlier. Martin says the victim, Charles Walker Jr., had been shot once in the back, or so it appeared, and collapsed facedown on the sidewalk. Though Walker didn't have a pulse and was not breathing, paramedics detected a faint electrical output from the boy's body, which meant they had to take him to the hospital. They told responding officers that the teenager stood little chance of surviving—in fact, they said they'd never seen anyone come back from such a dire wound.

Martin points to the opposite end of the street and says that Walker, a high school freshman, had left his apartment complex and was heading this way on Twenty-Eighth Avenue to catch a bus. According to relatives, he planned to visit his girlfriend and give her a present: the new pink Timberland shoes he was carrying in a plastic bag.

A witness called 911 to report the shooting and said it appeared that Walker had been thrown or had fallen from a white van. But Martin is skeptical. In his view, it's far more likely that the van's occupants spotted Walker on his way to the bus stop and tried to rob him of his bag of shoes.

"I think he is walking down the street, carrying the shoes, when some dudes see him," Martin tells Harris. "They pull up in the van, they try to take the bag, something happens, and our boy gets shot."

Gesturing to several spots of blood on the street about five feet away, Martin says he thinks the teenager ran a few feet, dropped the bag, and then turned and sprinted about a hundred yards in the opposite direction before collapsing. "He was heading home," Martin says. "He was running home."

For a moment Harris says nothing. He eyes the bag, at the bottom of which he can see the outlines of a shoe box.

"Fucked up," says Harris. "Might as well hold up a placard saying, 'Rob me!' in this neighborhood. There are some cold-blooded motherfuckers out here, and they take candy from a baby."

Harris looks up and down the quiet street, lined on both sides by red-brick duplexes with fake-grass carpet on their steps. Standing at either end of the block are squat apartment buildings; to the south, the detective can see the parking lot for Marlow Heights Shopping Center. It's a rough neighborhood, and Harris knows that he and his squad mates have their work cut out for them—partly because the residents are so accustomed to violence, partly because they fear being labeled snitches.

"They don't call when they hear gunshots," Martin says.

"They don't even call if they see a muzzle flash," says Harris.

Harris turns to his right, his attention suddenly drawn by an earsplitting scream at the far end of the street. Holding up a hand to block the setting sun, he sees a woman yelling and crying as she tries to push past several police officers in an attempt to get to the site where young Walker's blood was spilled.

"He's a good boy!" she wails. "He's just fifteen! Oh, my God! Oh, my God! He's a good boy! He goes to school!"

Harris, Martin, and the robbery sergeant watch as the woman is ushered from the small crowd, her screams becoming ever more distant until they are drowned out by the siren of a fire engine and the jingle of an ice cream truck.

Harris furrows his brow. *An ice cream truck? It's fucking February*. He shrugs—anything is possible in PG County.

The robbery sergeant directs the detectives' attention to a man in a green sweatshirt leaning against a street sign just beyond the police tape, not far from where the woman had been screaming. The man is one of the victim's uncles, the sergeant says, and he might know what happened. The sergeant provides the uncle's name, and Harris and Martin roll their eyes. The man is a notorious neighborhood character with a long arrest record.

"Why is he still here?" asks Harris, surprised that the uncle has remained in the presence of so many police officers.

The sergeant smiles, reaches into the right pocket of his jeans, and pulls out a plastic card. He hands it to Harris. "That's why," the sergeant says. "I liberated his ID. He's waiting to get it back."

Harris studies the ID, thanks the sergeant, and tells Martin he is going to chat with the uncle. A minute or two later, Harris is shaking the hand of the beefy twenty-nine-year-old street tough, and he's surprised to see that the man's eyes are red and puffy from crying. Harris hands back the uncle's ID and asks him what he knows.

"He was just going to drop off the shoes to his girl," the man says, wiping tears from his jaw. "He bought them for her as a gift. Then he was going to the mall to shop for new school clothes."

"How did you hear about it?" Harris asks, nodding back toward the bloody sidewalk.

"I heard police cars," the uncle says. "I looked out and saw a man running. So I headed that way, to see what the fuck is going on, and I see him on the ground."

Harris asks the man if he can tell him about his nephew's day leading up to the shooting. The uncle offers a detailed reply and ends by saying that after buying the shoes for his girlfriend and then returning home, Walker left the house at about 4:00 p.m., approximately twenty minutes before the shooting was reported to 911.

As he finishes his account, the uncle breaks down sobbing. "I mean, Chuck stays inside all the time. He plays Xbox—he doesn't cause no trouble. I'm hoping God can pull a miracle, but I doubt it. I've seen all the TV shows. I know how this stuff goes down."

Harris says nothing as the uncle cries.

Finally the man regains his composure and asks, "You have any witnesses?"

The detective momentarily considers the irony of the situation—this man, who in his time has surely intimidated more than his share of potential witnesses, wants to know if anyone has stepped forward to offer help.

"We have a couple, and they're at the station," Harris replies.

The uncle sighs, his gaze drawn to two evidence technicians who are scouring the scene and have begun taking photos of the blood and the shoe box.

Harris thanks the uncle. As he turns to leave, he feels the man's hand on his right arm.

"I know how everything goes," the uncle says. "Not everybody was raised perfect."

"No, they aren't," says Harris. "No, they sure aren't."

Harris again thanks the uncle for his time, shakes his hand, and heads back to the crime scene. There he rejoins Martin, who tells him that it's official: Charles Walker is dead. Martin adds that their squad mate Kenny Doyle has finished interviewing several young men who performed first aid on Walker. The officers were initially suspicious of them, but Doyle is convinced they had nothing to do with the shooting—they really had been trying to help.

"Really?" Harris says. "Good Samaritans? Over here?"

Another squad mate, Denise Shapiro, has joined Harris and Martin at the scene, and together the three detectives devise a plan for the rest of the evening. Harris and Shapiro will canvass the block while Martin remains behind to monitor the techs' progress.

The sun has fully set. It's now 6:30, and the temperature has already dropped several degrees. Blowing into his hands, Harris turns to Shapiro and says, "Let's do this quick."

While Shapiro heads for some houses down the block, Harris strides toward a brick duplex across the street. He climbs the front step and knocks on an iron security door. Hearing shuffling in the hallway, he knocks again, harder.

"County police!" he shouts.

The inner door opens a crack. Harris makes out a woman in her thirties or forties, her hair done up in curlers.

"Yes?"

Gesturing toward the crime scene, Harris explains that they are investigating a shooting that occurred about an hour earlier. The woman looks past Harris, toward an evidence tech who is taking photographs with a bright flash.

"I didn't see or hear anything," she says.

She starts to shut the door, but Harris reaches through the security gate's bars and prevents it from closing.

"Wait—you didn't hear anything?"

"No," she says, pausing. "Just gunshots."

*What the fuck,* Harris thinks. *Just gunshots?*

"Around what time?" he asks.

"I had just come home from work."

"Did you call 911?"

"No. We hear gunshots all the time."

Harris taps his pen on his notepad and purses his lips. "When was that, ma'am?"

"Maybe four or four-thirty," she says. "Well, I actually didn't hear the gunshots. I had my earplugs in and was on the phone. The person on the other end of the line heard the shots and was like, 'Was that a gunshot?'"

"So you didn't actually hear the shots?"

"No, my friend heard the shots and told me about it."

"What's your name, ma'am?" Harris asks.

"Do I have to give it? I don't want to be involved."

"Can I at least have your phone number?"

She thinks for a second, then glances over her shoulder into her house. The sweet aroma of barbecue enters Harris's nostrils, which leads him to wonder if the woman's evasiveness may have less to do with her fear of being labeled a snitch and more to do with her preparations for the arrival of a dinner date. When she turns back to the door, the porch light hits her face, revealing freshly applied makeup.

"If I give you my number, you're just going to keep calling me for information, and I don't want to give you any information."

Harris makes one last stab: "You didn't see anyone running?"

"No."

"Thanks for your time," he says.

Harris heads down the steps and walks quickly toward the adjacent house. After a second interview, he visits the next house and the next, getting mostly the same answer.

"No, I didn't hear anything."

"No, I didn't see anything."

"No, I didn't see or hear anything."

And so it goes: up and down the block, a whole lot of nothing.

HARRIS ROLLS INTO homicide at 11:30 the next morning, feeling semi-rested despite having left the office at 4:00 a.m. He had worked late for a good reason: around midnight, the squad had received a credible tip that Charles Walker had been killed by a thirteen-year-old boy over a pair of gray Air Jordans. Hours before the murder, Walker and the second teen had been engaged in a conversation on Instagram, the popular social-media site, about the sale of some sneakers. Rumor had it that this exchange suggested that the teen was setting Walker up to kill him for his shoes. As the existence of the Instagram conversation spread among Walker's friends and neighbors, the first tip led to two more. In the end, though, the rumor proved false—the Instagram conversation would wind up having nothing to do with the murder.

Late night or no, Harris is sharply dressed this morning: he's wearing a tailored gray suit, a light blue shirt, and a dark blue tie. The forty-six-year-old detective's attire has fueled his reputation as a lady's man. His wardrobe has also prompted his sergeant to insist that Harris question female witnesses, since they tend to offer him more information than they do his partner, Kenny Doyle, whose manner and taste in clothes is on the bland side.

Harris, a twenty-three-year veteran of the department, spent a decade as a sex-offense detective before joining homicide two years ago. Considered one of the unit's better interviewers, he used that skill to good advantage in the most recent murder he investigated, that of a twenty-seven-year-old drug user who was shot in a dispute with a friend and left for dead at a firehouse. It took twelve hours of intense questioning, but Harris finally cracked the key witness. The investigator had also gotten lucky: his suspect had dropped his wallet at the firehouse.

Harris settles into his desk in his squad's office, which is just down the hall from the larger homicide squad room. During a particularly brutal stretch of homicides a decade or so earlier, commanders had created the M-90 homicide squad and deposited the detectives in this small office. The room is bright and quiet—no rowdies like Mike Crowell or Joe Bunce—and it has its own conference table, chalkboard, dry-erase board, and coffeemaker. Members of M-90 like the space and consider their squad a Homicide Unit unto itself.

Soon Harris is joined by his sergeant, Greg McDonald. McDonald hangs his gray suit jacket on a coat rack and takes his seat in a row of workstations to Harris's right. After smoothing a wrinkle in his shirt, McDonald opens a desk drawer, retrieves a plastic dental pick from a small package, pops the pick into his mouth, and begins chewing it. The habit was formed a decade earlier, and he usually goes through a pick or two a day.

Tall and broad-shouldered with a shaved head, the forty-four-year-old wears a nearly constant smile and has an infectious laugh that can be heard far down the hall. A former marine who has spent sixteen years investigating homicides in PG County, the sergeant is known as one of the best interrogators in the department. He will

do whatever it takes—within the law or while making new law—
to get someone to talk. He is a contradiction: at once aggressive and
patient, he long ago mastered the art of extracting information from
the most reluctant witnesses and the toughest killers. "The first
eight hours belong to them," McDonald is fond of saying. "Then
they are mine."

Just a few weeks earlier, McDonald had spent two hours ver-
bally sparring with an obnoxious fifteen-year-old boy who the sergeant was convinced had witnessed a murder. Whereas other
detectives might have pushed the kid hard, McDonald never lost his
cool. At some point during the third hour, he noticed what looked
like pain in the teen's eyes and went silent—for one minute, two,
three, four. To a suspect in the box, four minutes can feel like four
hours, and soon the teenager began to gaze forlornly at his hands.
He sniffled, wiped away a tear, and then convulsed.

Once he stopped crying, the boy told McDonald about the worst
thing he had ever done. After seeing his best friend get shot, he had
cradled his friend's bloody head in his arms and watched as his
buddy struggled to breathe. He heard police sirens and grew frightened, at which point he laid his friend's head on the pavement and
ran, leaving his friend to die alone. The teen wept again, and as he
wiped his tears away with a shirtsleeve, McDonald gently put a
large hand on the boy's shoulder and said, "It's okay, son, it's okay.
Just keep talking—keep talking to me." And the boy did.

McDonald has seen almost everything in his years investigating
murders, which may explain why he is never in a rush. He believes
in carefully assessing evidence and letting a case develop. That's why
he sent his squad home at 4:00 a.m. to get some sleep, whereas other
supervisors might have pressed their detectives to work through
the night.

As Harris and McDonald review their notes, the sergeant's
phone rings. On the line is their lieutenant, Brian Reilly, explaining
that the previous night, not long after their murder and not too far

from the scene, a drug dealer had been wounded in a shooting. The suspects were seen fleeing in a white van that matched the description of the one leaving the scene of their homicide. Reilly tells McDonald that district-level detectives picked up a suspect in the other shooting earlier that morning; the detectives have finished interrogating him, and he now awaits them in the box.

After hanging up, McDonald signals for Harris to follow him. As the sergeant tells his detective about his call with Reilly, they leave the M-90 office, turn down the hallway, and proceed through a set of double doors to enter the office of the District 3 detectives, who investigate most serious crimes short of homicide.

McDonald and Harris pull a detective aside and get a detailed report on last night's shooting. The suspect in the box is twenty-two-year-old Tayvon Williams, of Oxon Hill. Williams and a few friends had arranged to buy marijuana from a dealer; when something went wrong during the transaction, Williams opened fire on the dealer, and the dealer shot back. Wounded in the left shoulder, the dealer was taken to the hospital. Under questioning, the dealer identified the man who had arranged the purchase and provided the detectives with his number. The detectives tracked the phone and picked up Tayvon Williams, who quickly confessed to shooting the dealer. He also confirmed that he and several friends had been driving around that afternoon and evening in a white van.

The District 3 detective tells McDonald and Harris he's fairly certain that Williams and his friends were actually plotting to rob the dealer instead of going through with the purchase. "Oh, and they had stolen the van from a church," the detective adds.

"Nice guys," says Harris.

The facts seem to suggest that Williams could have been involved in the murder of Charles Walker, but Harris wonders aloud whether it's plausible that someone would fatally shoot a fifteen-year-old at 4:20 p.m., line up a drug rip, and then ninety minutes later shoot a drug dealer only two miles from the scene of the homicide. Moreover, the notion that the gunman in both shootings is sitting in the box seems too good to be true, especially if he has confessed to one of the shootings after little prompting.

McDonald and Harris thank the detective for his efforts and a few minutes later enter the District 3 interview room. Waiting for them is a relaxed young man in a red-and-blue windbreaker, a black skullcap, and blue jeans. He is sitting at a small table, a half-finished bottle of Gatorade in front of him.

The detectives introduce themselves. Harris sits down across from Williams; McDonald takes a chair to Williams's left.

"We've heard you have been extremely cooperative," Harris says, smiling.

"Yes," says Williams, nodding.

"The people we spoke to believe you have been honest, and we want you to continue to be honest."

Williams take a sip of his Gatorade and looks at Harris expectantly.

Harris says, "We understand about the situation you got into yesterday. What did you classify that as—a drug deal gone bad?"

"I don't know what to classify it as," Williams replies.

Harris asks how the deal went down. Williams says he was picked up at his apartment by two friends in the white van between 3:00 and 3:30 p.m. They drove around for a bit, and just before they went to purchase the marijuana, one of his buddies handed him a revolver. When the dealer and some other guys emerged from a dark corner of an apartment building, Williams says, he opened fire.

"So you had a bad feeling about this thing?" Harris asks. "He didn't do anything aggressive? It didn't look right?"

"Yeah, that's what made me do what I did," Williams says. "I thought he was going to shoot me."

"It was supposed to be a legitimate transaction?"

"Yes."

Harris doesn't believe Williams—he was way too quick on the trigger for someone just looking to buy drugs—and again asks Williams to talk about what he had been doing before the shooting. Williams says that after he was picked up in the van, the group drove to Twenty-Eighth Avenue so a friend could grab some cash at his apartment. *That's right where Walker was murdered,* Harris thinks.

After thanking Williams for being so forthcoming, Harris tells him that the police have obtained surveillance video from apartment complexes in the area of Twenty-Eighth Avenue and that they have the van's license plate. It is a lie calculated to make Williams believe that the evidence against him and his friends is piling up.

"So we already know about the van," Harris says, adding that they also have witnesses' statements from their neighborhood canvass. He pauses to study the twenty-one-year-old, who seems more nervous than before, twitchy even.

"On Twenty-Eighth Avenue there was another robbery, and that's what he and I are concerned about," Harris says, nodding toward McDonald. "We're not concerned with the drug deal that went bad."

Harris explains that Williams is lucky—he is the first one to be questioned. "Once we start talking to everyone else, you just never know how this is going to end up," the detective says. "Our robbery also turned bad."

Williams nods and says, "Right. I understand what you're saying. But to be honest with you, I don't know what they were doing before they got me."

Harris shakes his head and says, "No, no, no, no, no. Let's hit the rewind button. Let's not even go down that road." Then he tells Williams that the robbery attempt on Twenty-Eighth Avenue occurred after 4:00 and reminds the suspect that he said he was picked up at 3:00. "You were with them," Harris says.

Williams dodges Harris again, claiming he had nothing to do

with the first robbery. McDonald, who up to this point has mostly been observing the interrogation, presses the suspect but gets the same response.

Harris can see that Williams is weighing whether to talk but is worried about being labeled a rat. "Dude, this ain't snitching," the detective says. "This is your life. I'm telling you right now, this ain't snitching. We have to clear this up."

"This is called self-preservation," McDonald says. "It is heavy on you, man. I am sitting here reading you like a book."

Williams scratches his forehead, then looks back and forth between the detectives and leans forward.

"All right," says Williams, his words barely a whisper. "I'm going to tell you—the honest-to-God truth."

After he was picked up, Williams says, the group collected two more friends and then went looking for someone to rob. They were driving along Twenty-Eighth Avenue in the van when they spotted a teenager they didn't know carrying a bag that clearly contained a box of shoes. The driver handed a revolver to one of the passengers and told him, "He wears your size." After passing the kid, the driver snapped a U-turn and halted abreast of him. The gunman opened the door, stepped out, and said, "You know what time it is. Give that shit up."

It should have gone down smoothly, but the kid was wearing headphones, Williams says, and did not grasp the seriousness of the situation. At first he actually laughed, but once he spotted the gun, he turned and ran. It was too late; he made it only a few steps down the sidewalk before the gunman opened fire.

"What provoked him to shoot?" Harris asks.

"I guess because he ran," Williams said, adding that the gunman seemed more upset about missing out on the loot than about shooting someone. "He was like, 'Damn, bro, I could have had shoes and money.'"

"He didn't care that he shot him?" Harris asks.

Shaking his head, Williams looks at Harris blankly and says, "Nope."

AT 4:15 P.M.—not quite four hours after Harris began questioning Williams—all five detectives in the M-90 squad gather in their small office to brief Captain George Nichols on their progress; also in attendance are Lieutenant Brian Reilly and Sergeant Greg McDonald. Nichols has called the meeting because he is about to provide a briefing to the department's chief about yet another big case. The chief, meanwhile, has scheduled a news conference that is due to start in just forty-five minutes.

Few things alarm police commanders and local politicians more than an unexplained and apparently unstoppable spate of murders of young people, and Charles Walker is the fifth Prince George's County high school student to be killed since classes started in August. Amber Stanley was the first; less than three weeks after her murder, another popular honor student, eighteen-year-old Marckel Ross, was slain in a botched robbery as he walked to school. The two killings that followed, both involving teens with gang associations, were cleared, but neither the Stanley nor the Ross murders have been solved, and they hang around the chief's neck like a noose. Now, with Walker's murder, the chief is under enormous pressure to explain the recent flood of homicides involving students.

Nichols starts the meeting by explaining the obvious: the chief wants to send a message that despite this string of murders of the county's youths, his department rules the streets. He will provide an update on the Stanley and Ross investigations, and he'll have to answer questions about the previous day's murder of Charles Walker. In particular, he is eager to tamp down rumors that the killing was orchestrated over Instagram.

The captain turns the floor over to Harris, who describes what

he and McDonald learned from Tayvon Williams during the interrogation. But Harris cautions that it's too early to entirely trust
Williams's rendition of events. "Frankly, I think Tayvon may have
been the gunman. He shot the drug dealer. And he was really
quick on the trigger."

For now, however, the squad has enough evidence to track down
the four men who were in the van with Williams, and all four will
be questioned intensively about their roles in the two shootings.

As Harris wraps up his briefing, Nichols takes a call on his cell
phone. On the line is his boss, Major Michael Straughan, who says
the time has come to announce that they have a suspect in Marckel
Ross's murder. A little more than six weeks after Ross was shot,
police recovered the gun used to kill him, and before long they were
able to tie it to the man they suspected of committing the murder.
The detectives and prosecutors working on the Ross investigation
want a few more weeks to solidify their case before bringing charges,
but Straughan tells Nichols that the chief feels he needs to release
some positive news on a bad day.

After hanging up, Nichols sighs, looks at McDonald, and says:
"Marckel Ross."

McDonald nods: having listened to Nichols's side of the conversation, the sergeant doesn't need to be told what the captain has just
learned. Nichols checks a roster of detectives taped to a desk, finds
the number for the lead investigator on the Ross case—it's Detective Paul Dougherty—and dials.

When Dougherty answers, Nichols explains that in a few minutes the chief will announce that they are close to making an arrest
in the Ross case. The suspect is already in jail on robbery charges,
so there isn't any risk of him hearing the news and fleeing.

But Nichols makes it clear that under no circumstances should
the victim's mother hear about the chief's announcement from news
reports.

"The major wants you to reach out to the mother immediately,"

Nichols tells Dougherty. "You can say we are really close and we had a break, something is coming down. Anyway"—Nichols pauses and exhales—"you know what to say."

THIRTY MINUTES LATER, at precisely 5:00 p.m., Chief Mark Magaw steps to the podium. A press conference in Prince George's County is typically a low-key affair, and this one is no different. The chief stands in the lobby of police headquarters, which features a restored 1931 black Model A Ford county police car and a white police motorcycle from the 1970s. To Magaw's left is Angela Alsobrooks, the county's state's attorney, and Michael Blow, director of school security; to Magaw's right is his assistant chief, Kevin Davis. Standing in front of this collection of officials are a half dozen respectful print and television reporters and a handful of cameramen.

Chief Magaw, dressed in a crisp white uniform shirt and gray slacks, is a balding, fifty-four-year-old former college linebacker who joined the PG force in 1984. The son of a former director of the Secret Service, Magaw is usually quiet and reserved in public. But he has been known to lose his temper. The previous fall, when the third student of the school year was killed, in the Lewisdale neighborhood, Magaw convened a meeting of his detectives, police officers, and their supervisors. After demanding updates on the investigation and details about the steps his department was taking to tamp down tension among rival Hispanic gangs in the area, the chief smacked the conference table with the palm of one hand and yelled, "*They* don't own Lewisdale! *We* own fucking Lewisdale!"

In the twenty-four hours since Charles Walker's death, Magaw's anger has been boiling. But Magaw knows that showing even a little of that fury at his press conference will send the wrong message. Instead, the chief wants to appeal for patience and calm, remind his audience that crime in PG County is dropping, and assure people that the county is safer now than it has been in many years.

Gripping the podium firmly with his left hand, Magaw nods to the assembled journalists and begins: "While the murder investigation into Charles Walker is still very active and just barely one day old, I want to first and foremost offer my personal condolences to the family during this difficult time."

Detectives have been working tirelessly, Magaw says, and have developed suspects. He appreciates the community's concern and urges witnesses to call with information. He cautions reporters that rumors about a social-media connection to Walker's homicide are "incorrect" and explains that the motive for the murder is the attempted theft of a pair of shoes.

"When a senseless act of violence takes a young person's life, this police department and community grieve," Magaw says. "When five high school students are killed within the 2012–2013 school year, we all demand both justice and accounting of circumstances that give rise to juvenile violence."

The chief goes on to say that the department, other county agencies, and various interfaith groups will soon announce a new strategy to address the problem, and the effort will focus intensely on conflict resolution. He also touts the Homicide Unit's success at having solved two of the five murders. He adds that there will be a "significant announcement" in the Marckel Ross investigation next week and that "significant leads are being vigorously pursued in the Amber Stanley case."

The chief looks at each of the reporters standing in front of him and declares confidently, "I anticipate all five of these cases to close with arrests."

After taking several questions, Magaw concludes the press conference. He and his commanders return to their offices and begin to discuss the department's plan to roll out the conflict-resolution program and a crime-suppression plan if the violence continues apace. The latter initiative will involve the deployment of officers in cars with flashing lights at the county's forty-four most violent street corners from 3:00 p.m. to 3:00 a.m. Though it is likely to prevent shootings within a several-block radius of each officer, the program will be expensive, costing the cash-strapped county about $130,000 a week in overtime.

Meanwhile, the press conference jinx has once again worked its dark power. Not thirty minutes after Magaw leaves the podium, a cascade of phone calls and text messages pours down on the chief, the assistant chief, and the other commanders in the department. The calls and messages all convey the same horrific news: a sixth PG student has been shot and killed, and another teenager has been mortally wounded.

### 7:50 p.m., Tuesday, February 19

Detective Billy Watts slips under the yellow police tape, his head bowed against the night's cold drizzle, his leather soles clacking against the wet, oily pavement. For a moment, he stands alone in a corner of this dreary parking lot, his face illuminated by the dull glow of a building's amber floodlights. If ever a homicide scene captured the atmosphere of the entire county, it is this one.

To his left, Watts sees Assistant Chief Kevin Davis and several commanders chatting with a group of officers. Davis—a short, stern man—does not look pleased, though that is hardly surprising, since his mouth is usually a frozen grimace and his cheeks are perpetually flushed crimson. It is never a good sign when Davis appears at a scene, and it takes little effort for Watts to imagine Davis growling under his breath about the murder of yet another teenager, this one reported to be just fourteen.

Watts, bundled in a black overcoat, walks across the parking lot. This is his case, and the double shooting took place outside the twenty-four-building Penn Mar apartment complex, which is located in the heart of Forestville, a four-square-mile, amoeba-shaped parcel of unincorporated suburbia nestled against the Beltway. When the detective reaches Brian Reilly, who is standing on the curb in the center of the crime scene, he shakes his lieutenant's hand and offers a quiet hello.

A tall and imposing man, Reilly has dark bags under his eyes. His colleague Lieutenant Billy Rayle has been out on sick leave while recovering from a burst appendix, so Reilly has responded to most of the crime scenes over the past two months. The forty-two-year-old officer starts with the good news. "Your victim isn't fourteen," he tells Watts. "He's eighteen."

As Watts jots down some notes, Reilly continues. The victim's name is Aaron Kidd, and despite his age, he's only a freshman in high school. The second victim is Kidd's friend Andre Shuford, also eighteen; later, Watts will learn that he is no longer in school. Shuford is dying at Prince George's Hospital Center: doctors say he is brain-dead and has only a day or two to live, which will make this a double homicide.

As Reilly finishes, he and Watts are joined by two more detectives, Ben Brown and Andre Brooks. Watts and Brown, longtime partners, exchange knowing nods: having caught the murders while on the evening shift, they are going to go sleepless again. Watts had been about to take a nap and Brown was just sitting down to a family dinner when they got the calls that will upend their lives for days to come.

Dressed in a tan overcoat, Brooks scowls downrange at the gaggle of commanders and officers. "This is a clusterfuck," he says. "But at least it will get the old-lady heat off me."

Reilly shakes his head. "No, it won't, Andre. This kid may be a freshman, but he's eighteen."

"Shit," says Brooks, realizing that his case, the murder of Geraldine McIntyre, easily trumps Watts's. "I thought he was fourteen."

Reilly shrugs and then glances over to the gathering of commanders and officers at the other end of the parking lot. As the lieutenant and his detectives watch, the group breaks up and the assistant chief speed-walks back to his car. It's obvious to Reilly and the others that Davis, too, has just learned that the night's victims are eighteen, not fourteen. In the cold calculus of red ball murders, a slain adult high school student is not nearly as tragic as a dead fourteen-year-old, and thus it does not require such a high-ranking commander at the scene.

Reilly turns back to his detectives and continues with his briefing. He points to his right; Watts and his two colleagues squint into the darkness and see evidence technicians scouring a grassy area by the light of a portable flood lamp. Reilly says both victims were shot more or less where the techs are working. Shuford fell near the site of the shooting, whereas Kidd turned and ran some three hundred yards before collapsing in a courtyard about one hundred yards to Reilly's left.

Reilly tells Watts and the others that one witness reported seeing the gunman sprint from the scene and then double back to collect shell casings. Another witness watched the gunman pedal away from the apartment complex on a bicycle. "There is a blood trail out of this development," Reilly says, pointing over Watts's shoulder toward the street. "It's like a drop every ten yards, or two drops. It's along the bicycle's path, and there is no other reason for it to be there. It's fresh." Reilly doesn't have to explain the significance of the blood: it is entirely possible that the shooter was also wounded during the altercation.

A third witness, the lieutenant says, is an elderly man who claims he heard three or four gunshots, looked out his window, and saw Shuford on the ground and a man firing a gun from behind a tree on the edge of the parking lot. Other witnesses reported hearing ten to twelve gunshots. "They hear three to four initially and then five or six more," Reilly says.

"How many casings?" Watts asks.

Brooks, who has already spoken briefly with the evidence techs, replies, "They haven't found any yet."

Watts frowns. "We should get some more lights—and metal detectors. He couldn't have collected them all, not in the dark."

"On it," Reilly says, setting off to find the county's top evidence technician.

Watts respects evidence technicians, but they sometimes need prodding, so he and Brown head across the parking lot to the area where the two victims were shot. In the glow of a portable light attached to a generator that sounds nearly as loud as a jackhammer, two techs are placing yellow numbered placards next to pieces of clothing and other items. Watts knows both techs well, and he is pleased to see that the lead on the scene is Alana Andrews. A redhead dressed in a black sweatshirt and black fatigue pants with a digital camera slung around her neck, Andrews is respected by PG homicide detectives.

Watts asks Andrews what she and the second tech have discovered thus far. She admits they haven't come up with much, despite extensive searching for bullets and casings. Later, she says, she'll scan the area with metal detectors, and she's weighing whether to summon a sufficient number of police officers to conduct a slow line search for potential evidence.

Motioning for Watts and Brown to follow her, Andrews gives the detectives a tour of the scene. She begins by pointing out what she and her colleague have cataloged: earphones, a hairbrush, a cell phone, a pair of shoes, clothing that had been yanked off by paramedics. Next she brings Watts and Brown to the spot where a large kitchen knife with a wooden handle and a six- or seven-inch blade is lying on the ground. "There is something smeared on its handle and blade," she says. "It could be blood, but I think it's dirt."

Brown stoops to inspect the knife. "Looks like dirt," he tells Watts, his voice barely audible above the thundering generator. "Someone brought a knife to a gunfight."

Watts squats down and studies the knife. He suspects that it belonged to either Kidd or Shuford. Maybe, Watts thinks, one of them used the knife to threaten a robber or rival drug dealer, who in turn pulled out a gun.

As he stands up again and surveys the scene, Watts hears music in the distance. It is difficult to discern over the generator, but it sounds like a gospel hymn coming from a second-floor window. *Perfect,* he thinks. *Maybe the music will summon God and help me close this case.*

"It looks like your one victim ends up here," Andrews says, pointing to the spot where Shuford was found, "and the other flees that way. You see the towels and the blood up there, in the courtyard?"

Watts shakes his head; he hasn't been to the courtyard yet. He looks into the distance but can make out only the parking lot and the dark forms of the apartment buildings.

"We walked that whole thing," Andrews says. "It looks like the suspect was shooting at the guy as he ran away." The tech then points to a building across the parking lot and tells the detectives that a resident there reported that her windowsill had been hit by a bullet. Watts finds this plausible: if the gunman had been firing at the sprinting Kidd, a shot could have sailed over the teenager's head and struck the building.

Satisfied that Andrews and the second tech are doing everything they can to find shell casings and collect other evidence, Watts and Brown head back to the parking lot. From there, they carefully trace Kidd's path to the spot where he collapsed in a courtyard. As they stand over the two towels mentioned by Andrews and a small spot of blood in the grass, Watts coughs and sniffles, as does Brown. Both are weathering heavy colds, their condition only made worse by a grueling week on the midnight shift that will not end for two more days.

Alone in the courtyard, the two detectives scan the area in hopes of finding a security camera or a new witness. They see nothing. As they head back to the parking lot, Watts and Brown run into a detective who specializes in gang-related crimes. The investigator explains that the gang operating out of this complex is called the National Society. The gang, of which Kidd was a member, is involved in assorted offenses ranging from drug possession and distribution to burglary. "'Gang' is kind of a strong term for the group, though," the detective says. He's watched a number of videos that show the gang members rapping, smoking weed, and brandishing guns for the camera. "They think they're tough," he says.

Watts thanks the investigator, and he and Brown divide up their duties for the next couple of hours. Brown will hit the office to write reports and review other investigators' notes; Watts will visit Prince George's Hospital Center to check on the victims' families and oversee the collection of evidence.

Brown walks to his car and drives off. Watts, after opening the door to his red Impala, pauses. Narrowing his eyes, he wonders what he might have overlooked during the last hour at the scene, but he can't think of anything. He coughs, then coughs again. He feels like crap, but he knows he will have to bull through the illness if he hopes to solve this case.

After he gets behind the wheel and starts the engine, Watts pulls out his phone, dials the number for the communications department, and gives the operator his badge and cell number, telling her he will be the detective getting all the callouts during the midnight shift. He hangs up, opens his notebook, jots down the time— 8:58 p.m.—and writes that he has cleared the scene. But his long night has only just begun.


AN HOUR AND a half later, Watts is standing in the bustling trauma bay of Prince George's Hospital Center. To his left is a dead teenager, to his right a dying one. Aaron Kidd's body lies on a gurney and is covered by a white sheet; across the room, a large breathing tube snakes from Andre Shuford's mouth to a machine. Watts overhears two frustrated nurses standing by Shuford's gurney complain to each other that they've paged a doctor six times in the last hour. They need a physician to tell the dying teen's parents how to fill out a "do not resuscitate" order; otherwise, they'll have to continue pumping him full of medicine to keep his heart beating. "He's going to crash at any moment," one nurse tells the other above the constant pinging of monitoring alarms signaling Andre Shuford's plummeting blood pressure.

Leaving the trauma bay, Watts heads for the waiting room and finds Detective Paul Dougherty in the hallway. Dougherty has the build of an aging power forward in basketball and a reputation in the Homicide Unit for being brusque, impatient, and opinionated. It makes Watts more than a bit nervous that Dougherty has been assigned to handle the victims' families.

Dougherty tells Watts that Kidd's family has left the hospital but Shuford's is behind the door of the waiting room to his right. "Andre's mom is very good people," Dougherty says in a rapid-fire whisper. "The dad is amazing—twenty-seven years military. Mom says Andre smoked marijuana. They have six kids. The youngest three are adopted. He was adopted. He dropped out of school before he turned eighteen. Since turning eighteen, he has been acting like a knucklehead and is the most fucked-up person in the family. He's homeless, sleeping in apartment hallways, laundry rooms. They all know he is breaking into houses."

Watts asks Dougherty whether Shuford's relatives have the passcode to his phone, which could contain a trove of photos, text messages, and social-media postings. Dougherty says he'll find out and ducks into the waiting room. After Dougherty leaves, Watts realizes he had no cause to worry about him: his colleague is doing a fine job.

A minute later, Dougherty pokes his head out and summons Watts inside. Dougherty politely introduces one of Shuford's sisters to Watts, telling her that his colleague is the lead detective on her brother's case. Watts gently asks if she has the code to her brother's phone; wiping tears from her eyes, she tells him that she doesn't know it and that her brother only used his phone for listening to music. Watts apologizes for bothering her, hands her his card, and asks her to call if she hears something or has any questions.

As he leaves the room, Watts looks back at the half dozen family members. They're all still wearing their winter coats, and without exception they are sobbing, crying quietly, or staring vacantly into space. Andre Shuford might not have been the world's most upstanding young man, Watts thinks, but it is clear that he was loved.

Watts returns to the trauma bay to wait for an evidence technician. He stops next to Shuford's gurney and watches as a nurse checks his victim's vital signs. The detective catches the nurse's eye and raises an eyebrow: *How much time does he have?*

"Not long now," she says, pointing to the base of Shuford's skull. "Brain matter."

Watts leans close and sees pus seeping out of a gauze bandage. He nods.

Realizing he hasn't heard from his partner since they left the crime scene, Watts calls Brown and learns that he was dispatched to a hospital in the District to check out a stabbing victim. Their sergeant had hoped that the victim might be the guy who fled the scene of their homicide on his bike. Brown answers his phone and tells Watts that, unfortunately, the stabbing is not related to their case.

After hanging up, Watts turns to find Detective Dave Gurry sitting on a chair by the rear wall of the trauma bay. Gurry, who came to the hospital with Dougherty to help handle the families, is clad in an oversized winter coat and has a phone pressed to his right ear.

"Um, she was facedown?" Gurry asks. "Pants around the ankles? Hmm. Money beside her? Okay."

When Gurry hangs up, Watts asks what's happening.

"Suspicious death," Gurry says. He goes on to tell Watts that other detectives from the unit had just arrived at a scene to find a fifty-five-year-old woman dead by her back door. Her death seems to indicate foul play, but until they roll the body and examine it more closely, they won't know whether she was murdered. Gurry is at bat for the next homicide, which is why he was called.

"It's probably a natural, but I'm ready to go if they find her throat slit," says Gurry.

"Sounds like it's either nothing or something," says Watts, who massages the dark patches under his eyes and his wan cheeks, then coughs into his right fist. *Fucking cold,* he thinks. At least his nose is so congested that he can't smell the room's heavy odor of disinfectant.

Gurry's phone rings again. "Hi, Sarge," the detective says into the receiver. "Yes. Yes. Uh-huh. Any witnesses on the scene? He is ten-seven? Almost? Okay. Going to United Medical? Seven-A recovered? Victim shot a couple times in the head? Suspect there? Okay. Cool."

The detective hangs up, a smile on his face. Gurry, more than most of the PG homicide detectives, speaks in police-radio 10 codes: 10-7 means "out of service"; 7A means a gun was recovered. During the conversation with his sergeant, Gurry learned that the victim at another scene is dying and on his way to the hospital; he also learned that a weapon has been recovered and a suspect has been arrested.

Watts knows why Gurry is smiling: he's caught a smoker. After investigating two murders that will probably never go down, Gurry desperately wants an easy homicide. His last case, the slaying of a drug dealer, is so barren of clues that he held a quasi-séance with a witness in the interview room because she claimed she could speak with the dead.

As Gurry gathers his things to head to the next homicide scene, an evidence tech finally arrives. Lugging a large equipment bag and wearing the all-black uniform typical of her tribe, Kelcey Miller looks slightly beleaguered; her squad has been hopping tonight. After adjusting her square-rimmed glasses, she strides up to Watts.

The detective gives Miller a quick update on what he has and then asks her to swab Shuford's hands for DNA and other trace evidence. Watts is in something of a hurry: he is concerned that they'll lose the opportunity to collect evidence from the dying teenager if the nurses and doctors keep working on him or he gets taken to surgery.

"Are you sure I'm allowed to do that?" Miller asks, looking over at the gurney, where two nurses are hovering. A twenty-four-year-old, she joined the police department the previous year.

"I'm sure, but go ask," Watts says.

Miller walks over to the gurney, and after a nurse tells her to go ahead, the tech swabs Shuford's hands. When she returns to Watts's side, he points to the second gurney and tells her to "bag" Aaron Kidd's hands—wrap them in large brown paper bags—so evidence can be preserved and examined for clues at the morgue. He also asks her to take detailed photos of Kidd's clothing and a small-caliber bullet that was discovered in the ambulance. Watts suspects that the bullet fell out of Kidd's clothes; after penetrating a body, a bullet sometimes gets caught in a shirt or jacket.

After Miller pulls back the sheet covering Kidd, she and Watts inspect the body for wounds. The detective is the first to notice a small bullet hole between the victim's right armpit and nipple and another small wound on his left elbow. Both wounds support Watts's suspicion that Kidd was hit by a small-caliber round, a theory that will be confirmed at the next day's autopsy.

Once they have cataloged all of what they call the "defects," Watts and Miller examine the corpse for other potential clues.

"What does that say?" asks Miller, leaning close to a tattoo that runs down Kidd's right arm.

"'Respected,'" says Watts.

Miller runs her gloved hand over a similar tattoo on the left arm. "R-E-G," she says.

"'Regarded,'" Watts says.

While recording the tattoos in his notebook, Watts hears a doctor loudly telling a nurse to make sure she keeps up the medications so Shuford can live long enough for them to harvest his organs. The detective looks up and sees Shuford's family shuffling into the trauma bay. With tears streaming down their cheeks, they crowd close to the gurney and begin saying their good-byes.

Watts watches them for a few minutes, feeling neither sadness nor empathy. He has witnessed countless similar scenes over the years; to him, the family members are no more than potential witnesses. Glancing down, he checks his watch—it is nearly 11:30 p.m. As the family grieves, Watts studies his notes, making sure he hasn't forgotten anything.


BILLY WATTS SWEARS he hears a telephone ringing. It rings and rings—somewhere, just out of reach. He cracks open an eye and realizes the sound is coming from his nightstand. He knows it can signal only bad news, and he groans as he contemplates the possibility that something awful has happened with just a few hours left on the final day of his week on the midnight shift.

He left the office two hours earlier, thanks to the generosity of Ben Brown, who'd volunteered to hold down the fort for his sick partner. Almost thirty hours have passed since Watts watched Andre Shuford's heartbroken family in the trauma bay, and since then the teenager has died, officially making his case a double homicide.

Yesterday, while tracking down leads, Watts was dragging badly and regularly popping ibuprofens. When Brown offered him the chance to get some rest, he eagerly accepted.

"Hit me if you need help," Watts said as he left the homicide office.

The phone won't stop ringing. It can only be Brown, and he must be too overwhelmed to handle whatever has happened. A typical death investigation or a suicide—even a run-of-the-mill homicide—would be no problem for his partner.

Watts struggles to open his other eye. He looks at the clock next to his bed—it's just shy of 5:00 a.m.—and then smacks his nightstand with his right hand until he feels his phone. After pressing a button, he puts the phone to his ear. Shari, his wife of sixteen years, doesn't stir; her nights have been interrupted so many times by such calls that this one doesn't even register.

"Yeah," Watts groans.

"You know I wouldn't call unless I needed your help."

As Watts expected, it's Brown. His partner tells him they've caught a tragic case: not an hour earlier, a fire swept through a single-family home not far from the office. Brown says that three people have died and a fourth is "circling the drain." He has also called their rookie, Jonathan Hill, but Hill can't make it to the office because he has a court date later that morning.

"Shit, you would think he would want to learn how to do this stuff," says Watts, frustrated that the rookie doesn't yet understand the importance of helping his partners out, even if only for an hour or two before court.

Watts hangs up and trudges to his closet, where he retrieves a dark suit, a light shirt, and a striped purple tie. He showers, dresses, and gets in his Impala, cursing his luck during the drive to the scene. He had looked forward to seeing his teenage son and daughter over breakfast that morning; now not only is he sick and exhausted, but he'll be investigating a fatal fire. Fire deaths suck—he thinks his colleagues would agree that there's no other way to put it. The scenes are often gruesome, and afterward the smoke clings to your nostrils, skin, and clothes. Worse, they're inevitably a slog of delivering death notifications, supervising evidence technicians, and filing reports. There's no adrenaline rush, no chasing down suspects.

An hour and fifteen minutes after being awakened, Watts is standing next to Brown and a county fire investigator on the melted fake grass that covers the front steps of the burned house. As the men look into the blackened remains, the investigator points to a spot a few feet inside the doorway where firefighters retrieved a thirty-six-year-old man who later died at a local hospital. Two of the man's four young daughters were pulled from the house and declared dead at Prince George's Hospital Center; the girls' mother and another daughter are being treated for serious injuries in the same hospital. The fourth daughter is dying at a DC hospital. All told, Watts and Brown are looking at four deaths—a father and three of his daughters—in a single blaze. That makes a total of six bodies for the partners in just two days.

The three men step back from the rubble. The fire investigator says it's too early to say for sure, but he doesn't think the blaze was intentionally set; the house had been under renovation, and the fire was most likely sparked by faulty wiring. "No smoke detectors, though," the investigator says.

Since Brown was the first at the scene, he will take the lead on the case and ensure that the investigation is properly handled. He huddles with Watts, and they agree that Brown will head to the office to gather more information from fire investigators and get started on the reports while Watts visits the hospitals.

Twenty minutes later, Watts is at Prince George's Hospital Center for the second time in two days. In a cramped examination room a dozen yards from the trauma bay, the detective is once again standing between two bodies—this time a four-year-old girl and her eight-year-old sister. In speaking further to firefighters, Watts has learned that the father may have bled to death, perhaps after severing an artery when he punched out a window and threw one of his daughters to safety. The details are murky, but Watts is convinced that the dad is a hero for saving one child and trying to rescue the others before collapsing from blood loss.

Joining Watts in the examination room is a forensic examiner, Angie Turcotte. A former paramedic, Turcotte sits in a plastic chair against the far wall. She is dressed casually in a blue sweatshirt, blue jeans, and boots, her long brown hair pulled back with a clip. She and Watts chat for a minute, and then the detective nods, signaling that it's time for the examination to begin.

Turcotte stands and steps up to the gurney bearing the smaller body. She pulls off the sheet, turns, and takes the sheet off the second girl. The room instantly smells of smoke and char. Watts holds back a sneeze as he watches Turcotte check the girls for signs of foul play. The four-year-old—a breathing tube still extending from her mouth, her eyes half open—is clad in a child's hospital gown decorated with blue penguins and whales and bearing the phrase "Splish splash I was taking a bath."

Watts leans close to read the adult-sized name tag on the girl's tiny right forearm. Suddenly his impassive expression softens, his face sags, and he sighs. More than any other kind of death, Watts hates investigating child fatalities. Some are easier to keep in perspective than others. This is not one of them.

"Sad," he says, shaking his head.

"No matter how long I do this," Turcotte says, "I will never get used to child deaths."

Watts blinks but says nothing, still staring at the four-year-old's oversized name tag.

Turcotte follows his gaze and says, "They didn't have any little ones."

Turcotte rolls the girl's body onto its side and studies it for a few moments. She points to skin slippage on the girl's bottom and tells

Watts that it suggests she had been sleeping on her stomach as the fire raged. "She probably never even woke up," Turcotte says.

Next the examiner checks the child's eyes. "Blisters," she says. "It was very hot."

Watts dutifully takes notes as Turcotte examines the girl's face and opens her mouth. There is soot on her tongue and in her nose. "Probably died of smoke inhalation," Turcotte says.

The two are silent for a moment, and Watts retreats to the far wall.

"God, I hate child deaths," Turcotte says again.

She pulls the sheet over the little girl and turns to the older sister, finding the same soot on the tongue and nose, the same blisters on the eyes. She observes skin slippage on the child's front and back and small cuts on her feet. "She may have been awake," Turcotte says. "She was walking around. There was broken glass in the room?"

"The father threw one of the other girls out that window," Watts replies. "That explains the glass."

They exchange a few words about the father and then go silent again. For two full minutes, neither speaks.

Finally, Watts breaks the spell and says he should try to find a family member. In the hallway, he encounters one of the girls' grandmothers. Her cheeks are streaked with tears; she seems to look through Watts as he introduces himself and asks how she and her family are holding up.

The grandmother doesn't respond to his question. Instead she says, "They had an evacuation plan and practiced it."

Watts nods.

"They knew how to get out of the house."

"Okay," says Watts. He pauses, trying to think of what he can say that will ease her pain. "We don't think there was anything suspicious," he says finally. It's the best he can do.

"It's God's time," the grandmother says. "It's God's plan."

"I'm sorry." Watts usually doesn't struggle in such situations, but this time he feels a knot in his stomach. He hands the woman his card and heads back to the examination room, his steps heavy and slow.

Turcotte has finished her work and placed both bodies in white bags for the trip to the morgue. She and Watts talk briefly about another problem: at the hospital where the father was taken, a nurse entered an incorrect birth date into the medical record. If it is not fixed—with official documentation—the father will be transported to the morgue as a John Doe. That could cause administrative headaches and possibly delay the release of the body to the family.

Watts grits his teeth, frustrated by the loose end. Another detective might go home and leave the problem to someone else, but Watts feels duty-bound to correct the mistake, especially given his respect for the heroic efforts made by this father. "I'll head over there," Watts says.

The detective winds his way through the emergency department, goes out a side door, and walks past three ambulances before getting into his Impala. Behind the car's tinted windows, his face loosens, his chest deflates, and he coughs into his hand. As he thinks about the two little bodies in the antiseptic examination room, he briefly loses his battle with fatigue and sorrow.

During his six long years in the Homicide Unit, he has mostly handled the murders of drug dealers and gang members and people who have been the unfortunate victims of robberies. Most of these killings have taken place in rough neighborhoods, and he has coped with this steady stream of violence by remaining intensely focused on the work at hand and doing his best to keep his job separate from his family life. He has convinced himself that his wife and two children are entirely safe: they live in a nice home in a nice neighborhood in an ultrasafe suburb. They aren't going to get hit by stray bullets during a drug robbery gone bad or a shoot-out in a dangerous apartment complex.

When he goes to work, his duty is to gather evidence, find witnesses, and solve murders. He's a homicide detective, and as he drove away from the Penn Mar apartment complex two nights ago, he promised himself to do his absolute best to arrest the person responsible for killing Aaron Kidd and Andre Shuford. That's the job, and that's what he owes the victims, the families, the county, the department. He doesn't owe them grief or tears.

But something about this fire has struck a chord. Maybe his psychological defenses have been worn down by a tough week on the midnight shift, a double homicide, and a bad cold. Maybe it was two trips to the hospital in two days; maybe it was the sight of that oversized name tag on that little girl's arm. Whatever the reason, his heart races as he sits in his dark car and thinks about the dead father he's about to visit at a nearby hospital.

Checking his watch, Watts is shocked to realize that it's nearly 8:30 a.m. Afraid that he's missed the chance to talk with his children before they leave for school, he unlocks his phone and punches the speed-dial icon for home. It rings once, twice; on the third ring, his wife picks up. He greets her and asks to talk to their son or daughter. He hears Shari call out to them.

Finally his thirteen-year-old boy comes on the line.

"Hi, Dad," the boy says.

The detective exhales. His shoulders relax, and he smiles. Now everything is okay, even if it's not.

1:50 a.m., Friday, February 22

Sean Deere stares at the corpse on the hospital gurney, wondering how such a tiny stab wound brought down such a hulking man. The hole, which is dead center in the man's chest, is the diameter of a pencil. The doctors said the killer had delivered a lucky and devastating blow—though it had penetrated less than two inches, the knife had clipped a major artery. With that, the six-foot-three, 250-pound man was done.

Deere records the official time of death for Charles Blyther Jr., age fifty-one, as 12:35 a.m. Then he notes what Blyther was wearing, down to his New Balance sneakers, and what he had in his pockets: a small bag of suspected crack and $25.30. While evidence techs take photographs, Deere finds a quiet spot near the ER to call his squad mate Allyson Hamlin, who is the lead detective on the case. When she answers, he relays what he has learned.

Hamlin tells Deere that she and her rookie, Jamie Boulden, have things under control at the crime scene, which is in a nearby apartment complex. She expects to wrap up there in an hour; meanwhile, two witnesses and a suspect have been taken to homicide for questioning by Mike Crowell and Joe Bunce. The murder, she says, seems to be relatively straightforward and involves a dispute between the victim and his ex-girlfriend's daughter.

"It was a lucky wound, and you got lucky, too," says Deere. Hamlin had been out sick with the flu for a week, and she'd returned to work only the day before. She could not have asked for an easier case.

"You know it," Hamlin says. "See you back at the office."

Hanging up, Deere heads to the ER to make sure the techs got what Hamlin needed. Half an hour later, he walks to his Impala, pulls out of the hospital's parking lot, and begins the drive back to the homicide office. But he doesn't get far; almost immediately, he stomps on the brake. Does he dare visit the crime scene? He very much wants to, and it's only a mile away.

Six months ago, the question wouldn't even have occurred to Deere. He is a homicide detective, after all; when one of his squad mates catches a murder, he almost always visits the scene. But the Amber Stanley investigation has scrambled everything. To keep him focused on that murder and that murder only, his commanders have barred him from visiting homicide scenes. Two weeks ago, in fact, Deere was reprimanded by Major Michael Straughan for going to Geraldine McIntyre's neighborhood to knock on doors and pass out reward flyers. But Deere misses crime scenes and the easy camaraderie between detectives as they try to sort out how a murder happened, and he is growing weary of working exclusively on a single, very frustrating case.

He checks his watch—it's 2:30 a.m. Drumming the steering wheel, Deere decides that there can't be any harm in swinging by the apartment where Charles Blyther was killed. Besides, there is little chance that he will get caught: it's the middle of the night, and no commander will visit the scene of a domestic murder in Oxon Hill, a fairly rough neighborhood in the southern part of the county and a sixteen-mile drive from police headquarters.

Deere turns south, guns the engine, and five minutes later is standing at the doorway of the second-floor apartment where Blyther was found dead. For a moment he watches the small crowd of detectives and evidence techs working to craft order out of chaos; it feels almost absurdly good just to be here. Then he walks across the beige carpet to where Joe Bergstrom is sitting at a small kitchen table. When he taps his sergeant on the shoulder, Bergstrom looks up, surprised. Deere shrugs as if to say, *Give me a break—I was next door.*

"Don't worry," says Bergstrom, patting the crime-scene log in his left hand and smiling broadly. "You were never here."

Deere grins and steps over to Hamlin, who is studying a sweatshirt, a towel, and some personal belongings scattered on the floor. He leans over and notices a couple of spots of blood and maybe some vomit on the sweatshirt and the towel.

"Not much blood," says Hamlin, whose short and chic haircut and puffy North Face vest make her seem younger than her thirty-six years.

"Small wound," says Deere. "Internal bleeding."

Hamlin tells Deere that they have already demolished the first story concocted by the mother and two daughters who live here. The women told the officers that Blyther, the mother's ex-boyfriend, must have been mortally wounded before arriving at their door; they claimed that he had entered the apartment, collapsed, and died. But Hamlin and Boulden had carefully examined the stairwell and the apartment's carpet and found no blood. That meant that Blyther could not have been stabbed outside the apartment, since he would have dripped some blood on the landing or on the carpet inside the front door.

The mother and her younger daughter, Hamlin says, have since provided a more plausible scenario to Crowell and Bunce while being interviewed at the homicide office. The ex-boyfriend had been drinking heavily earlier that night, and soon after arriving he and the mother had gotten into a raging argument. The woman's older daughter, twenty-eight-year-old Kimberly Smith, got involved and tried to persuade Blyther to leave. He refused; they tussled. Smith grabbed a small kitchen knife and stabbed Blyther once in the chest.

"He is a huge dude, and she is just tiny in comparison," Hamlin says. "I feel for the daughter. She certainly got thrown into a mess."

"You thinking second-degree?" asks Deere, referring to a charge for murder that is not premeditated or deliberate.

"I don't know," Hamlin says. "It's close to self-defense—very close."

As the two detectives discuss the case, Deere notices his squad mate massaging her right knee. He feels for *her*: Hamlin has had a tough time of late. In November, she led a complicated investigation into a drug-related execution. In December, after weeks of pressure from the unit's commanders, she closed a year-old stabbing case involving Hispanic gangs. In January, she began working out twice a day and preparing to lead her semipro all-female football team as its star quarterback and captain. Then, in early February, she was served with a baseless lawsuit—it was later dropped—

alleging that she had violated the rights of two witnesses in a homi-cide case. The stress finally took its toll. On Valentine's Day, Hamlin caught the flu, and the illness sparked an arthritic attack in her knee, which has been battered by years of playing sports, swelling it to the size of a pineapple.

After missing a week of work, Hamlin could have swapped spots on the board with one of her squad mates, but Deere knows that is not her way. Not only is she dedicated to the job and her squad, she's superstitious. Every PG detective knows that it's bad luck to skip your turn in the rotation, and Hamlin wouldn't dream of risk-ing it, since the homicide gods would surely punish her by making certain that she'd be assigned a nearly impossible case.

For another few minutes, Deere watches as Hamlin and Boul-den scurry about the scene, taking careful notes, debating the signi-ficance of a candle, some blood on the wall, men's shoes in the mother's room, cleaning supplies on the floor, blood in the bathtub. They are in the zone and treating what seems to be a smoker as if it were a real case. Perhaps he's jaded after six months of investiga-tive hell, but to Deere the murder seems routine. There was an argu-ment; the mother's older daughter stabbed the ex-boyfriend; he died; she goes to jail.

But this is not his case, and he will leave the resolution of it to Hamlin. It's time to head back to the office, where Amber Stanley and the vengeful gods await him.

IT IS AFTER 6:00 a.m. and Sean Deere—alone in the old evidence bay and taking a final drag on a Camel—is lost in thought. Frus-trated almost to the point of madness, he has spent the past three weeks racing in circles, and his investigation of Amber Stanley's murder is exactly where it was when the month began. He has grown increasingly pessimistic about the chances that his prime suspect, Jeff Buck, had anything to do with the crime. He and his

squad have tracked down a number of people in Buck's circle and
questioned them hard, yet he hasn't uncovered a single piece of
corroborating evidence that points to Buck as the killer. The DNA
test results, which Deere expects to receive next week, may surprise
him, but his guess is that they'll prove that the blood on Denise's
shirt isn't Buck's. There is still a chance that Buck did it, or more
likely knows who did it, but Deere's instinct is that his investigation has hit a wall.

He does have other leads to track down. In January, he asked
PG hospitals for the identities of people treated for stab wounds in
the hours and days after Denise was raped, the premise being that
her attacker might have sought help for the knife injury that left
blood on her shirt. After getting a mass of hospital records, Deere
selected 125 likely patients and ran their names through law
enforcement databases. One individual stood out: three days after
the rape, doctors treated a twenty-two-year-old man for a cut and
an infection. The man had been a suspect in a previous sexual
assault and had ties to a group of armed robbers known to kick
down doors of houses, storm inside, and rob their victims at gunpoint—an MO that seemed similar to the one used the night Amber
Stanley was killed.

Though this new angle looks promising, it hurts Deere's brain
to contemplate going down another investigative wormhole. After
putting out his cigarette, Deere walks back to his desk, grabs a copy
of a report he's written for Hamlin, and heads to the copy machine.
He presses a button; the machine says it's warming up. He waits
two minutes, then smacks the copier. When nothing happens, he
smacks it again.

"Come on," he says. The machine is temperamental and tends to
eat reports. Detectives have heard rumors for the past two years
that the department has ordered new copiers, but no one is holding their breath. They've also been told that they are moving to a
new headquarters building, but given that the county is chronically

strapped for cash, everyone is deeply skeptical that the move will ever happen.

The machine finally hums to life, and Deere makes a copy of his report. As he sits down at his desk again, his eyes fall on a printout of his recent e-mail exchange with Amber Stanley's older sister. He had shown the e-mails to his supervisor, Joe Bergstrom, so that the sergeant would be up-to-date with his ongoing effort to maintain good relations with Amber's family.

Keeping in touch with a victim's relatives can be a surprisingly vexing part of the job. It's a tough balancing act: a detective has to provide family members with meaningful progress reports while also withholding details that could harm a case if they leaked. Over the years, Deere has come to prefer e-mail to phone calls when dealing with relatives, for a host of reasons. E-mail is more efficient; more important, there tends to be less drama. When he carefully composes an e-mail, he's less likely to slip up and make a mistake. And it's often useful to have a record of his interaction with families. When progress on a case is slow, relatives sometimes get upset, and they have been known to falsely complain to commanders that a detective hasn't been in regular touch with them.

In this case, Deere has mostly dealt with Amber's older sister, thirty-seven-year-old Gevalle Gaither. She has always been polite but firm when attempting to find out how her sister's case is progressing. Over the course of the past several months, Deere has come to expect fairly regular e-mails, phone calls, and visits from her.

He printed out the most recent message from Gaither three weeks ago, but it has remained here, sitting on his desk next to a stack of notes and reports that he needs to file in one of his big binders. It's a reminder that the personal toll on Amber Stanley's family is far greater than his frustration at failing to solve the case. Whereas other detectives are sometimes annoyed by calls and e-mails from a victim's relatives, Deere doesn't fault Gaither. He admires her tenacity, because he knows he would be just as persistent if he were in her shoes.

"I haven't heard from you in quite some time," Gaither wrote. "I don't feel comfortable with you always saying that you don't have any information. It's been nearly six months and it's becoming more frustrating than you can imagine. There are a lot of people relying on your team to resolve this tragic event. I do continuously pray that Jehovah guides you to the necessary things that will help you solve my sister's case. Please don't take this the wrong way. I really need closure."

Deere spent several hours thinking about how to respond and then another thirty minutes composing a careful reply. His e-mail revealed nothing substantive about the ongoing investigation but offered Gaither every assurance that her sister's case remained the department's highest priority. He closed by thanking Gaither for her prayers and promising to remain steadfast in his attempt to achieve a prompt resolution of her sister's case.

Now, sitting alone at his desk, Deere organizes his paperwork, and the printout vanishes into the stack of notes and reports waiting to be filed. Though he is satisfied enough by his response to Gaither's e-mail, ultimately he feels that it's utterly inadequate. Only one reply would truly satisfy Amber Stanley's family, and it's a message that Deere worries he will never get the chance to send:

We solved it. We know who did it. *We got him.*

## · CHAPTER 6 ·

The homicide office is empty except for Detective Victoria Bracey, a very pregnant investigator on M-30 who is catching up on her paperwork before going on maternity leave. On Fridays, a single squad of detectives usually works the day and evening shifts, which often means that no one is actually in the office, leaving it dark and quiet except for the ringing of unanswered telephones. But today Bracey happens to be at her desk when a uniformed patrol officer appears at the open door.

"Can I help you?" asks Bracey, looking up from her computer in the second row of workstations.

The officer, who is lean, has a slight mustache, and wears a Russian-style winter hat, smiles and introduces himself as Michael Powers of District 3. "I'm looking for the detective handling the old-lady murder," he says.

Bracey mentally scrolls through a long list of homicide victims before hitting upon Geraldine McIntyre. "The one down in Capitol

Heights?" she asks, trying to remember when it occurred. "Maybe two weeks ago?"

"Yeah, that one."

"That's being investigated by Detective Brooks."

"I have an informant who approached my patrol car today," Powers says. "He claims he knows who has her television."

"Her television was missing?" asks Bracey.

"That's what he said."

Bracey assumes Brooks will want to hear about this tip, so she picks up her desk phone, checks a list of cell-phone numbers taped to her cubicle wall, and dials. When Brooks answers, Bracey tells him what Powers has told her and hands the phone to the officer.

Powers gets on the line but isn't given a chance to say anything beyond "Hello."

"Go get your informant and bring him in," Brooks says. "I'm on my way."

Thirty minutes later, Brooks walks into the homicide office and, without greeting either Bracey or Powers, puts his eye to the peephole of Interview Room 2, where the informant—a thin man in blue jeans and a thick black coat—has been deposited. Brooks turns, thanks Powers for his help, and asks how he came across the man.

Powers says the informant, a known drug addict and thief, approached his squad car at about 12:30. The officer was parked in an alley three blocks from Geraldine McIntyre's house, and after chatting with the hustler for a minute or two, Powers asked the man if he'd heard anything about McIntyre's murder.

"He wanted to know if we had found her TV," Powers says to Brooks. "I told him I didn't know her TV was missing. And he was like, 'Yeah,' and then he tells me the names of the guy who sold the TV and the guy who has it, but they meant nothing to me."

"What were the names he gave you?"

Powers tells him, and one of the names causes Brooks's natural scowl to turn into a smile. For the past two weeks, Brooks has been bitching nonstop about the lack of initiative and hustle by PG County's patrol officers. Now a patrolman has given him a huge gift, one that has the potential to break open his case.

"Nice work," the detective says.

Without another word, Brooks turns and takes four long strides to the box, opens the door, enters, and slams it shut. He sits down across the table from the informant, whose black coat still glistens from the remnants of a cold rain.

Beyond recording the man's first and last names, Brooks doesn't bother asking for basic information. He gets straight to the point. "Who has the old lady's television?" he asks. "Who sold it?"

The informant gives him the same names he passed to Powers. Brooks doesn't know the purchaser, but he is well acquainted with the seller, a street peddler named James Alphonso Ward, who goes by the nickname JuJu. A heavy heroin user and neighborhood handyman, Ward was an early suspect in Brooks's investigation into McIntyre's murder. Just ten days ago, in fact, the detective questioned Ward in this very room.

In that interview, Ward seemed strung out; when questioned, he told Brooks that he had taken heroin a number of hours earlier. Clad in a gray sweatshirt and black shorts over a pair of grubby long johns, he had recently shaved his beard and roughly cut his hair. Looking at the black-and-gray tufts covering the man's scalp, Brooks wondered if he had intentionally altered his appearance. Ward could not provide an alibi for the time of the murder and admitted that he had walked past McIntyre's house that day; he also said he considered her a friend and had once eaten dinner at her house.

Yet despite a marathon interrogation session, Brooks could not break Ward, and the suspect vehemently denied any involvement in the murder. The fingerprint lifted from the windowsill had also not come from him. Unable to prove that Ward was involved in McIntyre's murder, Brooks sent him to the PG jail to be held on unrelated burglary charges. The detective then turned his attention to other burglars, thieves, and addicts, but so far all of them either had alibis or for other reasons didn't seem good for the crime.

Now, sitting across from Powers's informant, Brooks cannot believe his luck. "I'm Detective Brooks, with homicide," he says. "I want you to know that I appreciate you coming to talk to us."

The informant nods and frowns. "That was really wrong what he did to the old lady," he says. "Killing that nice old lady."

"I know," says Brooks. "That's why we're working this so hard."

Brooks asks for more information about the informant's conversation with the man who purchased the TV.

"Did he say what kind of TV it was?" the detective asks.

"A flat-screen," says the informant.

Brooks allows himself a quick smile; in their briefings about the crime, the police have not mentioned this detail. He asks for more information about the buyer, but the informant has only a first name, and he doesn't have a phone number. "But I do know where he lives," the man says.

"Okay," says Brooks. "If I put you in a car right now and drove you around, could you point out where he is?"

"Think so."

"Good," the detective says. "Let's go."

Brooks can barely contain his excitement. To build a case and charge a suspect, he needs the television; as far as he knows, it's the only piece of tangible evidence that can link the killer to the crime. He also needs the man who bought the TV, since the purchaser can testify against the thief who sold it to him.

Brooks and the informant leave the box and are joined by Brooks's partner, Mike Delaney. But when the three men reach Brooks's Impala, the witness refuses to get inside, explaining that he doesn't want to risk being spotted in a police car.

Brooks hurries back inside and returns with the keys to homicide's battered Dodge minivan. Fifteen minutes later, he is driving through Geraldine McIntyre's neighborhood when the informant points to a house belonging to the purchaser of the TV. Brooks knocks on the door; a woman answers and tells him that the man he's seeking isn't home. But she gives the detective his phone number, so Brooks calls the man and tells him to get to homicide right away.

AN HOUR LATER, Brooks is waiting outside the front door to the criminal investigation division when a blue van pulls into the visitors' lot. A thickset man wearing a gray fleece pullover and blue jeans gets out of the van and saunters up to Brooks, and the detective briefly explains why he has been summoned. But the man says there has been a mistake: he didn't buy the television and doesn't have it. Then he smiles, and with the flourish of a salesman offering an irresistible deal, he tells Brooks that he knows who does.

Brooks doesn't like the man's attitude but says nothing as he leads him inside and takes him to the box. They sit down across the table from each other, and the man drapes his arm casually over the back of his chair. Joined by Delaney, Brooks asks for some basic information and learns that the man is sixty-one and operates an illegal taxi.

With the preliminaries over, Brooks tells the man that he would appreciate his help. "I need this TV," the detective says, "like yesterday."

"That's why they call me—they all confide in me," the taxi driver says, presumably referring to the neighborhood's addicts and hustlers. "This whole scenario is all fucked up."

"It is," Brooks agrees.

"Comes with a twenty-five-thousand-dollar reward?" asks the witness.

Brooks and Delaney exchange a glance—detectives are always suspicious of witnesses eager for cash.

"Up to twenty-five thousand," Delaney says. In a careful bit of marketing by the department and a nonprofit program called Prince George's County Crime Solvers that provides the funding, all rewards are "up to $25,000." Few tipsters get close to that kind of cash.

"So who told you they had it?" asks Brooks. "How did they get it?"

"I can tell you how—they got it from JuJu."

"How do you know that?" asks Delaney.

"That is what the person told me. He was pressed for money."

"JuJu was?"

"Yeah," the taxi driver says. "He had a bag, too, with something else in it. But my man didn't know what else was in the bag." He folds his hands across his stomach, a satisfied look on his face.

"Can you tell me who this guy is?" asks Brooks.

"I cannot. I gave my word. But I can get you the TV if you let me go, and I'll come back with it."

"What do you want?" Brooks asks.

"The reward," the taxi driver says with a grin.

"We don't just have a big bag of money to give you—there is a process," says Delaney.

*This won't do,* thinks Brooks. "Tell you what," he says, pushing both hands hard on the table, shoving back his chair, and motioning to Delaney. "Let me step out for a minute."

The two men excuse themselves, and Brooks closes the door and flips the lock. He has lost all semblance of patience; he doesn't understand how anyone can turn the murder of a seventy-one-year-old woman into a business deal.

"Fuck him," Brooks fumes. "We need the TV *and* the dude. Motherfucker—this guy thinks he doesn't have to give us the guy?"

Brooks steps back, forward, back. Shaking his head, pursing his lips, he breathes hard through his nose. He tries to speak but can't find the words. Finally, he sputters and says, "Fuck him." He says it again and again before growing quiet and turning to Delaney.

"We have to go old-school on his ass."

A little anxiously, his partner smiles; he has seen Brooks get worked up before, but never like this. "Could be trouble, Andre."

"Fuck him," says Brooks. "Old-school."

Delaney nods, and the two detectives reenter the room. Brooks stomps to his chair, yanks it from under the table, and drops into the seat like a wrecking ball. He rolls the chair close to the taxi driver and pins the man with his eyes.

"I need to talk to the guy with the TV," Brooks says, his voice a furious whisper.

The witness's bravado evaporates in an instant; suddenly he is too scared to speak. His chest rising and falling rapidly, he scoots his chair back as far as he can, until he is pressing against the gray wall.

"*Now,*" says Brooks.

"Um, ah," the taxi driver says. "Um, um." His eyes dart between Brooks and Delaney. "Give me a few minutes to go talk to him."

"No, no," Brooks says, leaning forward, his face now less than a foot from the witness's. "You are not listening; you are not hearing me. I cannot let you go talk to him, not unless we are there, too. I don't need the TV. I need the guy *and* the TV."

"I feel you," says the taxi driver.

"You feel me?" says Brooks, thinking, *Did this asshole really just say that?*

For a moment, Brooks considers yelling, breaking a chair against the wall, and letting his witness stew in the box for a few hours. Instead he glares silently at the taxi driver, his scowl growing more intense by the second.

The witness looks at Brooks, at Delaney, back at Brooks. He is cornered, and he knows it.

"It wasn't right what he did to the lady," the taxi driver says, in a tone clearly meant to convey empathy.

Brooks has seen this before: his witness needs a way out that doesn't signal disrespect or defeat, and feigning compassion does the trick. After all, doesn't everybody feel bad about the murder of an innocent old lady? Doesn't doing good always outweigh the reward? Brooks watches the man convince himself that he isn't surrendering, that he's doing the right thing for the right reasons.

"I feel so bad for that old lady," the taxi driver says. "I'll take you to his house. That's what I'll do."

TWENTY MINUTES LATER, Brooks and Delaney, still in the Dodge minivan, are trailing the witness's van when it pulls up to a ranch-style house just a few doors down from McIntyre's home. The taxi driver knocks on the door, and a woman answers; they talk for a bit, and the witness hustles back to his van. He phones Brooks and says that his friend is on his way home. The detective calls three waiting police officers on his radio, gives them the address, and a minute later their cars screech to a halt next to Brooks's. Leaping from their vehicles, the two detectives and three officers sprint for the front porch.

Brooks pounds on the door, and it's opened by a tall man—not the guy they're waiting for—whom the detective grabs by an arm and flings to one of the officers. Brooks and Delaney burst into a short hallway, sidestep a small kitchen, and race into the dining room, where a startled woman sits at a table. Towering over her, Brooks asks for permission to search the house.

As soon as she mutters, "Okay," Brooks thuds from the dining room to the living room and through to a bedroom, but he doesn't find the TV. Finally he reaches what appears to be a guest bedroom. Scanning it quickly, he sees a bed with a gray comforter, a green recliner, men's sneakers arranged in pairs along one wall, and, against the wall to his left, a wooden chest, on top of which is a flat-screen television.

Brooks takes two long steps and bends close: the TV is the same brand and size as the one missing from McIntyre's house. He dips his head behind the set; his eyes widen and he can feel his heart pounding. The back of the TV is coated with dirt. Brooks has always suspected that the killer lowered the set into the patch of bare earth below McIntyre's window. Amazingly, neither the thief nor the new owner had bothered to clean off the dirt.

Two young patrol officers enter the room. They spot the television, move closer, glimpse the smear of dirt, and break into a victory dance, slapping high fives and hooting.

Brooks is so pumped he can't think. He excuses himself and returns to the front porch, where he grips the railing and slows his breathing until his heart stops racing.

"Better than sex," he mutters to himself. "Better than fucking sex."

NOT TEN MINUTES later, the man who bought the TV appears. Thirty-six and heavyset, he is dressed entirely in black, except for gold highlights on his high-tops and a New Orleans Saints baseball cap. He takes a seat across from Brooks at the dining room table.

Brooks explains why he needs the television. "We can do this the hard way or the easy way," he says, meaning either the man cooperates and permits the police to take the television or the investigators can confiscate the TV after obtaining a search warrant.

"I understand," the man says. "I'm happy to sign. I'm happy to help."

After he scrawls his name on a form, Brooks loads him into the front passenger seat of the van for the ride to homicide. Delaney takes a seat in the rear. Brooks doesn't buckle his seat belt—he is too excited to bother—and as he drives the three miles back to the office, an alert *ding-ding-ding*s the entire way.

"Why'd it take you so long to find me?" asks the man.

Brooks grips the steering wheel so hard his knuckles turn white. "Why didn't you find *us* and tell us what you had?"

"I didn't know," the man says, staring out the windshield.

*Bullshit*, thinks Brooks. *You live a few doors down from Geraldine McIntyre, and you knew exactly where that TV came from.*

"So how long have you had the TV?" asks Brooks.

"Since the day of the situation," the man says.

Brooks shakes his head: *The situation.*

"I didn't realize it until a few days later, when I was speaking to a friend who said you guys hit that house and pulled out JuJu, and then my friend told me that you also were looking for stuff that someone stole from the old lady."

Except for the dinging seat-belt alarm, the van is quiet. It smells of gasoline and French fries and sweat; when the front window begins to fog, Brooks switches on the defroster. Disgusted, he stares stonily at the road ahead.

"That's when I put two and two together," says the man, clearly uncomfortable in the silence. "I talked to my girl about it, and she was like, 'Don't call the police.' And I didn't want to get myself in trouble, know what I'm saying?"

"Yeah, we know," says Delaney.

"We know," says Brooks. "We know."

"JuJu was just walking up the street that Saturday, and my girl was on the porch and she called me out and said this guy wanted to sell me something. So I spoke to him. And he has this big flat-screen, and I thought I could use it to play my Xbox on, so I asked JuJu how much he is selling it for, and he says, like, forty dollars. So I paid him forty dollars, and he left about his business."

*Forty fucking dollars*, thinks Brooks. *A life for forty dollars.*

Brooks asks a few more questions, and the man's answers make it clear that he bought the television from JuJu Ward soon after McIntyre was killed. Brooks goes silent again, and as he drives he experiences a wash of emotions: relief, joy, sorrow, anger. He thinks back to the murder scene and the cluttered house and the daughter's bed in the living room and the bloody, dusty floor and wonders why a drug addict would kill an old lady for forty dollars.

"So," Brooks finally says, not even attempting to quell the fury in his voice. "He was just like any other motherfucking crackhead?"

"Yeah," the man replies a little sheepishly, "like any other."

**10:00 a.m., Tuesday, February 26**

Sean Deere takes his place at the head of the long table as members of his squad file into the frigid conference room. To his right sit Joe Bergstrom and Allyson Hamlin; to his left, Mike Crowell and Joe Bunce. A minute later, Captain George Nichols enters the room, followed by Lieutenant Brian Reilly. Nichols grabs a chair between Crowell and Bunce, and Reilly sits next to Hamlin.

The previous morning, Deere got the news he'd been expecting: Jeff Buck's DNA test came back negative. Since then, Deere, Bergstrom, and the rest of the M-40 squad members have spoken at length about what they should do next. Despite the test results, the investigators are not ready to discard the theory that Buck or members of his gang played a role in the rape of Denise or the murder of Amber Stanley. But they know they'll have to expand the scope of their hunt for the killer, and they're well aware that their bosses are getting impatient. Yesterday, Bergstrom and Deere got word that the captain and the lieutenant wanted this briefing.

The room grows quiet as Nichols shuffles some papers. When he asks for a progress report, Bergstrom launches into a description of how hard the squad has worked and the long hours they have logged.

"We have been bringing in people, it seems, like every day and night," Bergstrom says. "We've been working around the clock."

He tells Nichols and Reilly that since December he and his detectives have been focused on Jeff Buck, his gang, and his neighborhood because it's the strongest lead they've got. He adds that the squad is convinced there's a connection between the rape of Denise and Amber Stanley's death. "It's the only thing that makes sense," Bergstrom says.

Nichols nods, jots down a note, and turns to Deere, who takes this as his cue to pick up where Bergstrom left off.

"It seems like everyone we bring in talks about more people that we have to run down," Deere says. "That guy might have raped Denise, this guy might have a gun. We pick up, we question, we pick up again."

Nichols and Reilly know this is true—they have watched the investigators at work and have approved their overtime slips. Nichols asks what Deere plans to do next, and the detective says the squad intends to keep rounding up people in Jeff Buck's gang and neighborhood.

Reilly asks for an update on the DNA results, and Deere shakes his head and mutters, "All negative, all negative."

"Even Jeff Buck?" asks Reilly.

"Yes," says Deere.

Nichols and Reilly frown. This is not what they had expected, but they also know that the DNA tests do not necessarily mean that Jeff Buck and his crew had nothing to do with the murder.

"We just need more time to work this angle," says Deere.

"Other avenues?" Nichols asks.

Deere mentions that the squad has recently developed a new theory involving a man who had been treated for a wound a few days after Denise was raped. Bunce has done the most research into this theory, and at a signal from Deere he describes the gang of thieves who kick in doors and rob residents at gunpoint. One of them may have raped Denise, had his hand cut during the assault, and then returned with his boys to punish her for the stabbing and for going to the police. The squad's hope, Bunce tells the captain and the lieutenant, is that the man's DNA will match the blood on Denise's shirt.

Nichols makes a note and asks Deere how he ultimately expects to link the murder to a suspect. Deere explains that thus far he has no physical evidence beyond the shell casings. "We can get to the rape through the blood," Deere says. "But there isn't really anything tying anyone to the murder, unless we get them with the gun."

"So it's the rape," says Nichols. "It comes down to the rape."

"It's the rape," confirms Bergstrom.

Nichols asks if they are planning to revisit Denise and interview her again.

"Absolutely," Deere says, adding that they are currently making plans to travel to her mental-health facility.

"That is important," says Nichols, jotting down a final note and looking around the room. He thanks the detectives for their efforts and says he believes he has enough information to persuade the chief and the assistant chief to give them more time to continue investigating Jeff Buck's crew and to pursue their new theory about the gang of robbers and the man with the cut on his hand.

"They don't know all the work you've done and all the stuff you've dug up," Nichols says. "This will buy you some time." But then the captain mentions the news—announced the previous day by the chief—that the police have charged a twenty-year-old in the murder of Marckel Ross, one of the six PG high school students slain since August. Calling this development "both a blessing and a curse," Nichols says that the high-profile arrest will remove some of the immediate pressure to solve Amber Stanley's case. But with the Ross murder solved, the focus is now squarely on them.

The meeting ends, and Nichols and Reilly get up to leave. After they're gone, Bergstrom and his squad remain at the table and talk for a couple of minutes about Hamlin's murder from the early hours on Friday and how quickly they wrapped it up over the course of the day. They laugh about how drunk some of them got that Friday night over a sushi dinner. Finally, their focus returns to the case at hand. Bergstrom asks Deere to compose a memo about the Amber Stanley case that lists the suspects and witnesses whose DNA has been tested and the results.

Deere screws up his face and laughs. "I can do that now," he says, jotting something on his pad. He holds up his note: "All negative."

"All right, all right," says Bergstrom.

Bunce excuses himself, saying he wants to run some background checks on the gang of robbers. Bergstrom leaves next, then Crowell.

Deere is slow to rise, and Hamlin can sense the doubt in his stooped shoulders.

"We'll solve this," she tells him. "You know, it's probably something we haven't even thought of yet."

11:05 a.m., Wednesday, February 27

Four of M-40's five detectives are slumped in the fifth row of folding chairs in the department's auditorium, waiting for what promises to be a sleep-inducing lecture on the prevention of domestic violence. It's not that the issue is unimportant or that the detectives don't care about domestic violence; it's just that the PG police department has the ability to transform almost any topic into a mind-numbing slumberfest.

The auditorium buzzes with gossip and griping in the minutes before the lecture begins. As a major takes the podium, Crowell feels his smartphone vibrate, pulls it out, and sees that he's received a text from Sean Deere: "Mike, sign me in and meet me in SAU. We have news." Crowell studies the phone's screen, blinks, scratches his chin. He knows this must be a big deal if Deere is summoning him out of a mandatory training session.

Crowell turns and whispers the news to Bunce, who elbows Hamlin, who smacks Jamie Boulden's left thigh. They huddle in the row and whisper about the meaning of Deere's message. It must have something to do with Amber Stanley, says Crowell; the others agree. They stand, and Hamlin waves good-bye to the major, who says, "There must be something big in CID."

A minute later, the detectives enter the Sexual Assault Unit, where they find Deere chatting with two other investigators. Deere calmly delivers the good news: the department got a DNA hit linking the blood on Denise's shirt to a rape suspect in the PG jail. The hit was generated by a state database that compares DNA evidence from crime scenes to the DNA of offenders. Their new suspect, Deere says, is David Upshaw,* a twenty-year-old who has been charged in two sexual assaults and an armed robbery, all of which recently occurred in PG County. Upshaw's name means nothing to the squad's detectives; until today, they've never heard of him.

Deere has reviewed an SAU report claiming that Upshaw kicked down a door and raped a girl he had befriended online; another document alleges that Upshaw sexually assaulted a prostitute. A third incident was more ambiguous. About six months ago, a fifteen-year-old girl reported to police that she had been raped by Upshaw behind a library. The teen later recanted the accusations, however, and no charges were filed. After reading the report and

---

*Not his real name.

speaking to the investigators, Deere strongly suspects that the rape actually occurred.

The detective has also seen paperwork from the Robbery Unit that describes an incident in which Upshaw and another suspect, armed with a gun, robbed a man in the basement of an apartment building.

"So he kicks down doors, rapes women—including prostitutes—and carries a gun?" says Crowell, his voice rising in excitement. "Wow. I really like this guy."

Bunce, Hamlin, and Boulden nod in agreement—everything seems to fit. But Deere is cautious. After spending the better part of three months building a case against Jeff Buck, he has just abandoned the idea that Buck is his prime suspect. Now he's suddenly changing directions and pursuing someone who wasn't even on his radar until a couple of hours ago. And although he is pleased to have physical evidence that seems to tie his new suspect to Denise's rape, he's anxious about whether he'll be able to prove the connection to the murder.

Still, he has long believed that the rapist—angered at being cut and worried that Denise would report the crime to the police—went to her home five days later and killed Amber Stanley by mistake. In just a few hours, this theory will finally be put to the test.

FOUR HOURS LATER, Deere and Crowell enter the office of Major Michael Straughan, who has heard about the DNA hit and requested an update on the investigation. The higher-ups are understandably worried that the news about this development in the Amber Stanley case might leak to the media. The detectives, aware of their bosses' concern, feel a not-so-subtle pressure to pick up Upshaw right away.

Since learning about his new suspect, Deere has been busy compiling a dossier on him. From sex-offense and robbery detectives, he has learned that Upshaw is cagey and smart, an alleged sexual predator who has admitted nothing. That means he is not likely to break easily, and Deere would prefer to spend the next day or so preparing for the biggest interrogation of his life. Since that probably won't be an option, Crowell has completed the necessary paperwork and visited a judge to get permission to "writ" Upshaw out of the PG jail. But before they can grab Upshaw, they're obligated to provide their no-nonsense major with a briefing.

Joining the detectives are their supervisors: Nichols, Reilly, and Bergstrom, the same trio who sat through the strategy meeting a day earlier. Deere, his face stern, drops into a comfortable chair next to Nichols; Crowell, smiling and fidgeting, takes the couch between Reilly and Bergstrom.

Major Straughan—a sinewy man with a crew cut that makes his bony face look even more severe—leans back in his chair and laces his fingers behind his head. He gazes across his big desk at Deere and then Crowell, then back at Deere, his eyes blank, betraying no hint of enthusiasm or concern. He has been investigating murders or supervising homicide detectives for nearly twenty years, and to him this is just another case. Nothing would surprise him.

"So," he says, his eyes locked on Deere, "what do you have?"

Deere explains the DNA hit, the blood's link to Amber Stanley's foster sister, and their plans to pick up Upshaw this evening and question him aggressively.

"This is it," Deere says. "It comes down to this."

"When the judge asked what case it was," Crowell adds, "I told him, 'Amber Stanley.' And he just immediately signed that paper and looked at me and winked and said, 'Good luck.'"

Crowell then tells the group that Upshaw is represented by the same defense lawyer who handled his prior cases. Crowell also reports that the judge told him that since this is a fresh offense, they are free to interrogate Upshaw about it, but they cannot question him about his earlier crimes without his attorney present.

"Those rules tie our hands somewhat," says Bergstrom.

"Fucking Constitution," quips Deere.

Straughan nods for Deere to continue. The detective delves into Upshaw's history, Denise's background, and his theory that the rape is tied to the murder.

As the major mulls this summary, his eyes drift to the ceiling. Finally he looks back at Deere and says, "He sounds good."

Deere begins to say something, but Straughan holds up a hand, cutting him off.

"Why did he rape her if she was selling it?" the major asks.

"We don't know," Crowell says, jumping in. "Maybe he didn't want to pay, and that's when he just took it. Maybe he didn't pay, and she kirked out."

"Possible," says Straughan, turning back to Deere and asking if he's confident there really was a rape. The major is well aware that prostitutes sometimes seek charges of sexual assault when their clients refuse to pay.

"We're pretty sure there was an assault or a sexual assault," says Deere. "She was kind of beat up—cuts on her legs and stuff. I believe her."

Straughan clasps his hands and places them on his desk. "But he does three rapes, right? So why does he do a fourth and start killing?"

Deere doesn't respond. The major has raised a good question: why didn't Upshaw try to silence his other victims—why just Denise?

"That's the leap here," Straughan says, "that he rapes her and returns five days later to kill her. Why?"

"She was all over Facebook talking about it," Deere replies.

"He might have been worried she called police," says Crowell. "She reported it."

"She cut him up," says Bergstrom. "Revenge."

The major goes quiet for a moment.

"Maybe," he finally says.

The room grows hushed, all eyes on Straughan.

"You track his phone?" the major asks, his eyes back on the ceiling.

"It was shut off at the time of the murder," says Deere.

"You have any prints at the murder scene?"

"No," says Deere.

"What physical evidence do you have?"

"Shell casings."

Straughan's questions make plain what Deere has understood from the beginning: to successfully pin Amber Stanley's death on Upshaw, the detective must get a confession.

"Well, it sounds like you have a very good rape case," Straughan says as the briefing concludes. "Good luck with the murder."


AT 8:30 P.M., DEERE and Crowell bring David Upshaw through the back door of police headquarters into the Criminal Investigation Division. His hands are cuffed behind his back and his ankles are shackled, but even so their new suspect has an athletic bounce to his step. He is wearing the jail's inmate uniform: orange pants, an orange shirt, and white basketball shoes.

Escorting Upshaw down a long hallway, the detectives pass the door to the Homicide Unit and turn right into the Sex Assault Unit. Upshaw has been here before, and Deere and Crowell don't want him to know they are from homicide—not yet. After removing his handcuffs, they lock him in the first interview room to the left. Deere switches on the audiovisual recording system before he and Crowell head back to their desks to review their notes and prepare for the interrogation.

As he takes a seat, Deere scans the squad room, which has been hopping all day. Detectives on M-10, including Billy Watts and Ben Brown, have been trying to identify three armed gunmen who stormed into a house in Capitol Heights that morning and robbed a mother and son. As the masked men fled the house, they were fired upon by police. No one was injured in the incident, but homicide is required to investigate all such shootings—to the vocal frustration of Watts and Brown, who feel they have much better things to do, like solve a double homicide.

Deere looks to his left, down the last row of work stations, and studies Bunce and Hamlin. Both are working intently at their computers. Bunce is banging his keyboard with his thick fingers, digging into databases in the hopes of learning more about Upshaw. With large headphones over her ears, Hamlin is listening to recordings of Upshaw's jail calls, all between him and his mother.

Deere asks the two detectives what they've come up with so far. Bunce says he's found reports linking Upshaw to a series of burglaries and an armed robbery several years ago that apparently landed him in juvenile detention. Hamlin says that Upshaw's calls from prison reveal little beyond the routine frustrations of jail life. She also reports that Upshaw seems careful and does not discuss his alleged crimes over the phone. Bunce and Hamlin agree that Upshaw seems like a loner, a description that fits with the sex-offense detectives' assessment of him. This will undoubtedly make the squad's job harder: they are not likely to find friends or associates to dime Upshaw out.

Deere turns to his own computer and loads a file containing Denise's Facebook account; the previous fall he obtained the file from the California-based company through a court order. Looking for Upshaw's name or any content that may have come from him, Deere begins scrolling through six hundred pages of postings, musings, messages, photos, and links. He gives up after fifteen minutes, concluding that Denise and Upshaw hadn't communicated over the popular social-media platform.

During a final pass through the data, Deere stops at an array of twenty-five *Kama Sutra* positions Denise posted to her page in April.

He tilts his head to the right, to the left, trying to find the best angle to appreciate the sexual contortions. His movements attract the attention of Crowell, who wheels over in his chair.

Crowell examines the screen for a few moments. "I like number eight!" he says.

"I've definitely done that one," says Deere.

"I've done every single one on that list," brags Crowell, leaning closer to Deere's monitor and pointing at one of the graphics. "I like that one: the wheelbarrow."

"That looks like a lot of work," says Deere.

They both break into raucous laughter. Crowell stands, stretches his arms toward the ceiling, and heads for the men's room and a smoke break. A moment later, Deere follows him, and soon the two detectives are standing outside the back door, smoking one cigarette after another and plotting strategy. They agree that at first they'll go easy on Upshaw, in an effort to convince him that they are on his side and are merely seeking to clear up rape allegations from an unstable prostitute. Once they get him to confirm that he raped Denise, the hard work will begin: somehow, they'll have to persuade Upshaw to confess that on August 22 he went to her house, kicked in the door, and shot Amber Stanley. Crowell proposes that they lie to Upshaw about having discovered his DNA in the house, and Deere agrees that it's probably a good idea.

Deere suggests that they use the good cop, bad cop routine when it's time to bear down. Though Deere doesn't say so, it's clear that Crowell will be the one who gets in Upshaw's face. It's their usual approach in such sessions, and Deere has so much faith in Crowell's abilities that he's willing to yield control over the interrogation at critical moments.

As he puffs away on his second cigarette, Deere acknowledges that his emotions are a jumble—he's nervous, apprehensive, optimistic. He says he wishes they could have waited a day to bring Upshaw in, so they could have done more research and gotten some rest before beginning the interrogation. But he also notes that he and Crowell have done their best work under pressure, and he finishes by expressing a rare note of confidence. "We can break him," he says.

"We will," says Crowell.

Deere flicks his cigarette butt to the ground. He motions to his partner, and they head through the door.

THE DETECTIVES SLIDE into the SAU's Interview Room 6 at 9:25 p.m. and find Upshaw seated at the wooden table, which has been pushed into the far right corner. Sitting with his left elbow next to the wall, he has buried his face in the crook of his right arm. *The felony nap,* Deere thinks. *But which felony?*

Deere scoots his chair next to Upshaw's right side, taking a position so close to the twenty-year-old that his left knee nearly touches the suspect's right knee. Crowell takes a seat to Deere's right, facing Upshaw from the far end of the table.

Deere unclips his smartphone from his belt, checks the time, and jots, "21:27 CID/SAU" in his notebook.

"Spell your last name for me," Deere says to the back of Upshaw's head, which remains buried in his elbow. Upshaw sits up a little and answers the question; the detective then asks for more background information: the spelling of Upshaw's first name, his date of birth. Deere leans closer, trying to engage Upshaw's eyes, but the man stares vacantly at the room's gray wall.

Deere asks Upshaw where his mother lives.

"Man, you ask a lot of questions," Upshaw says.

Deere pauses for a moment before saying, "We are just getting started."

Upshaw's face is stone, his eyes wide and empty. No fear, no loathing, no apprehension, just irritation at being asked to repeat the same information he's already given to other detectives.

"I know what you are incarcerated for now, and I have nothing to do with that," Deere tells the suspect. "I want to talk to you about something new, something different. We just want to straighten it out. Your name came up in something, kind of along the same lines of what you are charged with now."

Deere chooses this moment to introduce himself as "Officer Deere," hoping the title has a softer edge than his real one. Upshaw nods, and Deere takes him through the "Advice of Rights" form, a written version of the Miranda warning.

After the suspect consents to be interviewed, Deere explains why they're in the box. "We got a report of a sexual assault, all right? Back in August."

Upshaw looks at him steadily, his face a blank.

"I know you have other charges," says Deere, his right arm perched casually on the table. "This is a different one. This one is more like, uh . . . The girl making the claim is—well, the story doesn't seem right."

Deere tells Upshaw that the victim was a prostitute; the clear implication is that her word cannot be trusted. "Does this sound familiar to you?" the detective asks. "I'm giving you a chance to explain."

"Who is this person?" says Upshaw.

"A girl that hangs out in Mitchellville Plaza," Deere says, naming the shopping center near Amber Stanley's home. He is being vague, providing just enough detail to let the suspect know he's in their crosshairs but not enough to scare him. The detective also doesn't want to feed him information.

Deere asks Upshaw if he has ever spent time at the shopping center, and the suspect mumbles that, yes, he has occasionally visited Mitchellville Plaza.

"Who in that area have you ever had sex with?" Deere asks. "The stuff we have is indisputable. There is no question that something sexual happened. But just because something sexual happened doesn't mean it's a crime."

Upshaw mutters, "Uh-huh," and goes no further beyond saying that he is "not recollecting." A minute later, however, he admits to having had sex with a woman near the plaza and provides a brief description of her.

It's immediately clear to Deere that the woman is not Denise.

"I want you to be more forthright in what you are saying to me," the detective tells Upshaw, explaining that if the girl is a prostitute, there's no basis for a real complaint. "But if she's not, and you deny it, then there is going to be an issue. Do you follow what I'm saying?"

"Yeah," says Upshaw.

Hoping to provoke the suspect, Deere describes Denise as a "chick who wore fucking shorty shorts and no bra and walked around with fishnet shirts on and shit like that, and wigs, high-heeled shoes."

When Upshaw doesn't respond, Deere studies the man and decides to give him another way out: how could he resist such a woman? "You banging her out, well, that could happen to anybody," Deere says casually.

This tactic works, and Upshaw eventually admits that he had sex with a girl who told him her name was Candy. After hearing Upshaw's description of the girl, Deere feels confident that Candy and Denise are one and the same. Upshaw says he met Candy after he spotted her getting off a bus near another shopping center about a mile and a half west of Mitchellville Plaza. She gave him a fifteen-dollar blow job behind some nearby town houses.

"A fifteen-dollar blow job?" Deere says, pretending to ponder the price point. "Was it any good?"

"It was all right," Upshaw replies.

"The evidence shows it was more than just oral," Deere says. "That is no big deal, but I don't want you to half-step it. Sex is sex. Pussy sex is sex."

For nearly another hour, Deere and Crowell push and cadge,

digressing into questions about Upshaw's life before returning to the sexual assault. Finally the suspect relents, confirming that he had intercourse with Candy. After the blow job, Upshaw says, he and Candy walked to Mitchellville Plaza and then negotiated sex for nineteen dollars; he had only twenty dollars left and had to purchase a one-dollar condom at a gas station. Under prodding from Crowell, Upshaw provides specifics of the sex act. After finishing, the suspect says, he refused to pay Candy the nineteen dollars.

"Was she mad?" Deere asks.

"She threw a little fit," he says. "I wasn't going to argue with her. She said, 'It's fucked up. You are a broke-ass nigga.'"

Upshaw shrugged his shoulders. "I mean, I am. So I just left."

Deere decides that this is a good moment to confirm that Candy is Denise, so he slides a photograph of the foster sister across the table.

"Is this who you're talking about?" Deere asks.

"Yeah."

Crowell asks the suspect to stand and remove his orange shirt to see if he displays any injuries from stab wounds. Upshaw complies, turning around as the detectives inspect his torso. Deere notes that he has a couple of scars on his back that appear to be a few months old and could be the result of knife wounds. Deere thinks that one or both of the scars could have resulted from his struggle with Denise.

"How did you get that scar right there?" Crowell asks, pointing to a mark on Upshaw's lower back. "It looks like you were cut."

"Don't know," Upshaw says.

For the next twenty minutes, the detectives push Upshaw to reconstruct what happened after he had sex with Denise and argued with her about money. They appeal to his better nature, to logic, to anger; they "call bullshit" on his evasions in a more or less friendly way. Finally Upshaw admits that his back may have been scraped while he was having sex with Denise on the ground. He also says he walked her back to her neighborhood and admits that he stood on a street corner and watched Denise head down her street toward what he assumes was her house. He even says he watched her walk up her driveway, and he appears to correct Crowell when the detective intentionally places the house in the wrong place on a hand-drawn map.

Still going easy on their suspect, the detectives press Upshaw gently until they sense resistance. They back off and try another route, then another. Just after midnight, they declare that it's time for a break.

SMOKING CIGARETTES IN the old evidence bay thirty minutes later, the detectives agree that when they resume the interrogation, Crowell should squeeze Upshaw, allowing Deere to study the suspect and jump in if he spots an opening. They dissect Upshaw's probable lies and truths. Though their suspect hasn't admitted it, both detectives are certain he raped Denise. More likely than not, he knew where she lived—and that is the key point, the one they must nail down. After finishing their cigarettes, they check on Upshaw through the peephole and on the video monitor. Spread out across two chairs, he seems to be dozing, so Deere decides to wait a bit before continuing.

By 2:30 a.m., the situation has changed. Upshaw is now pacing around the box, his orange shirt pulled over his head, arms crossed on his chest. For a moment he stops and stands as still as a statue; then he yells, "Hey, Police!" and "Hey, Detectives! Investigators! Mr. Officers!"

He pounds on the thick door and then looks straight into the video camera in the corner of the interview room. "This nigger is going to get thirty years to life, locked up. Fuck it," he shouts.

Deere knows it is time. Upshaw is fully cooked; if he is going to confess, he will do it now.

Deere and Crowell reenter the box at 2:43 a.m. Crowell apologizes for the long wait, saying they were just trying to figure a few things out. Deere retakes his seat next to Upshaw; Crowell sits at the opposite end of the table. Hoping to boost Upshaw's energy, Deere gives his suspect some gummy worms, which he devours.

At first Deere leads the interrogation, asking Upshaw about friends and associates, women he may have had sex with. Deere is relaxed, nearly lethargic—deliberately, he establishes the calm before the storm.

When the moment seems right, Crowell launches into a spiel about the importance of DNA. He then tells Upshaw that his blood was found on Denise's shirt; boldy fabricating, Crowell also says that his DNA was discovered in her house. The detectives focus on these two points for a good thirty minutes, repeatedly asking their suspect to explain them.

Upshaw says the blood probably came off his back while he and Denise were having sex. But he denies ever having been in her house, and he will not budge.

"Your DNA is in the house," Crowell says, his voice rising. "The only way your DNA is in that house is if you are in that house."

"I was not in her house," Upshaw says again.

Deere looks hard at his suspect: he feels reasonably sure that Upshaw isn't telling the truth, but he's not 100 percent certain.

"Evidence doesn't lie," Crowell says, leaning across the table and staring hard at Upshaw. "Evidence doesn't discriminate. Evidence doesn't know anything about you. It is what it is. The reason people lie is because they are afraid of what the consequence might be or they are afraid of the truth."

"I'm not," Upshaw says calmly.

"You should be," Crowell says, a hard edge in his voice.

"The only thing you should be afraid of," Deere says, "is sitting there denying stuff that we know is right, okay? That only makes you look worse because it makes you look smaller."

"David, you are making this way harder than it needs to be," says Crowell.

"*Way* harder," agrees Deere.

"Saying my DNA is in her house is crazy," Upshaw says.

"Let's start small," Deere says. "How did you get bleeding?"

Upshaw says he must have been scratched on his arms and back. The detectives again inspect his back. The scars are not the result of scratches—they clearly come from a cutting.

"How did those happen?" Crowell asks. "If she stabbed you, let's make her accountable for it."

Upshaw leans back in his chair. He takes a deep breath, and Deere is sure he is about to concede this point.

"Did she cut you?" Crowell asks.

"Yes," says Upshaw. His breathing is slowing, becoming more labored; his head is angled down.

Deere feels a surge of energy. His suspect seems defeated. The interrogation has reached a critical point; he and Crowell have to keep Upshaw rolling, not give him time to think too much and build a defense. It has been an hour since they reentered the box, and Deere senses the momentum building. This is how it often happens: they ride a river of lies that finally ends in a waterfall of truth.

"How many times did she cut you?" asks Crowell.

"Three or four," Upshaw says.

"How did she cut you?" asks Crowell.

He makes a slashing motion.

"She slices you?"

"Yeah," says Upshaw, adding that he was holding her while she was flailing at him with a knife.

"If you went back there, or you had been there before, now is the time to tell us," Deere says, referring to Denise's house. "If you went back there to talk to her, that is fine."

"You saying you have never been in that house is wrong, dead wrong," Crowell says. "Being in her house don't make you a bad dude. Not being honest is what jams you up."

"Yeah."

"Did you go back to her house that night to try to apologize or something like that?" Crowell asks.

Upshaw mumbles, his words unintelligible.

"David, please," Deere says. "Be honest."

"We have your DNA in the house, bottom line," Crowell says.

"Were you afraid she was going to call the police?" Deere asks. "Did you try to talk her out of it?"

"About what?" Upshaw says.

"About making up some bullshit rape," Deere says.

"Did you go there for that purpose?" Crowell asks.

"I went there to try to make it right."

"Did you all go into the house?"

"I didn't go in with her."

"You went in the house?" Crowell asks again.

"Yeah," Upshaw says quietly.

Deere is startled by this sudden reversal. *Did he just say that? Did he just admit going inside the house?*

"Where do you go?" asks Crowell. "Explain it to me. Go in the house and sit on the couch? Go in the house and go downstairs?"

Upshaw hesitates—and then once again claims he didn't enter the house. He says he went with Denise to her street and then watched her standing at her front door, yelling at him and taunting him, threatening to sic her friends on him. He says that after listening to her for a bit, he walked to the corner and smoked a cigarette. A few minutes later, he says, he saw a tall stranger emerge from the darkness, go to the front door, and speak with Denise. Then the stranger walked from the house to where Upshaw was standing and beat him up. After losing the fight, Upshaw says, he ran away.

Deere is skeptical. *A stranger appears out of nowhere and beats him up?* Denise never mentioned asking a friend to go after her attacker. He's not even sure Denise has such a friend. The story sounds bogus.

As Deere considers this new twist in his suspect's account, Crowell presses ahead.

"Okay, you are pissed," Crowell says. "You got cut up and your ass whupped. She is going to call her people—what do you do?"

"I call my people," Upshaw answers.

"So, at some point, you go back over there," Crowell says. "The problem we have is that your DNA isn't in the house yet. How the fuck is your DNA in the house? I am going to tell you. You went back over there mad. Am I right?"

"Right," Upshaw says.

"And when do you go back to the house?" Crowell asks. "Do it right, David. Do it right."

"Couple days."

"What is a couple? A couple to him"—Crowell nods toward Deere—"might be two. Couple to me might be five."

"Three or four days," Upshaw says softly, his eyes glued to his hands, which are resting on the table.

*Jesus,* thinks Deere. *The timing fits just about perfectly.* "How did you get there?" he asks.

"Bus."

"Went by yourself?" Deere asks.

Upshaw shakes his head and says he was joined by a friend named Vincent, whom he'd contacted through his Facebook page.

"Both of you went in the house?" Crowell asks.

"Yeah."

"How did you get into the house?" asks Crowell. "Be straight. You should see your chest, the way it's going up and down, a lot faster than ten minutes ago. This is your chance to make it right, David."

"The door was unlocked. She was at the door."

Deere glances at Crowell and sees him shaking his head. Tightening his grip on his pen, Deere thinks, *Careful, Mike. Be careful.*

"Uh-uh," Crowell says, his voice practically a growl. "Stop. Stop. Stop. Did you kick in the door or did your boy kick in the door? David, did you kick the door or did your boy kick the door?"

Deere's stomach knots: he hates feeding lines to suspects. Besides, not many people know the door was kicked in, and Deere believes it would be far better to get their suspect to confess that point without prompting. But he knows he cannot stop this train—the interrogation is now in Crowell's hands.

"I didn't kick the door," Upshaw says, sounding resigned.

"Who kicked the door? Vincent?"

"Yeah."

"Both of you went in?"

"Yeah."

Crowell barely pauses before saying, "Who has the gun?"

"The gun?" asks Upshaw. His eyes narrow, his back stiffens. His expression suddenly changes. It's as if he's just been jolted by a Taser.

Deere leans back and rubs his cheek. Looking at Upshaw's bright, angry eyes, he feels overwhelmed by dread. They've lost control of the interrogation: either Upshaw knows where their questions are going because he killed Amber Stanley or he has just realized that he's on the verge of falsely confessing to a murder. One word keeps passing through Deere's mind: *Fuck. Fuck. Fuck.*

"I didn't have no gun," Upshaw says vehemently.

"I didn't say you did," says Crowell.

"Vincent didn't do nothing," says Upshaw.

And with that, Upshaw abruptly changes course. He claims that he is under the influence of marijuana, that he is not thinking straight. He says he has no idea what the detectives are talking about. He has done nothing wrong. He has never been to Denise's house.

"I'm still high, my man," he says. "This shit is crazy."

Before Deere or Crowell can respond, Upshaw buries his head in his arms.

It's over.

TEN MINUTES LATER, just before 4:30 a.m., Deere drops into a rolling chair, leans back, and stares at the tiled ceiling of the old evidence bay. He leans forward, blinks, then closes his burning eyes. He listens as Joe Bunce and Allyson Hamlin chatter about how they were watching the interrogation on the monitor; when Crowell was hammering Upshaw with questions about the door and the gun, they were sure he was about to confess. Deere hears Joe Bergstrom say that Upshaw is cornered, that he has walked himself into a murder charge and is now trying to back away from his earlier admissions. Crowell is raving about how well the interrogation has gone.

"Sean, he's our guy!" Crowell says. "He did it! This is our guy. He kicked in the fucking door!"

Hands between his knees, Deere opens his eyes and looks at his colleagues for a moment. His gaze shifts to the floor.

"He's there, but he's not," says Deere. "He's playing dumb because he's tired as fuck. He is just throwing a name out there. He's just making shit up to make other shit fit."

"You don't think he's there?" Hamlin asks.

"No," Deere says. "No—that's my gut."

"What do you mean, Sean?" Crowell asks. "He did what I told you. He put someone else there."

"You almost had him," says Bunce.

"He *is* playing dumb," says Crowell, taking a deep drag off his Marlboro, savoring it, exhaling. "He did it. We have enough to charge him. He admits to kicking in the door!"

Deere squeezes his eyes shut and tries to clear his foggy mind.

Again he wonders: did they lose Upshaw because he realized he was implicating himself in the murder he committed or because he realized he was making a false confession? He can't tell. He is pissed at Crowell for feeding the suspect too much information, but he knows that if Crowell hadn't pushed Upshaw they would probably still be in the box, circling him and never getting any closer to the truth.

"He is trying to make shit fit, and we don't know if the shit fits or not," Deere says, looking up at his partner. He can see that Crowell has no doubts. That is not his way.

"The bottom line is that he killed this girl because he got punked," Crowell says. He argues that Upshaw got spooked by their questions because he finally understood what they were after—a murder. He reminds Deere that Upshaw admitted that he went back to Denise's house.

Deere shakes his head. "He backed off all of it."

The conversation goes on for another ten minutes, until Deere slowly gets up from his chair and leaves the evidence bay. The other detectives fall silent; after a minute or so, they return to their desks.

Bergstrom goes into the computer room, where a video of the interrogation has been playing on a monitor. He eyes the live feed and grimaces: Upshaw is doing push-ups. He walks back into the office and signals his detectives. "Guys," he says, "you need to get back in there."

Deere and Crowell return to the box. Over the next two hours, they take several more runs at Upshaw. They get nowhere.

"You said somebody kicked the door in," Crowell pleads.

"I wasn't serious," Upshaw answers.

"You were lying?"

"Yeah."

"Why would you lie about that?"

"I want to get back to my bed," Upshaw says. "I have cooperated as much as I can. I have nothing to do with this shit."

Finally the detectives run out of steam and leave the box. Though he knows it's futile, Deere agrees to let Boulden take a crack at Upshaw.

At 6:30 a.m. Deere is sitting at his desk, staring at a blank page in his notebook. He turns and spots Hamlin putting on her wool coat; she says she's heading home, but something on her desk catches her attention, and she sits down again. Then exhaustion exerts its inexorable pull, and a moment later she rests her head on a large case file and falls fast asleep.

Bunce tells Deere he has to help his wife get their kids to school. He stands up, pushes his chair under his desk, and moves carefully past Hamlin. Boulden returns from the box at 7:15 a.m. and says that Upshaw isn't changing his story. After gathering up his coat, the rookie slips out the door. Bergstrom leaves next; before he goes, he tells Deere that they will all meet that afternoon to discuss the interrogation.

Now it's just Deere and Crowell. They argue for a few minutes about the interrogation and what it means. Crowell continues to insist that they have enough to arrest Upshaw, and he wants to push their commanders to let them file charges. Deere disagrees, saying he needs to review the interrogation before deciding whether Upshaw actually confessed. He hopes that watching the video will change his mind, but instinct tells him it won't.

Crowell volunteers to brief the major after going out for breakfast; Deere says he'll arrange for one of the day-shift detectives to take Upshaw back to jail. Crowell nods, forces a brief smile, and then heads for his Impala and a quick trip to McDonald's.

This is Deere's case, his burden, but the weight of the interrogation of David Upshaw will not fully land on his shoulders until he has had some time to think about how it went wrong. Already, though, a swirl of questions are racing through his mind. What if Crowell hadn't fed Upshaw that detail about the door and then frozen him with the question about the gun? What if he had taken the interrogation away from Crowell when he'd first sensed that his partner was going too far? What if he had handled the interrogation better only to get a false confession from an innocent man? And worst of all: what if he has just let a killer off the hook?

Shaking off his doubts, Deere decides that he is certain of one thing: he and the squad gave it all they had. If they made mistakes, they didn't do so out of negligence or incompetence or dereliction. They slipped up only because he and Crowell and the others shared a burning desire to solve an unsolvable case.

Deere closes his notebook, pushes it to the middle of his desk, and stands up. He sighs, suddenly remembering that his day isn't done. *Jesus,* he thinks. *I've got the fucking midnight shift.*

Donning his coat, he takes a last survey of the empty office. He smiles at the slumbering Hamlin, then walks out of the Homicide Unit, down the long hallway, and into the back parking lot. He squints in the bright early-morning light. It's the last day of February, and before a new day begins, another body will fall in PG County, the twelfth homicide of the shortest month of the year.

Now feeling nothing beyond pure exhaustion, Deere gets behind the wheel of his Impala. He sits for a moment, rubbing his face. He switches on the ignition and checks the clock radio: it's nearly 8:00 a.m. After lowering the window a few inches, the detective lights a cigarette, puts the car in drive, and begins the long ride home.

## · EPILOGUE ·

Lieutenant Billy Rayle's prediction proved to be accurate: February 2013 was indeed a good month for murder. PG County's Homicide Unit tallied twelve killings over those twenty-eight days, a harrowing challenge that pushed the unit's detectives to their limits. Over time, they solved ten of these homicides, an impressive feat. Five ended in guilty pleas, and two others led to a federal indictment that has not been completely resolved. One case went to trial but resulted in a hung jury; prosecutors have pledged to retry the case. A suspect in another was charged, but due to legal maneuvering he has yet to go on trial. The gunman in the tenth murder committed suicide.

For the remainder of that year, PG's homicide detectives continued their successful run, making arrests in thirty-three of the fifty-six murders that occurred in 2013 and arrests in fifteen murders that took place in previous years. Including six murders closed by exceptional means—such as those in which the suspect has been killed—the unit posted an overall clearance rate for 2013 of 96 percent.

The people killed that February were fairly typical of other victims of violence in PG County. One was white, three were Hispanic, and the remaining eight were black. One was a woman; the rest were men. The manner of death was also typical: nine of the victims were fatally shot and three were stabbed.

The February spree put the county on pace to record nearly 120 murders for the year. Facing the onslaught, Chief Mark Magaw and Assistant Chief Kevin Davis implemented a crime-suppression program that was both aggressive and expensive: every day for weeks, they placed officers in marked squad cars at forty-four high-crime spots throughout the county from 3:00 p.m. to 3:00 a.m. It's impossible to determine whether the initiative worked or violence ebbed for other reasons, but the facts are these: the department logged just three murders in March and then went thirty-four days straight without catching a homicide, the longest such streak in memory. Despite the bloody start, the department finished 2013 with eight fewer murders than the previous year. The county posted similarly low numbers in 2014 and the first six months of 2015, even as violence escalated in nearby Washington, DC, and Baltimore.

Besides deploying police officers in high-crime locations in the spring of 2013, the department continued working closely with other county agencies to target trouble spots. Further, Magaw and Davis were convinced that homicide detectives helped stem the spate of murders by making prompt arrests following many of the killings that occurred that year. In their view, the arrests dampened the chances of retaliatory violence and also sent the message that it is not easy to get away with murder in Prince George's County.

DETECTIVE EDDIE FLORES managed to solve the murder of Salaam "Slug" Adams, the drug dealer from North Carolina who was fatally shot in a park in Hillcrest Heights. The rookie's instincts had been correct: his chief witness, Harvey "B-Gutter" Gunter, had lied repeatedly. After initially thinking that Gunter was a witness, Flores came to believe that he may have shot Adams and then tried to shift the blame to others when confronted by the police. Gunter eventually pleaded guilty to first-degree murder; he admitted to playing a key role in Adams's death, though he did not confess to pulling the trigger. Gunter was sentenced to life in prison with all but thirty years suspended, meaning he could theoretically be eligible for parole someday.

Flores also concluded that both Brandon Battle and Robert Ofoeme were involved in Adams's murder and charged them in the slaying. But state prosecutors eventually dropped both cases, telling the detective it would be difficult to win convictions because the case would be based heavily on Gunter's shaky word. Even so, Flores enjoyed a modest courtroom victory: Battle was sentenced to ten years in prison for possessing an illegal handgun and a stash of marijuana, both of which Flores had seized during the search of his apartment. Throughout the court proceedings, Battle and Ofoeme maintained their innocence with respect to the murder charges, and Ofoeme asked the court to expunge that charge from his record. A judge in 2015 denied his request.

After solving the murder of Adams, Flores went back into the rotation, eager to catch his next case. He soon found himself the at-bat detective, but then the county went quiet. Every day, he hurried into work, checked the murder board, and saw his name right there. After every shift, he kept his work phone on his hip so he wouldn't miss the call for his homicide. He eventually realized that it wasn't a nightmare or a trick being played on him by his colleagues. (In the end, it proved to be the historic thirty-four-day lull.) Surely, he thought, all of the suspense meant that his next case would be a doozy. And it was: though the murder he caught was eerily similar to his first—a drug dealer shot dead in the woods— he couldn't crack it. Despite countless hours of hard work, the slaying remains the only unsolved homicide of the eight Flores has investigated since Adams's murder.

Mike Ebaugh won similar success. His labors ensured that Nicoh Mayhew's grand jury testimony was entered into evidence during the 2014 prosecution of Mayhew's nephew Brian "Block" Mayhew for the 2011 slayings of Sean Ellis and Anthony McKelvin. Brian Mayhew was ultimately convicted of first-degree murder and sentenced to life in prison. To Ebaugh's consternation, however, Brian Mayhew's codefendant, Kenan Myers, was acquitted of all charges, in part because the prosecutors were not able to persuade a judge to allow them to use Nicoh Mayhew's testimony during Myers's separate trial.

Ebaugh charged six people in Nicoh Mayhew's killing, including Brian Mayhew and his girlfriend. For her role in arranging the calls that led to Nicoh Mayhew's death in December 2012, the girlfriend pleaded guilty to conspiring to retaliate against a witness. Ebaugh did not charge Kenan Myers in Nicoh Mayhew's murder because the detective was never able to establish a link between the suspect and the crime. Charges against two of the other suspects were dropped. In June 2015, prosecutors took Brian Mayhew, Anthony Cannon, and Stanley Winston to trial. But after a series of surprising rulings that limited the evidence the prosecutors could present in court—including a decision that prohibited any mention of the key recording in which Winston appears to have informed Brian Mayhew that his uncle had been slain—the jury failed to reach a verdict on any charges. Prosecutors have pledged to retry the case.

While continuing to investigate the Nicoh Mayhew case, Ebaugh caught a fresh killing on February 23—that of Nicolas Gonzalez, a thirty-four-year-old El Salvadoran day laborer who was hacked to death with a machete early one morning in front of the house where he lived. The detective quickly linked the murder to the notoriously violent gang Mara Salvatrucha, also known as MS-13; as Ebaugh knew, the gang's members often wielded machetes. Federal authorities soon became involved, and in 2014, U.S. prosecutors unsealed an indictment alleging that nine MS-13 members played roles in the killings of Gonzalez and four other men in Prince George's County. Among those men was eighteen-year-old Meyder Bladimir Yuman, the final murder victim in February 2013. A third case involving Hispanic gangs, the fatal shooting of twenty-year-old David Avelar on February 24, was also solved, and Avelar's killer pleaded guilty to first-degree murder and is awaiting sentencing.

Ebaugh's work on the Mayhew case earned him the respect he had been seeking from his superiors and his fellow detectives. But his outlandish personality sometimes continued to grate, as when he made a show of dousing his thinning hair with growth formula or bragging about achieving a very high score on the written portion of the sergeant's exam in 2014. His comeuppance came during the exam's oral assessment: while he was being drilled on how to respond to a multicar accident, a fire alarm began sounding in the classroom. It wasn't part of the test, and Ebaugh grew so frustrated that he screamed, "Fuck!" His colleagues teased him relentlessly for losing his composure, and he was later passed over for promotion.

Even the best investigators can be stymied by a challenging case, and two of the Homicide Unit's most respected detectives failed to solve the murders of Aaron Kidd and Andre Shuford. Billy Watts and Ben Brown worked the case assiduously through February and March, tracking down witnesses and persuading a particularly reluctant one to identify the suspected killer. That witness, as well as several others, told Watts and Brown that a teenage armed robber had been responsible for a number of holdups in the neighborhood. In the days before the double homicide, the robber had ridden his bike into the apartment complex and tried to mug Kidd and Shuford. According to the witness, the two friends spotted the robber a few nights later; after confronting him, they got into a fight with him and then were fatally shot.

In early March, Watts brought the seventeen-year-old suspect into homicide and questioned him for hours. But the teen would not confess, and it was later determined that his DNA did not match blood drops recovered near the scene, a puzzling development. Even so, Watts remains convinced that the teenager—now an adult—did indeed kill Kidd and Shuford, and he continues to plug away at the case.

Over the next two years, Watts became increasingly burned out, and in 2014 he decided it was time to put investigations behind him. He studied hard for the sergeant's exam and scored high enough to win a promotion. He expects to remain in the Homicide Unit, as does Brown, who is also due to become a sergeant soon. Both men look forward to imparting their knowledge to fresh investigators while no longer bearing the direct responsibility of speaking for the dead.

Jonathan Hill survived his rookie season and remains in homicide, where his love of video games and *Star Wars* continues to vex his veteran colleagues. He also managed to identify the victim of the police-involved shooting on February 8. Her name was Tonya Buggs; she was the forty-three-year-old daughter of the apartment's leaseholder, who had moved to New York City to care for her own mother.

After tracking down Geraldine McIntyre's stolen television, Andre Brooks charged James "JuJu" Ward, a heroin-addicted handyman, with fatally stabbing the seventy-one-year-old homebody. Successfully prosecuting Ward will be difficult: Brooks and evidence technicians discovered no forensic evidence linking him to the murder scene. Further, the suspect's lengthy interrogation was thrown out by a judge after Ward alleged that he had been roughed up by Brooks during a break in the interview. This is not an uncommon allegation—most judges view it skeptically—and Brooks vigorously denies it. Prosecutors also dispute the claims and are appealing the judge's decision to disallow the interrogation. Even if they win the appeal, Brooks's session with Ward may be of limited value at trial, since Ward admits only to having walked past McIntyre's house on the day of the murder.

In the two years following the McIntyre case, Brooks's luck did not improve, and he became known as the detective who caught the saddest cases. A few months after McIntyre's death, he investigated the murder of a toddler. In 2014, he arrested a mother who killed her one-year-old son and three-year-old daughter by wrapping their heads in plastic bags. Brooks says the murders of so many innocent victims took a toll, making it nearly impossible for him to distance himself from the more routine violence and emotional tumult that accompanies his job. After twenty-five years on the force, he claims he is finally ready to retire.

Spencer Harris and Greg McDonald were correct to be wary of Tayvon Williams, the first witness they interviewed in the murder of fifteen-year-old Charles Walker Jr., shot for a pair of new pink Timberland boots. Although Williams's information helped detectives from the unit round up the four other men in the white van that night, they later determined that Williams had been the triggerman. Williams pleaded guilty to second-degree murder and is awaiting sentencing. The four other men have all pleaded guilty to various charges stemming from the robbery and shooting.

In late 2014, with the murder rate holding low and steady, commanders decided to eliminate Harris's squad, M-90, and scatter its detectives to other assignments. Harris and McDonald were transferred to the cold-case squad, and they now spend most of their days digging through dusty case files and answering calls from relatives curious about the status of investigations.

The detectives of M-40 have remained as intense and jocular as ever, though the tight-knit group has broken up. Sergeant Joe Bergstrom retired a few months into 2015; Joe Bunce won promotion to sergeant and is expected to lead a robbery squad. Allyson Hamlin charged Kimberly Smith with the murder of Charles Blyther Jr., her mother's ex-boyfriend; Smith pleaded guilty to manslaughter and was sentenced to five years in prison. Hamlin continued to devote much of her spare time to football, and in 2015 she led her team, the D.C. Divas, to victory in the league championship.

Jamie Boulden, after investigating scores of natural deaths and seven slayings, says he finally feels like he belongs in homicide. Whenever he runs into Trasee Cosby at a scene, he teases her just like any other veteran, and they still joke about their first encounter shortly after her examination of the overdose victim.

Mike Crowell is eyeing retirement in late 2016 so he can focus his prodigious energy on growing his security business and spending more time with his very understanding wife. As the winter of 2013 went on, he stuck with his pill-assisted diet and lost twenty pounds; later that year, however, he put fifteen back on. Over the past two years, Crowell has investigated everything from gang-related disputes to the beating death of a nine-month-old boy.

ON A HOT summer evening in August 2013, Sean Deere returned to Chartsey Street in Kettering and knocked on door after door, still seeking evidence in the murder of Amber Stanley. Sweating heavily in his dark blue suit, Deere hoped to turn up a new clue by interviewing Amber's neighbors, but he was not optimistic. The subdivision had been canvassed and recanvassed since that tragic night a year earlier, and Deere knew that not a single doorbell had been left unrung.

In truth, Deere's visit to Chartsey Street was not so much a canvass as a theatrical appearance. His audience consisted of half a dozen journalists who were filming him and his fellow investigators as they talked with neighbors and passed out flyers. Deere was more than happy to play his part in this scene: a story on the evening news might bring in a tip that could ultimately lead to the honor student's killer.

By the first anniversary of Amber Stanley's death, Deere had ruled out the possibility that his first solid suspect, Jeff Buck, was involved in the murder. He had spent several months learning as much as possible about David Upshaw, the alleged serial rapist he and Crowell had questioned well into the final morning of February. Deere had examined Upshaw's cell-phone records, questioned dozens of fellow jail inmates, searched his mother's town house, reviewed scores of social-media postings, and interviewed the two women he had been charged with raping. But despite all that work, Deere had failed to uncover a single fact that linked Upshaw to the killing.

That fall, Deere was elated when he was finally permitted to return to the murder rotation. Not long after he became the at-bat detective, he caught and quickly solved the fatal shooting of a motel clerk in an armed robbery. But the Amber Stanley case remained his first priority, and in September he and Crowell visited Denise at her mental-health facility in the Midwest and interviewed her again. When presented with a photo array of mug shots, she identified Upshaw as her rapist. Deere was on the verge of charging Upshaw with sexual assault when he learned that the judge responsible for the case had reviewed a handwritten motion submitted by Upshaw and thrown out one of the two existing indictments against him.

When state prosecutors told Deere they felt confident that the judge's ruling would not stand, Deere decided to hold off on charging Upshaw. In late 2013, Upshaw pleaded guilty to second-degree assault in the robbery he was accused of committing; he was sentenced to eight years in prison. And in July 2015 the Maryland Court of Special Appeals reinstated the indictment that had been thrown out by the judge.

Deere expects to charge Upshaw with Denise's rape soon; after he does, he intends to bring his suspect back to homicide and take a final run at him in the box.

Del Quentin Wilber, August 2015

## AUTHOR'S NOTE

My lifelong fascination with police work most likely started in grade school when I began swiping crime novels off my father's nightstand. It continued during two long stints as a crime reporter in two of America's most violent cities, first in Baltimore for the *Baltimore Sun* and then in Washington, DC, for the *Washington Post*. In particular, I was drawn to the work of detectives, especially those who investigated murders. A major influence on my reporting career was *Homicide*, a singular book by David Simon, a former *Sun* reporter who chronicled a year (1988) in the life of Baltimore's vaunted homicide unit.

In late 2011 I began looking into the ways that detective work had changed in the two decades since *Homicide*'s publication. I soon decided to focus my research on a place that would be at once foreign and familiar: Prince George's County, Maryland. In early 2012, I approached PG County's police chief and asked if he would be willing to let me embed with his Homicide Unit. Chief Mark Magaw, a veteran officer who believes in transparency, told me I could write about whatever I saw as long as I allowed his department to review the manuscript before publication. This would give PG police an opportunity to question the inclusion of any information that might harm a witness or a prosecution, though I would retain full editorial control and the final say on what was published. This arrangement made sense to me, so we agreed to go forward.

I began my reporting in November 2012 and soon was trailing detectives as they interrogated suspects, finessed witnesses, delivered death notifications, and toiled at their desks. Within two or three weeks I knew I had gotten lucky: it was obvious that PG County's homicide detectives were as competent as they were colorful. In particular, I remember feeling fortune's warm touch on the afternoon I watched Andre Brooks arrive at the scene of a murder, snarl at a corpse, and then venture into a side room, whereupon he spotted a guitar, picked it up, and began strumming a tune.

Twenty-five detectives worked in PG County's Homicide Unit during the months I was reporting this book, so naturally I couldn't be everywhere at once. My firsthand observations provided the grist for most of the scenes in these pages; when necessary, I re-created events I didn't personally witness after conducting extensive interviews of the investigators who were present at these events.

Due to space constraints, I was not able to describe every homicide and police-involved shooting that occurred in February 2013. In particular, I did not write about the murders of Charles Thompson, twenty-seven, shot during an argument on February 8 in Forestville and found dead in a car outside the Ritchie Volunteer Fire Department in Capitol Heights; Stephen A. Rane, twenty-two, slain by his University of Maryland roommate (who then killed himself) on February 12 in College Park; and Eric Walker, twenty-seven, killed by a deranged PCP addict on February 19 in Temple Hills.

After reading a complete draft of the manuscript, PG County's police department raised only a handful of concerns. All dealt with the protection of witnesses, and I addressed each issue accordingly. None of the resulting minor changes altered the character, tenor, or scope of the book. Even before showing the manuscript to the police department, I decided to give pseudonyms to five witnesses and two suspects interviewed by PG detectives, thus obscuring their identities. Otherwise, every name used in the book is real.

For the record, I did not originally intend to write an account of a single month in the life of PG County's Homicide Unit; in fact, as I started into my research I wasn't at all sure how the book would ultimately begin or end. I only knew that a compressed and particularly intense period of time inevitably tests the mettle of those who live through it, and I hoped to stumble upon a story that fit that mold. After nearly six months of exhaustive research, however, I had scores of notebooks filled with terrific stories, but I was struggling to find a cohesive narrative arc.

One day in April it struck me that I had actually been a first-hand witness to precisely the sort of crucible I hoped to find: the twenty-eight days and nights of February 2013. Why it took me so long to perceive a narrative architecture that now seems obvious remains a mystery to me. Perhaps it was sleep deprivation; the pace of events that February was so demanding that one night I nodded off while waiting at a red light; another time I fell asleep while pumping gas. Only later did I realize that the bloody month of February had been brutal and exhilarating, frantic and revealing—and that it provided exactly the arc I had been looking for. By June I stopped reporting and started writing, and the result is this book.

# HOMICIDES IN PRINCE GEORGE'S COUNTY

## • FEBRUARY 2013 •

**FEBRUARY 4:** Salaam Adams, age twenty. Killed in a drug-related shooting in the 2600 block of Oxon Run Drive, Hillcrest Heights.

**FEBRUARY 8:** Charles Thompson, age twenty-seven. Shot during an argument in the 2500 block of Timbercrest Drive, Forestville; found dead in a car in the parking lot of the Ritchie Volunteer Fire Department at 1415 Ritchie Marlboro Road, Capitol Heights.

**FEBRUARY 9:** Geraldine McIntyre, age seventy-one. Stabbed to death during a robbery in her home at 1209 Chapel Oaks Drive, Capitol Heights.

**FEBRUARY 12:** Stephen A. Rane, age twenty-two. Shot to death by his University of Maryland roommate at 8706 Thirty-Sixth Avenue, College Park.

**FEBRUARY 18:** Charles Walker Jr., age fifteen. Shot to death in a robbery in the 4000 block of Twenty-Eighth Avenue, Hillcrest Heights.

**FEBRUARY 19:** Aaron Kidd, age eighteen, and Andre Shuford, age eighteen. Killed in a double shooting in the 3700 block of Donnell Drive, Forestville.

**FEBRUARY 19:** Eric Walker, age twenty-seven. Shot and killed by a deranged PCP addict at Branch Avenue and Colebrooke Drive, Temple Hills.

**FEBRUARY 21:** Charles Blyther Jr., age fifty-one. Stabbed to death during a domestic altercation at 1116 Kennebec Street, Oxon Hill.

**FEBRUARY 23:** Nicolas Gonzalez, age thirty-four. Hacked to death during a gang-related attack at 8109 Riggs Road, Langley Park.

**FEBRUARY 24:** David Avelar, age twenty. Shot to death during a gang-related dispute at 9137 Baltimore Avenue, College Park.

**FEBRUARY 28:** Meyder Bladimir Yuman, age eighteen. Shot to death in a gang-related dispute at Fordham Street and Twenty-Fourth Avenue, Lewisdale.

# ACKNOWLEDGMENTS

This book could not have been written without the cooperation of the Prince George's County Police Department, and as such I am deeply grateful to Chief Mark Magaw and then-Assistant Chief Kevin Davis for granting me unfettered access to the detectives in the Homicide Unit. In addition, I owe thanks to Julie Parker, the department's communications director, as well as County Executive Rushern Baker and his staff for permitting me to ride along with the detectives. At the Prince George's County State's Attorney Office, Wes Adams and Christine Murphy never hesitated to provide valuable insights into their cases.

My agent, Rafe Sagalyn, always offered sage advice and was willing to provide me with a stiff Scotch when needed. Henry Holt's publisher, Stephen Rubin, took a significant risk by giving me a contract based on the broad outline of an idea, and every single page of this book benefited from the critical eye of my fantastic editor, John Sterling. Maggie Richards, Pat Eisemann, Tracy Locke, and Richard Pracher helped me package and market the book; Kenn Russell, Molly Bloom, and Emi Ikkanda provided crucial help along the way; and Bonnie Thompson gave the manuscript an exceedingly thorough copy edit.

While laboring on this book, I was fortunate to be a reporter for two of the world's leading news organizations. The *Washington Post* graciously granted me an extended leave to pursue this project. At the newspaper, I worked with some of the best journalists in the business: Don Graham, Marcus Brauchli, Kevin Merida, Maria Glod, Steven Levingston, Chris Davenport, David Marino-Nachison, Allison Klein, Freddy Kunkle, Ann Marimow, Peter Finn, Clarence Williams, Lynn Medford, and Frances Sellers. I owe special thanks to Vernon Loeb and Mike Semel, two of newspapering's most encouraging and thoughtful bosses.

In January 2014, I joined Bloomberg News, where I have been blessed to work with wonderful colleagues: Steven Komarow, Michael Shepard, Craig Gordon, Justin Blum, Mark McQuillan, Laurie Asseo, Clark Hoyt, Joe Sobczyk, Nick Johnston, Megan Murphy, John Walcott, David Lynch, and Marty Schenker. I owe them all a great debt for their understanding and patience.

My family provided unflagging encouragement. Without my mom and dad, Kay and Del Wilber, and my sister and her husband, Lindsay and Philip Gutherie, there would be no *Good Month for Murder*. My two amazing boys, Quinn and Ryan Wilber, provided me with needed distractions. Laura Sullivan provided critical counsel and backing. I have also enjoyed the constant support of wonderful friends, including Jason Longwell (cochair of the Wednesday Night Social Club), Zachary Coile, Lincoln Schroth, Scott Woodworth, Annie Linskey, Jonathan Allen, Andrea Messina, Mike James, Wesley Woo, Doug Murray, David Greene, Ken DeCell, Trevor DiGirolamo, Michael Consilvio, Carolyn and the late Jerry Parr, Brian Roth, Michael de Riesthal, and the patrons and managers of Signature Cigars and W. Curtis Draper Tobacconist in Washington, DC. To the members and coaches of the Bethesda Chevy Chase Nationals and Phillies, two great youth baseball teams, thanks for a pair of terrific seasons that provided relief from book-related stress. In addition, I would like to express my gratitude to the 2013 World Series champions, the Boston Red Sox, for providing such a thrilling diversion at a time when I really needed it.

Finally, my most important thank-you is reserved for the women and men of the Prince George's County Homicide Unit. You allowed me into your world and trusted me to write about it fairly, factually, and objectively. You let me trail you everywhere and always answered my questions, even though I never gave you a proper Miranda warning. I hope you recognize the words in these pages as the truth, or as close as I could get to it.

# INDEX

## ABOUT THE AUTHOR

**Del Quentin Wilber** is the *New York Times* bestselling author of *Rawhide Down*, an account of the attempted assassination of Ronald Reagan. An award-winning reporter who previously worked for the *Baltimore Sun* and the *Washington Post*, he now covers the Justice Department for the *Los Angeles Times*. He lives in Bethesda, Maryland.